Raising a
Left-Brain Child
in a Right-Brain World

Raising a
Left-Brain Child
in a Right-Brain World

Strategies for Helping Bright,
Quirky, Socially Awkward Children
to Thrive at Home and at School

Katharine Beals, PhD

TRUMPETER
Boston & London
2009

The names of the individuals described in this book have been changed to protect their privacy.

Trumpeter Books
An imprint of Shambhala Publications, Inc.
Horticultural Hall
300 Massachusetts Avenue
Boston, Massachusetts 02115
www.shambhala.com

9 8 7 6 5 4 3 2 1

First edition
Printed in Canada

⊗ This edition is printed on acid-free paper that meets the American National Standards Institute z39.48 Standard.
♻ This book was printed on 100% postconsumer recycled paper. For more information please visit www.shambhala.com.

Distributed in the United States by Random House, Inc., and in Canada by Random House of Canada Ltd

Interior design and composition: Greta D. Sibley & Associates

Library of Congress Cataloging-in-Publication Data
Beals, Katharine.
Raising a left-brain child in a right-brain world: strategies for helping bright, quirky, socially awkward children to thrive at home and at school/Katharine Beals. —1st ed.
p.   cm.
Includes index.
ISBN 978-1-59030-650-5 (pbk.: alk. paper)
1. Gifted children. I. Title.
HQ773.5.B425 2009
649'.155—dc22
2009011382

Contents

Acknowledgments   vii

Introduction   1
Is This Your Child?

1. *Adrift in Today's Classroom*   13
   The Unsocial Child at School

2. *Playdates, Friends, and Family Life*   57
   The Unsocial Child at Home

3. *Hindered by Reform Math and
   Other Major Trends in K–12 Education*   86
   The Analytic Child at School

4. *All-Absorbing Interests and Other Quirks*   143
   The Analytic Child at Home

5. *Helping Our Most Extreme Left-Brainers*   160
   Understanding and Supporting the Mildly Autistic Child

6. *How to Change Right-Brain Attitudes*   189
   Useful Talking Points

Conclusion   203
The Best of Both Worlds

Resources   218

Index   223

Acknowledgments

I'm grateful to the many people who helped me out in various ways and at various stages of this project. For stimulating conversation on key issues and controversies, I thank Suzanne Allen-Weise, Nancy Beals, Sue Bennett, Hilary Bonta, David Bushell, Liz Ditz, Kathy Dowdell, Caroline Ebby, Steve Fischer, Kevin Fisher, Jennifer Freed, Ros Hartigan, Laura Hawley, Laurie Heusner, Heather Hicks, Kathryn Howard, Felicia Hurewitz, Jeanne-Marie, Catherine Johnson, Miles Kronby, Devi Ghosh Mazumdar, Angela McIver, Patricia Moore-Martinez, Manuela Noske, Kim Pelkey, Teresa Pica, Veronica Ramirez, Becky Wall, Judy Weinstein, Shel White, and correspondents at www.kitchentablemath.blogspot.com.

For feedback on various versions of the manuscript, I thank Anne Dubuisson Anderson, Jane Avrich, William Benemann, Nancy Bea Miller, Clara Claiborne Park, Gwynne Sigel, Emily Sims, Mary Jane Thompson, Sheila Tobias, and Caroline Williams. For mathematical feedback in particular, I thank mathematicians Richard Beals, Roger Howe, and Stephanie Frank Singer.

Most especially, for countless hours of their time—whether reading multiple drafts, writing out detailed feedback, combing through thousands of sentences, playing devil's advocate, and/or helping me conceptualize and strategize—I thank Emma Jean Baudendistel, Fran Bennett, Jacqueline Raphael, Rachel Simon, Stella Whiteman, and my husband, David.

In addition, I thank Susan Senator for introducing me to my agent, Rosalie Siegel, and Rosalie for her abiding faith, wisdom, and perseverance as this project evolved. Finally, I'm tremendously grateful to my editor, Eden Steinberg, for her wise and extensive feedback, and for keeping me focused on my ultimate goal: helping left-brain children in a right-brain world.

Introduction

Is This Your Child?

I scan the yard, searching for my son. Ms. Johnson, his first-grade teacher, points toward the far corner. Under a maple tree, as far as you can get from all the other kids: a splotch of blond in the dark grass, a faint tangle of pale, skinny limbs. Ms. Johnson shakes her head.

I turn to her. "Are you worried about him?"

She nods. "A little."

I watch her face, her furrowing brow, the flecks of green in her narrow eyes. "Hmm . . . ," I say, nodding back. Then I run across the yard, past the kids on the jungle gym, the kids in the sandbox, the kids playing ball on the field. My son sees me and springs up.

"What were you doing under that tree?" I ask as we head out the gate.

"I was dividing seven into twenty. With seven it starts repeating after the sixth decimal—2.85714285714285714, and so on."

I smile in awe at my seven-year-old boy.

"And did you play with anyone today?" I ask, patting his white-blond head.

"Not really." He looks up at me with his large, clear-green eyes and smiles.

This book is about a type of bright, quirky child who is often mis-understood and under-appreciated in today's world. To understand, appreciate, and nurture this child, it helps to begin with a fresh, non-judgmental label, and the one I prefer is *left-brain*. But I don't intend this term literally; that is, I don't wish to imply anything about the activity of brain hemispheres. Rather, I'm using the term *left-brain* in the everyday sense, to convey a specific collection of traits that include thinking abstractly and logically; analyzing and systematizing; processing things linearly (one at a time); attending much more to verbal than to nonverbal communication; preferring to work independently; and being shy, socially awkward, and/or introverted.

And I'm contrasting all this with the everyday connotations of *right-brain:* thinking holistically, applying intuition and emotion, processing many things simultaneously, being sensitive to nonverbal communication (e.g., facial expression, gesture, and tone of voice), being gregarious, and preferring to work with others. These contrasting bundles of traits, regardless of the underlying brain biology, arise together frequently enough that it's useful to draw a dichotomy between right- and left-brain personality types.

The British psychologist Simon Baron-Cohen describes this dichotomy in terms of Systemizers versus Empathizers. Systemizers (left-brainers) are captivated by rules, patterns, and how things work. They prefer nonfiction to fiction, libraries to parties, strategy games to games of chance, and, in general, doing things alone to doing them with others. They are bad at reading facial expressions. They find social situations confusing, dislike small talk, and have trouble putting themselves in other people's shoes. Empathizers, by contrast, are attuned to others' emotions and thoughts, they're skilled at reading them rapidly and correctly, and they tend to respond with care and sensitivity.

Of course, most people aren't so easily classified as one personality type or the other because their traits are moderate or inconsistent: a person may be somewhat intuitive and somewhat analytical, or sometimes social and sometimes not. My focus is on those children who, along most of these dimensions, consistently come out as left-brain.

How large is this group? Perhaps the best evidence comes from the thousands of people who have taken Baron-Cohen's online Systemizer Test. Approximately 17 percent of male respondents and 8 percent of females score as "very high" Systemizers. This suggests that left-brainers constitute somewhere between 10 and 15 percent of the population, and include significantly more boys than girls.

In school, they are the five-year-old who won't put down his science book and join the kindergarten circle; the eight-year-old who insists on doing group assignments on his own; the ten-year-old who solves math problems in her head instead of chatting with her classmates; the sixteen-year-old who writes long, thoughtful essays but finds class discussions too chaotic and intimidating to participate in. As adults, they are our mathematicians, scientists, engineers, computer programmers, economists, linguists, lawyers, analysts, and research associates. Some are talented writers, poets, visual artists, and composers, but create their work using strategies that, in comparison with their fellow artists, are much more analytical than intuitive.

I am the mother of three left-brain children, each of whom presents a different array of challenges and eccentricities. I am also an educator, having taught left-brain subjects like math, computer science, linguistics, expository writing, and English grammar to students from second grade into adulthood. (I've spent time not just in American classrooms but in classrooms abroad as well—in France, as a student, and in China, as a teacher.) This book is the culmination of six years of research, visiting classrooms, interviewing parents and left-brain children, and studying trends in education and popular psychology. In the process, I've discovered pervasive misunderstandings—here in America—about left-brain children, and significant biases against their behaviors and inclinations. And so I've written this book, above all else, to help parents and those who work with children better understand, appreciate, and nurture our young left-brainers.

Though left-brain children are in the minority, and though they present real challenges for parents and schools, they also possess wonderful gifts, and they greatly enrich the diversity of our schools, homes, and communities. However, their very particular learning styles include idiosyncrasies that our culture seems increasingly reluctant to accommodate. Left-brainers are also often aloof, awkward, and shy, so they struggle socially both in and out of school. Parents are often left wondering if there isn't something terribly amiss, and feel increasing pressure to submit their children to psychological testing and medical diagnosis. My hope is that this book will help parents see their kids, with all their strengths and weaknesses, as fundamentally okay. I also wish to offer, to parents and educators alike, strategies for nurturing left-brainers and advocating for them in a world that can often be hostile to their traits and temperaments.

A QUICK ASSESSMENT

By now, you're probably getting a sense of whether the term *left-brain* fits your child's behaviors, inclinations, and learning style. Here's a longer list of the common characteristics of left-brain children. If many of these characteristics describe your child, this book is for you.

Common Characteristics of Left-Brain Children

- Shy, aloof, and/or socially awkward
- Prefer to play and do schoolwork alone
- Tend to keep feelings to themselves
- Interact more easily with adults than with peers
- Have trouble reading facial expressions and body language
- Easily distracted by sensory clutter
- Detail-oriented; difficulty organizing large amounts of material all at once
- Learn better from abstract symbols and concepts than from hands-on activities
- Good at math, science, verbal argumentation, and foreign language grammar
- Good at calculating numbers in their heads
- Need and strive for precision
- Weak in handwriting, graphic arts, and/or visual representations
- Highly critical, skeptical, and argumentative
- Difficulty adjusting to new situations
- Deep, all-absorbing interests or seemingly encyclopedic knowledge of particular topics
- A tendency to lecture or "talk at" others
- Not susceptible to peer pressure; don't feel compelled to do what the other kids are doing

- Sometimes suspected of having selected mutism, social phobia, Nonverbal Learning Disability, or Asperger's syndrome

PARENTING A LEFT-BRAIN CHILD

Parenting a left-brain child brings many rewards and challenges. As I'll explain throughout this book, we're living in a right-brain world—one that strongly prefers right-brain qualities and often misunderstands and marginalizes our left-brain kids.

However, what is true of the larger culture may not be true within our homes and families. For many of us parents of left-brain children, left-brainers are the people who most persistently surround us. They include not only our own kids and the kids that our kids choose to play with but also, often, the parents of these kids—for the unsocial, analytical disposition may be strongly hereditary. Indeed, lots of us are left-brain ourselves and, accordingly, so are many of *our* closest friends. As a result, the personality type that most people consider at least somewhat unusual can seem quite normal to us.

And vice versa: to us, right-brain children can seem quite alien. Strolling along with our own children, who might be contemplating the pattern of odd- and even-numbered houses on either side of the street, analyzing the structure of the locust tree seed pods, or, withdrawn into their own secret worlds, just plain staring off into space, we may be mystified by those "other" children, the ones who run over and look up into our eyes even if they barely know us. "I have a new doll," says one. "Do you want to see my belly button?" asks another. Who *are* these kids, and why do they approach us with wider arms and bigger smiles than our very own offspring do?

But not all parents of left-brain children are themselves left-brain, and for those of us who aren't, it's our own kids who often strike us as alien. We might feel frustrated and embarrassed that our child has so much trouble making eye contact with others or engaging in the simple social exchanges of daily life. Why won't our son, so animated at home, respond to a friendly "hello" from a neighbor on the sidewalk? Why does our daughter, happily playing for hours with imaginary friends, so rarely ask for playdates with actual children?

Whether the outgoing and gregarious counterparts to our kids seem normal or abnormal to us, when we find ourselves making the inevitable comparisons, we may feel the occasional pang of disappointment. Much of what happens out there in the real world is social; most other children can seem much more engaged in general than their left-brain peers do. It's not just that they're constantly attending playdates and birthday parties. As part and parcel of their drive for social connection, they speak more articulately; their faces show more animation, and their bodies more poise. Their heads are constantly turning toward different social cues, their eyes fixing on other eyes. Comparing them to our left-brain introverts, with their often dreamy, inscrutable faces, unfocused gazes, and idle fidgets, it's easy to conclude that these other children are not only more social but generally more mature, intelligent, and lively than our own.

Gradually, as our left-brainers grow older, and they share more and more of their analytical introspections, their positive, wonderfully unique traits start emerging: their sharp minds, their creativity, their out-of-left-field insights, their immunity to peer pressure and openness to fellow eccentrics, and their growing ability to connect with others in their own unusual ways.

But even as we parents increasingly appreciate them, our children face growing challenges from the broader social forces, emanating primarily from school yards and classrooms, that impinge more and more on their private lives. Compounding these challenges, in modern-day America, is a single, sweeping, societal bias that afflicts all left-brain people.

IT'S A RIGHT-BRAIN WORLD

For all the lip service our society pays to individual genius, we've long favored social skills over academic accomplishments, extroversion over introversion, and group cooperation over independent thinking. Emblematic of this is the hugely popular and influential book *Emotional Intelligence* by the psychologist Daniel Goleman—enthusiastically cited as a manifesto about how real-life success depends more on social skills than on IQ, and about how schools should educate children accordingly.

Our culture also favors intuition and "following your gut" over logic and rigorous analysis. Emblematic here is the final installment of the *Stars Wars* films in which a Jedi knight counsels young Anakin, the hero, on how to win in battle and gain entry into the legendary Jedi Order. "Concentrate on the moment," he tells Anakin. "Feel, don't think—trust your instincts." In a *New York Times* opinion piece, the science fiction writer Neal Stephenson observes how odd this is as advice on qualifying oneself for an order that builds its own laser swords from scratch, but our culture seems eager to believe that a Jedi accomplishes this "not by studying calculus but by meditating a lot and learning to trust his feelings."

The more our culture favors intuition over analysis, the more we disfavor analytical subjects such as math and science. Increasingly, American students are avoiding upper-level math and science courses. David Anderegg, the author of *Nerds: Who They Are and Why We Need Them*, offers one reason: the growing antipathy that Americans in particular direct at so-called nerds or geeks, one of the few remaining groups whom it's still socially acceptable to mock. A psychotherapist who works with young children, Anderegg observes bright students shunning hard work and tough math and science classes to avoid being ostracized as nerds. Corroborating this is a 2008 study published by the American Mathematics Society, which observes that, among girls in particular, the top achievers are almost all immigrants, or daughters of immigrants, whose cultures value mathematics much more highly than does ours.

The Anglo-American distaste for math, science, and math-and-science nerds has a long pedigree. Even among intellectuals, it has for decades been much more socially acceptable to proclaim disinterest in numbers than in novels, to admit ignorance of the second law of thermodynamics than of the plays of Shakespeare. But now, Anderegg argues, stereotypes in American popular culture convey more strongly than ever that studying math and science makes you unattractive.

Worsening things further for the mathematically and scientifically inclined, math and science classes themselves, the ones in grade school and high school that students can't avoid, are increasingly skewed by America's right-brain bias—in ways we will discuss in chapter 3.

Finally, while our society continues to revere its top mathematicians and scientists, its views of them have become similarly skewed. For example, what is our mental image of Albert Einstein? Not the tidy, hardworking young patent clerk, but the scraggly eccentric of his later years—even though he developed his groundbreaking theories while clerking. Our image of Einstein speaks volumes about our conception of scientific geniuses. We view those we most admire more as intuition-driven, mold-breaking, wild-haired artists than as meticulous researchers and rigorous analyzers. We imagine their greatest mathematical and scientific breakthroughs occurring not at desks or in laboratories; instead, we see Archimedes in his bathtub, Newton under an apple tree, and Benjamin Franklin in a storm with his kite. In other words, our most esteemed scientists tend to strike us as classic *right*-brainers.

So, as we can see, some societal trends have us favoring extroversion over introversion. Others have us preferring intuitive judgment to analytical reasoning. Still others have us revering the artistic over the scientific. But nothing marginalizes the entire left-brain mindset more than do the forces of political correctness. Most Americans now, quite reasonably, concede that our society has long favored white, Western males to the detriment of everyone else. But some take this argument a step further, seduced by a chorus of intellectuals proclaiming that white, Western males, in effect, are quintessentially left-brain, and that women, non-Westerners, and nonwhites are contrastingly right-brain.

Some of these claims are purely speculative. Various academics and education theorists, for example, have simply asserted that females and/or non-Westerners prefer cooperation over individualism, holism over linear thinking, and spiritualism over logical analysis. Other claims—specifically those based on gender—are more empirical. The sociolinguist Deborah Tannen, for example, cites case studies showing that girls prefer social relationships and cooperation while boys prefer independence and competition. And the psychologist Simon Baron-Cohen cites statistics showing that men tend to be Systemizers and women Empathizers. But regardless of the basis for this partition of left- and right-brain traits between white, Western males and everyone else, arbiters of political correctness have argued that our white-male bias can be redressed only by making our society, in effect, more right-brain.

And more right-brain it has become. Most of us now consistently rank intuition over analysis, art over science, creativity over systematicity, spontaneity over structure, cooperation over independence, and extroversion over introversion. "Go with your gut," don't analyze. "Color outside the lines," forget that creativity requires structure. "Follow your dream," for example, become a painter, actor, singer, or novelist, not a computer programmer, number theorist, or molecular biologist.

A school principal's letter to parents states, "The search for excellence is best achieved cooperatively, rather than by individual effort," and no one questions this statement because it seems obvious. We forget that the most creative innovators still work in solitude. "He's very social and outgoing"—this is our new standard for childhood health and happiness. But is it the only form that psychological and developmental health can take? Haven't the standards of childhood normality become too narrow? And how does this affect our children?

Perhaps nowhere is our culture's right-brain bias stronger than in the setting in which our children spend the majority of their time outside the home: their grade-school classrooms.

Recent trends in education funding and school accountability, however, would suggest otherwise. With school districts relentlessly cutting back on arts programs and spending increasing hours preparing students for ever more frequent, state-mandated, No Child Left Behind tests in math and reading, haven't the latest trends favored the left brain? Aren't our schools, in fact, emphasizing rigorous academics at the expense of the arts?

In fact, current practices threaten rigorous academics at least as much as art and music. No grade-school subject has escaped today's right-brain trends in education, and the most affected subjects are the more academic and analytical ones. As we will see in chapter 1, the promotion of extroversion and cooperation over introversion and independence pressures children to participate orally in class discussions, and work in groups rather than independently—in all subjects. As we will see in chapter 3, the bias against rigorous analysis and toward holistic learning, personal reflections, and artistic creativity, together with the view of traditional math, science, and foreign language classes as overly dry and abstract, has shifted these subjects away from the analytical material that once defined them. As for the mandatory tests, we'll observe how pressures to leave no child behind have set the bar so low that, far from making the math curriculum more rigorous, they've inspired today's test-conscious schools to water it down even further.

Group work and oral class participation, as chapter 1 will show, are neither how left-brain children prefer to learn nor how they learn best. Similarly disadvantageous are the shifts in the math, science, and foreign language curricula. These changes, as chapter 3 will show, have disengaged our children from the subjects that earlier would have suited them best. They've also made it more and more difficult for left-brain learners to distinguish themselves academically and, in many cases, they actually lower these children's grades relative to those of their classmates.

These classmates, meanwhile, challenge our children even further. American culture has long been unfriendly to many left-brainers—for these are the kids it most often derides as "nerds" and "geeks." But an increasing antipathy toward such stereotypes, David Anderegg argues in *Nerds*, have made it less hospitable than ever. Worse, with students spending increasing amounts of class time working in groups, schoolyard social dynamics, as we will discuss in chapter 1, have found their way into the classroom.

The consequences of the right-brain bias extend beyond primary and secondary school toward higher education. As we will see in chapter 1, and as Malcolm Gladwell discusses in a 2005 *New Yorker* article "Getting In: The Social Logic of Ivy League Admissions," unsociability can impede a child's admission to selective colleges. As we will see in chapter 3, the impoverished math and science curriculum that today's schools now offer, together with the mediocre grades they often assign our children, make it difficult for the more mathematically and scientifically inclined of them to compete, in college and beyond, against the growing number of math and science students from overseas.

Besides its educational effects, the right-brain bias has a psychological dimension. As I'll explain, educators and psychologists are increasingly pathologizing unsocial children, assuming that lack of sociability is a problem to be solved. This attitude surfaces, as well, in some of the advice books that purport to help such children—books that tend to assume either that unsocial children want to become more social or that parents should coax them into sociability even if this goes against their nature.

ABOUT THIS BOOK

In order to fully explore the characteristics, challenges, and needs of left-brain children, I'll be dividing them into three categories: the unsocial child, the analytic child, and the mildly autistic child. These categories are not mutually exclusive. Many within the left-brain minority are predominantly analytical: mathematically, scientifically, mechanically, linguistically, or otherwise logically inclined. Others are predominantly unsocial: aloof, socially awkward, and often very shy. But many left-brainers are both analytical and unsocial.

The most extreme left-brain child might lie somewhere on the autistic spectrum. Indeed, Simon Baron-Cohen's tests and surveys find strong Systemizers to include large numbers of high-functioning people with autism. In chapter 5, I'll discuss the standard criteria for an autism diagnosis, as well as special considerations and suggestions for supporting mildly autistic children.

Chapter 6 lists talking points that readers can use in campaigning for left-brain-friendly education reform. The book concludes by discussing how American society can better balance its right- and left-brain priorities.

In the course of the book, I hope to inform you of potential problems facing your son or daughter; to validate your concerns and frustrations; to reinforce your appreciation for your child's left-brain quirks; to help you cope when these quirks are pathologized; to advise you on how best to nurture and advocate for your child; and to empower you to challenge right-brain biases. Throughout the book I will bring to bear not just my own research and personal experiences but the stories and wisdom of over a dozen fellow parents and left-brainers.

You are not alone, and there is much we can do to combat the biases against our children and help them thrive at home, in school, and in life.

1

Adrift in Today's Classroom

The Unsocial Child at School

In the hallway of a well-regarded private school, Angela waits for her five-year-old daughter, Monica, who is being interviewed for admission.

"I'm so sorry" are the first words out of Ms. Morris's mouth, as she and Monica emerge from her office. Monica smiles and sidles up to her mother, but Angela barely notices her daughter's bright smile.

"I'm so sorry," repeats Ms. Morris as she slowly shakes her head. Angela looks hard into her eyes, straining for clues. For months she will remember how the rims of those eyes gleamed with wetness. "I tried. I really did."

What could have so distressed this veteran of kindergarten admissions, who has interviewed hundreds of children for dozens of years? "Ms. Morris can get even the shyest child to talk to her," the admissions director had assured her. "She has ways." What could have so nonplussed Ms. Morris that she stands here, the crisp, self-assured, professional demeanor with which she first greeted them now melted away, apologizing for her failure — if that's what it is — to interview this five-year-old girl?

Gradually the picture unfolds. "I couldn't get her to say a word to me . . . I tried gentle inducement, I tried being firm . . . Every time I asked her to do anything, she'd turn her back on me . . . I've never met a child like Monica."

"We are a very social, verbal school," says the director of admissions when she calls with the official decision.

Verbal? "If you could read Monica's stories," Angela thinks to herself. "If you'd had any interest in seeing actual examples of what Monica can do when left to her own devices." Page upon page of elaborate writing: meticulous letters and punctuation, creative spellings, elaborate plots, intricate illustrations. But, so far as a "social, verbal" school is concerned, none of this verbal output counts if it happens only at home or in writing.

Sadly, Angela knows of no schools, public or private, that don't demand sociability from kids; she'd applied to this private school because she thought its smaller classes might take the edge off. Ever since becoming a mother, she'd look back on her own past as an unsocial child in an impersonal public school system—adrift and disengaged—and swear that she would somehow avoid inflicting all this on her unsocial daughter. But how?

———

"Benjamin, Caleb, and Oscar," Ms. Grant said as she walked around the classroom assigning the day's math groups.

"I'd rather work alone," muttered nine-year-old Benjamin.

When she hears about this later, Carrie, Benjamin's mother, can see it all: Benjamin's dark eyes glancing away, his mouth twisted in a half-sheepish grimace. Benjamin would always rather work alone, especially when it comes to math problems.

"Come on, Benjamin," Ms. Grant said.

Benjamin sighed and sat down with Caleb and Oscar. He looked at the math problem on the table and, he later tells his mother, was filled with an almost irresistible urge to complete it himself.

"Remember, everyone, you're supposed to work cooperatively and encourage one another."

Oscar described a strategy. Benjamin described a different one. They argued. Benjamin knew that his was better. Caleb said he didn't understand what they were talking about. Oscar tried to explain it. Caleb still didn't get it.

As Benjamin recounts this, Carrie starts bracing herself.

Benjamin decided to complete the problem on his own. Just as he started writing down the answer, Ms. Grant walked over and asked what he was doing.

"I'm doing the problem."

"You're supposed to be working with your group."

"I know, but until . . ." He closed his mouth and waited till Ms. Grant moved on.

Oscar was still trying to explain his strategy to Caleb. Benjamin said that he had the answer. Caleb asked him to explain it. Benjamin began, and Caleb stopped him with a question. Benjamin answered the question. Caleb asked another question. Benjamin answered that question. Caleb repeated the first question. Benjamin started to answer it. Caleb interrupted him with another question. Benjamin got up from his seat and shouted out the words he could suppress no longer.

"You idiot!"

Carrie first hears about this scene several hours later when Ms. Grant calls her at home. It's not the first time she's heard about Benjamin's weak social skills and negativity. The phone calls, the teacher's notes, and the quarterly report cards, all relentlessly drive home the same messages:

"Benjamin has a negative attitude about working with other children."

"He rarely shares, or even makes eye contact, during class discussions."

"He spends all of Circle Time staring at his watch."

"Our students do most of their class work with partners or in groups, and Benjamin is refusing to cooperate."

"Working with others is just as important as knowing your multiplication facts."

"Benjamin is significantly delayed in his social skills, and has made little social progress all year."

Carrie, a Spanish professor who shares Benjamin's strong preference for solo work as well as his impatience at explaining things to weak students, understands her son's frustration. But the school's persistent complaints are starting to make her feel like something is deviant, even pathological, about Benjamin. "Is he really the only child this frustrated with the many mandatory group activities?"

"Yes, he is," insists Ms. Grant. And so with each complaint Carrie's worries grow stronger. She starts entertaining every parent's worst nightmare. What if Benjamin is some sort of sociopath? Might this be how the world's Ted Kaczynskis and Dylan Klebolds start out in elementary school? How would she know? And what can she possibly do about *it? It's one thing to talk a child through his multiplication facts, quite another to talk him into being more friendly, patient, and positive.*

Especially since he's friendly, patient, and positive most of the time he's with her. At home Benjamin makes eye contact, shows affection, and talks about his frustrations at school. He spends most of his time devouring science fiction and fantasy books (several per day), rough-housing with his brother, and inventing and enacting intergalactic adventures with his few close friends. Who knows — maybe if her own teachers had insisted on so much group work and sociability, she'd have been as frustrated at school as Benjamin is.

———

A ninth-grade English class discusses The Lord of the Flies. *The conversation crisscrosses the circle in rapid exchanges: "A conch shell symbolizes unity." "No: tyranny." "No: civilization!"*

Janet just sits, confused and shy. Too many people, too many ideas all at once, a conversation that changes course abruptly whenever she starts to follow it. Sometimes she thinks she has something to say, but she's not sure. Does she have the right idea? Is this the right moment? And then it's too late — someone has beaten her to it, or everyone else has changed topic. She has to participate, somehow, if she's going to do well: as Mr. Thompson keeps reminding her, a quarter of her grade is class participation.

She catches him watching her again, and she knows he's increasingly dismayed. "How can you have so much to say in the papers you write," he's asked her time and again after class, "and have nothing to say in class?"

Revisiting all the ways she's disappointed him, she loses track of the discussion. She has no idea what's going on. And next thing she knows, this teacher, who had made a point of never calling on anyone — it was up to each student to decide when to participate, he'd insisted from the beginning — is saying "Janet, what do you think of what Erica just said?"

Silence fills the room. All eyes turn to her. She starts to panic. How on earth does she get out of this? The more ashamed she feels, the redder she turns; the redder she turns, the more ashamed she feels. All she can manage is a quiet mumble—"I don't know"—and hope that he, that everyone, will just leave her alone.

———

In this chapter we'll begin exploring the first of our three types of left-brain children: the unsocial child. This child has particular difficulty interacting with peers, adjusting to new people and situations, and working collaboratively, and tends to be withdrawn in public. In discussing the characteristics and needs of each type of left-brain child, we'll begin by looking at their experiences at school, because it's here where our kids are first measured against other kids and begin to stand out as different, and it's here where the first alarm bells are sounded about our left-brain child's emotional and cognitive health and development.

At school, as we'll see in this chapter, our unsocial children face new classroom practices, grading standards, and social expectations that particularly ill suit, marginalize, and pathologize them. As a result, they tend to dislike school more than we did, receive lower grades, often inspire calls for psychological evaluation, and generally face worse prospects for admission to competitive high schools and colleges.

"WHY DOES MY INQUISITIVE CHILD DISLIKE SCHOOL?"

Why is she so anxious whenever we head off to school? Why is he so sullen whenever I pick him up?

Until we visit a classroom, most of us know little about the recent changes in educational practices that might be disturbing our children: the shift toward student-centered class discussions, the growing pressure to participate in them, the rising calls to share personal feelings in writing as well as in discussions, and the increasing time that students spend working in groups.

Walk into any classroom, and you'll see the first signs. The seating arrangement that was once specific to kindergarten now persists throughout elementary school: desks pushed together in clusters with children facing their classmates rather than their teacher. A large open area in one corner often hosts "Circle Time," also called "Carpet

Time," when everyone sits on the floor together. Contrary to what we still see in movies and sitcoms, circular seating predominates in more and more high school courses as well, particularly social studies, English, and foreign language.

Stick around, and you'll see further symptoms of change. In elementary school, the typical protocol for all subjects is a "mini-lesson," followed by an informal class discussion, and then a small-group activity in which students read together, work on problems, give each other feedback, or play educational games. Time permitting, the class reconvenes for a collective summing-up. Informal class discussions and group activities similarly predominate in more and more middle and high school English, social studies, and foreign language classes.

Classroom discussions, of course, have been around for generations, but two things have changed that particularly shortchange left-brain children. First, there's the growing amount of time they consume at the expense of less socially fraught practices such as lectures and blackboard demonstrations. The "mini-lessons" that stand in for lessons are, at most, ten-minute affairs in which the teacher mostly asks questions rather than explicitly teaching new material and then quickly transitions to the much lengthier class discussion.

Second, there's the altered nature of the discussion itself. Back in our day, what predominated, particularly in elementary school, was a sort of "call and response" between teacher and students, with the teacher (as the "sage on the stage") asking a question, a student providing an answer, the teacher asking a follow-up question, and so on. Here it was natural for children to sit in rows facing their teacher, for though the discussion encompassed the entire classroom, it consisted of a series of two-way exchanges between teacher and individual students. Now, with students in circles, we have the teacher as the "guide on the side," encouraging them to respond directly to one another, and taking a seat as an equal, or even a backseat, once the discussion gets rolling. This, indeed, is the pedagogical ideal that today's student teachers learn to strive for.

It's an approach to teaching that prevails even in math class, because, as we'll see later, the new math pedagogy stresses multiple solutions and communicating about math. Math teachers are supposed to have numerous students share different strategies and comment on those of others and, in order to avoid favoring one method over another, are supposed to retreat once students begin talking directly to one another.

How does this teaching style affect our children? Shy children, of course, have always fretted about speaking up in front of groups. But now, instead of being called on by the teacher to respond to a question that has a specific answer and then receiving the teacher's feedback, today's student may be asked a more open-ended question about something said by one of his classmates—*Aidan, what do you think of Taylor's idea?*—and then, after making his reply, is expected to field reactions from other children.

This puts the shy student—who is characteristically much more at ease with adults—in the unnerving position of having to converse, on the spot and in front of the class, with one of his peers. Unlike in the call-and-response model, in which only the teacher replies to his answer, he's now exposing his ideas to the entire class. For many of us, challenges and corrections are more humiliating when they come from our peers rather than from teachers or other purported experts. For a shy person, being challenged or corrected by peers while the rest of the class is watching can be downright mortifying.

Even if Aidan isn't shy but merely socially aloof or awkward, asking him to judge Taylor's idea poses a range of problems. Once he is evaluating a classmate's answer rather than simply answering a teacher's question, Aidan needs to respond not just accurately, but diplomatically. Left-brain children are notoriously direct in their assertions; diplomatic criticism requires a level of social sophistication that many of them lag behind in attaining. Should Aidan think that Taylor's idea is completely unreasonable, two parties may end up hurt: Taylor, after Aidan speaks his mind, and Aidan, after he is taken to task for doing so.

Once the teacher takes her backseat, she expects students to continue the discussion without being called on. But this distresses our unsocial children even further. Sociolinguistically speaking, there is a huge difference between being asked to speak and speaking voluntarily. When the teacher calls on you, everyone knows that it wasn't your choice to say anything, and that in replying you aren't presuming your contribution to be correct or interesting. You are simply doing your best to answer your teacher.

When, on the other hand, you voluntarily jump into an informal discussion, you inevitably communicate to the rest of the participants, as they stop talking and collectively turn toward you, that you believe that you have something to say that is both worthwhile and relevant. This presumption—only implicit, but forceful nonetheless—makes you much more accountable for your words than you are when called on, and much more vulnerable to your classmates' reactions.

While most social children may be comfortable with large groups and adept at participating in them—the more so as they continue practicing this both inside and outside of school—shy and socially awkward children, who tend to avoid large groups whenever possible, have much more difficulty jumping in at appropriate moments, saying the right thing, and not feeling highly nervous while doing so. By the time they're old enough to appreciate how much their grades depend on this, the pressure can be downright unbearable.

Further challenging our children are the oral presentations that now are assigned as early as third or fourth grade. While most unsocial students prefer presenting prepared material to participating in class spontaneously, many are still far too shy at the ages of nine or ten to stand up in front of their classmates.

Yet another educational priority adds pressure to written work as well as to oral participation—namely, the personal connection. In class after class, and assignment after assignment, students are expected to share personal information and feelings (in what are sometimes called "reflections"), or interview others about theirs. In language arts classes, teachers may specifically require them not to invent stories but to write about things that actually happened to them. Because many classes use a "writing workshop" model, in which students read and comment on one another's work, they end up sharing personal details not only in writing but orally as well.

As for reading, a popular new teaching method called "text-to-self" has students relating what they read, orally and in their "reading-response journals," to their personal lives. The first years of social studies commonly center on friends (what if our child has none?), family (about which he may feel too private to comfortably share much), and community (sometimes through interviews he may be too shy to conduct).

Secondary-school English and social studies discussions, as well, increasingly have students expressing personal connections, opinions, and feelings, while French and Spanish classes have them pairing up to talk—in French or Spanish—about their home and social lives. Most personal of all is health class, with whole units on peer pressure and romantic relationships.

Thanks to the widespread conviction among educators that the best way to interest students in new material is through connections "to self," even math and science classes turn personal. A geology unit at one elementary school begins with students selecting a favorite rock and writing about why they like it. The first assignment in a popular new middle school math book asks students to pick out a favorite number and write notes about it throughout the first unit (e.g., "a multiple of five," or "not divisible by three"); the final assignment in another has them selecting a favorite work sample from their math portfolios and writing about why they're proud of it. Other math assignments ask students to gather data by surveying members of their family or community. The belief, popular with education specialists, that communicating about math is essential to learning it has some teachers requiring students to log in "math journals" their problem-solving strategies and "reflections" about mathematics.

All this especially unsettles the more introverted of our children. But some schools go farther, placing so much value on social interaction, emotional development, and the sharing of personal feelings that they spend taxpayer dollars on one of the many social and emotional curriculum packages now on offer, which Daniel Goleman's best-selling *Emotional Intelligence* has helped to popularize. These include the Social Competence Program, the Child Development Project, PATHS (Promoting Alternative THinking Strategies), and Lions Quest. The latter features activities like "What Bugs You," whose purpose is "to help students learn to give helpful feedback when others are annoying them." Students are asked to name specific annoying behaviors and then to pair up and role-play the behavior along with constructive responses to it. The teacher then reads various situations aloud, invites volunteers to stand up and demonstrate a response, and asks others to explain how constructive they thought the response was. Imagine how Janet or Benjamin would fare as participants.

Further unsettling our children are all the group activities that dominate today's classrooms. During the mini-lessons, teachers often ask students to pair up and discuss particular questions before sharing answers with the rest of the class; after the mini-lessons, students spend the bulk of their time in groups ranging from two to five classmates. Sometimes these groups are assigned by teachers; at other times students must form them themselves. Both contingencies can distress our child, who faces either the embarrassment of finding a partner or group who will accept him, or the unpleasantness of being grouped with some of the many students who don't especially like him. Then there's the actual activity, which, whether it involves reading together, giving feedback, working on problems, or playing games, confronts her with social dynamics that may confuse and overwhelm her. Inevitably, her vulnerabilities emerge, setting her up to be teased or ostracized—whenever the teacher is out of earshot. As we will see in the next chapter, certain types of group activities do help the unsocial child flourish, but they do not include those that currently prevail in our schools.

Unsocial children, of course, have always been teased, shunned, and otherwise victimized by classmates for their aloofness and awkwardness, and school yards are notorious arenas for such bullying. But in recent years, as David Anderegg observes in *Nerds*, this has worsened significantly. And now, with more and more classroom activities occurring within peer groups that no teacher can monitor either continuously or comprehensively, our unsocial children are increasingly harassed in their classrooms as well. In one room a visiting mother observed a whole group, unnoticed by the teacher, ganging up on one of its members: "You're a liar, Jimmy"; "Yeah, Jimmy, you're the biggest liar there is." At some point between the time when we left school and the time when our children arrived there, the proverbial school yard has been let through the front door and into the classroom.

Today's classrooms can sometimes foster more ill will toward unsocial children than school yards do. At least outside of class, loners may go their own way. In class, in a group where they are forced to cooperate, anything they say—as soon as the teacher moves on—may incur mockery, even if technically correct. Thus, an awkward honors student, attempting to explain via ruler and ratios how out of proportion her group mates' drawings are, manages to alienate them for the rest of the school year. Gone is any solitary refuge for the child who knows the right answer but lacks the patience and charisma to win over her peers.

The school yard intrudes even on teacher-supervised, whole-class discussions. Where the earlier "call and response" model kept teachers in continuous control, the modern ideal, where they sit back and let students take over, is easily hijacked by the boldest, most popular, charismatic kids, whose views then triumph over all others. The school yard's social hierarchy, thus reenacted in the classroom, stifles the quiet, insecure, or dissident voices. Making matters worse is how today's informal discussions favor multiple solutions, personal opinions, and personal connections over single correct answers. In previous generations the best answer, exerting an absolute veto power, favored the studious over the merely charismatic; now that there is no best answer, extroversion is king.

To fully appreciate the degree to which today's classrooms challenge our children, we should consider how they might have fared in more traditional schools. Imagine how much more at ease they might be in general, and how their attitudes toward school might improve, if they enjoyed the privacy of quietly listening to teachers lecture instead of having to talk to classmates. Imagine if they could keep most of their thoughts and feelings to themselves. Imagine if they could write fictional stories far removed from their personal lives that only their teachers would see. Imagine if they could read to themselves instead of to a group, do math problems on their own, and find, in the classroom, a safe haven from school yard dynamics. Even in the dullest, most tedious of traditional classrooms, the unsocial child had the privacy of her mind in which to daydream, and her notebook in which to doodle.

Most children emerge from today's educational practices fairly unscathed. Most, after all, are sociable early on, and widespread enrollment in day care and extended-day preschool exorcises the shyness and unsociability from many mildly shy introverts before they start kindergarten. But then there are our children: the ones who are more deeply, stubbornly shy and unsocial, and who remain so throughout their school years. When schools expect them to spend most of their time working cooperatively, talking to classmates, and baring their thoughts, feelings, and personal lives, they expose them to huge social pressure. Forcing them out of the privacy of their own minds into peer-dominated arenas in which they feel too confused or intimidated to participate not only makes classrooms stressful and unpleasant but also impedes rather than facilitates their learning—whether they are shy students like Janet, who suffer in silence, or aloof ones like Benjamin, who act out in frustration and refuse to cooperate.

"WHY IS MY INTELLIGENT CHILD GETTING LOW GRADES?"

Many of us parents of unsocial children are taken aback by their first report cards. It's only elementary school, our child seems bright, her schoolwork solid; where are these mediocre grades coming from? Inevitably we compare them to those we once earned back when we were little, before all that grade inflation we keep hearing about.

Most of us, a generation ago, were graded primarily on our solo, written work. But a recent sea change is ending what's now called "summative assessment," or assessments based on final products, such as papers and tests. The new convention is "formative assessment," based more on students' learning processes, as perceived by their teachers, rather than on their ultimate achievement. Formative assessments include effort, attitude, and performance in classroom activities.

Factor in all those new pedagogical priorities we've just explored that so discomfit unsocial children—group work, class participation, sharing feelings—and you have a recipe for low grades. Whether they simply don't like working in groups, participating diplomatically in class discussions, and sharing their feelings, or also find it difficult to do so, their performance often falls shy of teacher expectations.

Many report cards have specific ratings for class participation, "socially appropriate behavior," and "cooperating well with others"—all of them inherently punishing of the socially inept. But more insidious than this is the way that teachers factor all these considerations into the grades they assign for specific subjects.

Reading

Back when we were in school, teachers based reading assessments on decoding words and reading with fluency. Sometimes this would trip up the shyer students, who might be nervous enough about being assessed to stumble over the words. But today's teachers assess fluency not just by how quickly, smoothly, and accurately the student reads things aloud but also by whether she does so with expression. Reading with feeling doesn't come naturally to the more reserved introverts, and can be downright painful to the shy. With their flat, muted, mumbled delivery, they may fail to convince their teachers that they comprehend what they're pronouncing.

And perhaps sometimes they don't. Some students may be too nervous during these oral assessments to pay close attention to content. Whether or not they attend to what they're reading, they may feel too shy to give sufficient oral answers to the follow-up comprehension questions that today's teachers ask to further probe reading skills. Most intimidating of all are the new "text-to-self" questions discussed above, which ask students to link what they read to their personal lives—at which even the braver of our unsocial children may balk.

Also included in today's formative assessments are reading-response journals, in which students are supposed to make additional personal connections. The frequent resistance of unsocial children to questions like "How did it make you feel when . . . ?" lowers their reading grades even further.

Writing

Many quiet introverts channel their thoughts into writing. Even before they enter grade school, they may already be churning out long, imaginative works of prose. It's particularly surprising, then, when they start taking home mediocre grades in writing.

A generation ago, writing assessments were based primarily on spelling and punctuation. Today's teachers have been tasked with looking beyond this for "fully elaborated" details and descriptive words that "paint pictures in readers' heads."

It's one thing to produce colorful prose in your own private journals and stories. But hamming it up for an audience is another matter—particularly if it's to be read aloud and discussed with classmates, as the writing-workshop format of today's classrooms entails. One mother reports praising her seven-year-old for striking details in her home stories—"enormous thighs," "cinnamon-colored leaves"—and encouraging her to use such words when writing in the classroom. Her daughter replied that it was too embarrassing to use words like *cinnamon* and *thighs* at school.

Making matters worse, today's obsession with personal connections has our children writing personal narratives instead of the objective nonfiction or fantasy fiction that they often find more comfortable and interesting. For all these reasons, their classroom prose may be as flat and uninspired as their classroom reading.

English and Social Studies

While the trend toward discussion-based English and social studies classes began when many of us were still in high school, today's formative assessments of classroom performance have elevated oral participation to an ever higher percentage of students' grades. This percentage now typically lies somewhere between 10 and 25—enough to make the difference between an A and a B. Meanwhile, the ever more personalized nature of these discussions increasingly intimidates and disengages the shy and unsocial, further lowering their propensity to participate. Similarly intimidating and disengaging are the many written assignments that solicit more personal reflection than objective analysis.

Our introverted wordsmiths and history buffs are thus routinely marked down for failing to speak up or make personal connections. Even if she has enough insights and analyses to fill a long paper, they may go largely unnoticed. The more so, as we will see in chapter 3, as it's increasingly unlikely that an in-depth, analytical paper will even be assigned.

Math

One of the new grading priorities—and a litmus test for mathematical comprehension—is having students explain their answers. While shy students may be comfortable doing this in writing, teachers, especially during discussions, may solicit oral explanations as well. Here, even if a shy student has the right answer, she may be too nervous to convince her teacher that she understands how she got it.

As we saw, the personal connection that bedevils unsocial children in reading and writing also creeps into some of their math assignments. Many unsocial children will complete such assignments halfheartedly, if at all, further lowering their grades.

The New Importance of Attitude

Perhaps the most negative influence on our child's grades is the unprecedented attention to attitude—a consequence of formative assessment's focus on in-class activities. Attitude includes things like willingness to cooperate, enthusiasm, initiative, and curiosity. Under current practices, "cooperativeness" largely reflects how well students work in groups. "Enthusiasm" means being engaged by, and comfortable with, the social activities that predominate, contributing frequently to group activities and class discussions, and sharing personal connections. "Initiative" and "curiosity"—described in some report cards as "independently exploring" ideas that extend beyond the expected standards for mastery—means asking questions and requesting permission to explore things further. All of these are at once prerequisites for top grades and areas of weakness for unsocial children, particularly the shyer ones. In general, it's hard to be shy or otherwise unsocial and also display the extroverted, eager-beaver, go-out-and-get-'em attitude required to avoid being downgraded.

In particular, never before has pleasing the teacher been so important. But it takes social savvy to accomplish this. Here the most charismatic kids and the budding social manipulators leave our children far behind in the dust.

Strong academic skills can trump some of this to some degree. But two additional trends we will address in chapter 3—the watering down of academic subjects and a grading practice known in some circles as "grade compression" (akin to grade deflation)—has made it all the more difficult to do so. Furthermore, with fewer opportunities to distinguish themselves on paper, the quieter, more withdrawn of our unsocial children may look less academically able than they really are. Their frequent blank stares and expressionless faces may give the impression that their public passivity reflects an inner one: a deep deficit of ideas, creativity, and curiosity, all of which today's top grades now require.

A generation ago, a socially aloof child might never say a word in class and still earn academic distinction through high test scores and well-written papers. No matter how much his teacher disliked him, she still, however grudgingly, had to give him grades that matched the quality of those end results. Now all that has changed. Collectively, our child's in-class cooperation, participation, enthusiasm, gregariousness, initiative, and public inquisitiveness wield a far greater influence over his grades than does his academic achievement.

"WHY IS EVERYONE TELLING ME THERE'S SOMETHING WRONG WITH MY CHILD?"

Many left-brain children, early on in their school careers, are suspected of having emotional or cognitive problems. Not all of our kids arouse concern in teachers and other school staff. Those who are quietly shy may not raise any red flags, even at school. However rarely they speak up, they still are nominally compliant, obediently getting into groups and not disrupting their classes.

But with today's emphasis on social and emotional development, not all quiet, rule-abiding students escape suspicion. One mother reports getting constant feedback about how withdrawn her kindergartener was at school. He never disrupted class or demonstrated any problems learning, but the lower-school learning specialist singled him out early on for his aloofness and kept a close eye on him throughout the day. She was especially concerned about his behavior during recess, which, she kept reporting, he'd spend alone, running around the edge of the school yard pretending to be a train. Her concerns soon spread to his parents, who found themselves being called into school for meetings with her and the teacher.

The less compliant, more outspoken of our children, of course, upset the professionals even more. Remember Benjamin, whom we saw earlier in the chapter staring at his watch during Circle Time, calling his group mate an idiot, and prompting his teacher to phone his mother repeatedly.

Then there's Max, a smart ten-year-old with a special interest in science fiction and zoology, who first sounded alarm bells in kindergarten. Refusing to sit through Circle Time, he'd retreat to the book corner. "I want to read instead," he'd call out. His teacher, true to her pedagogical training, kept making him return to the group. Sitting there thoroughly disengaged, he'd grow increasingly disruptive — talking, making funny noises, picking his nose — ever more frequently as the year wore on. Desperate to escape the classroom, he'd repeatedly ask to go to the bathroom. Twice when his teacher refused him, he turned violent and hit her. Infractions like these had the principal suspending him for the rest of the school day, phoning his mother at work to tell her to take him home, and asking the school psychologist to evaluate him.

Even before our children start school, some of us parents have had to field constant concerns from aunts, uncles, and grandparents — particularly if they've bought into the high social expectations of today's teachers, developmental psychologists, and society at large, or are themselves highly social. But typically, as with Max, the real trouble starts in kindergarten — and continues, for years, to center largely on school. In the fall of our child's sixth year of life, we suddenly find ourselves bombarded with notes and phone calls from teachers, principals, and school psychologists. Following these are more official behavior slips, with their litanies of antisocial conduct, complete with consequences (time out in the principal's office; loss of recess or field-trip privileges) and calls for parent-school conferences.

Making their criticisms more painful yet, some teachers cast them in moral terms. So indoctrinated are they in the new standards for normality that they assume that all children can meet their social expectations, and that those who don't aren't socially behind or impeded but rather deliberately "inconsiderate" and "unkind." It's painful enough to hear that there's something morally wrong with our child, but such remarks inevitably carry an additional implication: that there's something correspondingly wrong with our parenting. Good parents, surely, know how to raise good children. Equally upsetting, as we try to convince teachers that we're doing our best yet things fail to improve, is the suggestion that comes next: No, we aren't at fault after all; instead there's a deeper problem with our child—some sort of psychiatric or neurological aberration. Accompanying this notion is a growing chorus of calls that our child undergo neuropsychiatric evaluation.

Much of it hails from our schools' psychological support staff. Particular to the Anglo-American educational establishment, and intimately connected with its social priorities, these professionals have been accumulating since the middle of the last century. In 1958, America's school counselors totaled twelve thousand, and school psychologists were rare; our public schools now house over ninety thousand counselors and thirty-five thousand psychologists. Because of the overall social expectations of the schools they serve, and because their professional reputations depend on how many abnormal children they identify and on how early they intervene with them, these people have been imposing ever stricter standards for psychiatric health and normality, and scrutinizing ever more closely those who deviate.

Aiding and abetting them is the official handbook of psychiatry, the *Diagnostic and Statistical Manual of Mental Disorders*, or *DSM*, which has been expanding and loosening up its diagnostic criteria for the various social illnesses. Roughly speaking, these come in two flavors: the shy/introverted, which the *DSM* calls "social anxiety disorders," and the aloof/asocial, which the *DSM* calls "autistic spectrum disorders." The first change occurred during the 1980s when, as Christopher Lane discusses in his 2007 book, *Shyness: How Normal Behavior Became a Sickness*, the *DSM* broadened the definition of social anxiety disorder to include a wider spectrum of shyness and introversion. Then, in 1994, it added Asperger's syndrome—a relatively mild but still, by today's standards, infamously debilitating subtype of autism—to its list of autistic spectrum disorders. Criteria for Asperger's are based largely on "impairments" in things like eye contact, body language, "appropriate" peer relationships, and "social functioning"—all of them fuzzy and open to interpretation.

Advances in pharmaceuticals complete the cycle. While there's no accepted chemical treatment for Asperger's syndrome, the world of psychiatry is teeming with treatments for social anxiety disorders. These, in turn, raise social expectations even further. As a result, Lane argues, there has been "a growing consensus that traits once attributed to mavericks, skeptics, or mere introverts are psychiatric disorders that drugs should eliminate," and "psychiatrists are now licensed to regard as ill those manifesting even vaguely ungregarious behavior." So, in effect, are school psychologists.

The upshot of all of this is that more and more unsocial children, often as young as five or six, are identified as socially aberrant and diagnosed with a disorder. Yes, we learn, there is something deeply wrong with our child—a social anxiety that requires daily medication or, worse, an autistic spectrum disorder like Asperger's. The latter, to his mother's despair, was the professional verdict on Max. However skeptical we are, we all have our worst fears, and the medical/psychological evaluation of our child's unsociability too often ends up confirming them.

"WHAT ARE MY CHILD'S PROSPECTS FOR COMPETITIVE HIGH SCHOOLS AND COLLEGES?"

The changing times make it more difficult for our children to get into competitive high schools and colleges than it was for us, even if we were just as unsocial. The applicant pool has swelled in recent years due to the cumulative effects of the "baby boomlet" (the children of baby boomers, the largest generation of young people since the 1960s), growing numbers of overseas students applying to American schools, and increasing American preference for selective schools over local ones. Top grades are more important than ever, and yet, as we've discussed, it's become harder for unsocial children, in particular, to earn them. Most private schools and colleges, meanwhile, haven't yet caught on to the new public school grading practices—and the connection between good grades and sociability—and may assume that grades from American public schools are as good an indicator of academic strength as they ever were.

Many competitive high schools and colleges, furthermore, are just as biased as local public schools against unsocial students. In the course of their selective admissions, they can prescreen for markers of sociability, for example, through their often mandatory interviews. A great way to pick up on a child's shyness or social awkwardness, after all, is to put her in a room with a stranger. Even the bolder, more talkative of our children may falter: eager to impress the interviewer, but lacking the social grace to soften his boasting, he may steamroll her with his accomplishments and intellect, lecture her, or zealously correct any mistakes she makes. As one parent remarks, "If Will reports that the interview went well, then it probably didn't go well at all."

When it comes to selective colleges, a single aspect of sociability has become almost as important as grades—namely, leadership qualities. As Malcolm Gladwell discusses in his 2005 *New Yorker* article "Getting In: The Social Logic of Ivy League Admissions," America's top colleges increasingly favor "best graduates"—those they predict will have the most impressive careers—over "best students"—those likely to perform best academically. Naturally, the careers that most impress people—in particular, wealthy donors and future applicants—are those involving leadership. This has colleges increasingly seeking students with proven charisma and leadership skills.

While poor leaders—those lacking in charisma—are easily spotted in interviews, it's extracurricular activities that positively identify good ones. Student council president, debate team captain, director of the school play, editor-in-chief of the school newspaper—these are the pursuits that most impress college admissions committees, and that unsocial children are least likely to engage in. Paling in comparison are music lessons, Web design, and engineering camp.

Mediocre grades, awkward interviews, and a dearth of leadership activities, unfortunately, too often trump markers of intellect such as high SAT scores and extracurricular intellectual accomplishments, erecting barriers to the kinds of schools that once might have welcomed our children. But these barriers aren't insurmountable and, later in this chapter, we will discuss various ways to help our children scale them.

LISBETH'S STORY

Lisbeth is a kind-faced athlete with blue eyes and strawberry blond hair. At nineteen years, she is old enough to have experienced both traditional and modern classrooms, and to explain why she prefers the former. Her account of her school days is therefore particularly illuminating.

In formal settings such as interviews, and with adults she knows well, Lisbeth speaks in measured, articulate paragraphs. You'd never guess, from her social grace and friendly demeanor, how shy and anxious she feels in most social settings, particularly those with peers. When she's among sympathetic adults, the only hint is the quiet of her voice. "I was the only one who never spoke inside or outside of my class," she says with a smile. "That's just who I am, my role: I'm the one who never talks, but who's really smart and plays lacrosse."

Not that Lisbeth is completely withdrawn. She appreciates people passively, observing them and guessing their thoughts. But she's always found it difficult to strike up a dialogue, and harder yet to join group conversations. As with many unsocial people, the larger the group, the more anxious she feels, and the more difficult it is for her to keep up with the banter, let alone join it; a whole classroom full of peers is as stressful as it gets. On top of this, she worries constantly about what people will think of what she says. Even if they react nicely, perhaps they are only pretending. So at school, while the other children would gather and chat, she'd be off in the corner doing algebra in her head.

Lisbeth attended public schools in an upper middle class suburb of York, Pennsylvania, and joined the top high school track that leads to colleges such as Haverford and Georgetown. In some ways the social scene couldn't have been more hospitable to a shy, studious girl such as herself. She'd known half of her classmates since grade school, and describes them, without exception, as unusually friendly and accepting. Her cohort was so academic that even the most studious were at least "somewhat cool," and parties were rare until the end of senior year. So even though Lisbeth stood out as the least social kid, her classmates never stigmatized her.

Lisbeth's anxiety at school stemmed instead from the dynamics of specific classrooms. Her favorite subjects were math and chemistry, where teachers continued to lead lessons to which they didn't expect students to volunteer ideas, and students (except during chemistry lab) continued to face the blackboard at school and work independently at home. In general, indeed, high school math and science appear to be the last holdouts for traditional, teacher-centered instruction. Only after she graduated did the new math methods start advancing toward Lisbeth's high school. Her humanities classes were another story. By the time she reached eleventh grade, both social studies and English amounted mostly to class discussions and group assignments—skits in French; mock trials and Kabuki theater pieces in social studies; four-day literature presentations in English.

From the moment a teacher called for groups, Lisbeth would feel the pressure, as her classmates jockeyed to be with friends or cool kids. "Well, I already said yes to her," Lisbeth would often be told. Eventually she'd find a group that would accept her. But however nice her group mates—even if working with them "wasn't horrible"—she still wished she could work alone.

The most awkward part about groups, of course, was the cooperative activity, especially when it unfolded as homework. Spanning many open-ended hours at students' homes, unsupervised by adults, it would easily devolve into free-form socializing, constituting what Lisbeth describes as some of her worst experiences in high school. "The other kids all liked it because they were all friends," she remarks. "But I would have preferred it if we could have split up all the work and I could have done my part by myself." Because no one else shared her preference, any divvying up would wait until the meeting's end, with the first two and a half hours, Lisbeth estimates, comprising little more than chitchat. And so she would sit, in quiet boredom and discomfort, amid three or four classmates who bantered back and forth as if she weren't there. Because she spoke up so rarely, it was easy and natural for them, without malice, to simply ignore her.

Since most of the projects included presentations or performances, students would strive to be funny and creative. This had them competing as much over their entertainment skills as over their academic insights. While they brainstormed ways to amuse their classmates, Lisbeth, for whom such humor didn't come naturally, would feel all the more uncomfortable saying anything.

If only, she'd wish, she could have brainstormed her ideas in the privacy of her mind, instead of among classmates in someone else's living room. If only she could have elaborated and defended her views in written essays seen only by her teacher, instead of orally in front of peers who seemed to prize entertainment and charisma over argumentation. And if only she could have attended lectures instead of class discussions where, once again, she'd sit on the sidelines while everyone else participated, feeling too shy to expose her thoughts orally and extemporaneously—the more so here, where the audience was now the entire class.

Class discussions, aggravating things, would focus primarily on students' personal opinions on broad political and philosophical issues. In both English and social studies, questions like "What do you believe?" and "What do you think about the world?" were, in Lisbeth's words, "what it almost always came down to." And yet, for all this vague open-endedness, there was always the intimidating possibility of being dismissed, challenged, or otherwise overridden by peers. Indeed, the more open-ended the conversation, the more readily the school yard dynamics crept in. Both class discussions and group activities, Lisbeth reports, exactly mirrored the social hierarchy outside of class, with those who were most confident and charismatic in purely social situations also doing most of the talking, leading, and winning of arguments in class and during group work.

More challenging still was when participation in these discussions wasn't merely expected, as it was in social studies, but actually required, as in English. The English teacher told students that 15 to 20 percent of their grades would be based on it, and she made sure they didn't forget this. Sitting in the circle along with them while they talked, Lisbeth recalls, "she would write down how much we spoke. . . . You were graded purely on how much you said. And that was very, very stressful." Indeed, senior-year English, the last class in her daily schedule, was one, Lisbeth says, "where I was concerned that I could actually fail." She spent much of the school day dreading those final fifty minutes, and would sometimes return home almost in tears.

In reaction to Lisbeth's reticence, the teacher sometimes called on her. Because the question was usually an open-ended one, with no obvious correct answer, Lisbeth found it far more intimidating than a straightforward math or science question would have been. "I don't know," she'd typically reply, only to hear back, "Come on, you have to have an opinion on this." It wasn't that Lisbeth didn't have plenty to say; indeed, she would often come home bursting with ideas to share with her mother. But facing her teacher, and dreading the pressure to defend her views before classmates, she'd simply repeat, "I don't know, I just don't know." "I remember my face getting really red and just feeling twisted in knots, and if I was having a bad day, I was probably getting close to tears."

But most stressful of all was how the teacher expected students to participate without prompting. For Lisbeth, finding the right thing to add at just the right time to an unstructured, large-group conversation was not only much more intimidating than answering a teacher's question, it was also much more cognitively challenging. "What set me apart from the other kids was that it was very difficult for me to formulate answers off the cuff," particularly when the questions were open-ended and the discussion fast-moving, Lisbeth notes. And because she was so shy about presuming to have something interesting and relevant to say, she'd set the bar impossibly high: finding just the right words, getting "everything right."

Occasionally she'd manage. "I'd think, 'I have an answer, I have an answer' . . . And then it was like, 'I don't want to do this. . . . I'm not going to make myself miserable.'" She explains, "I was scared of the repercussions," scared of how her classmates would react, particularly the more vocal and charismatic. She would focus her fears on the most intimidating one of all, the boy at the very top of the social hierarchy: the class president and valedictorian-to-be, now a sophomore at Harvard. Exposing your opinions to him was "like throwing your-self to the wolves." Thus, though Lisbeth would spend much of English and social studies class trying to follow the discussion so that she "might find that bravery to raise my hand," she never actually did.

Without the pressures for participation, English class in particular would have been "a completely different story." "I wouldn't have participated," Lisbeth adds, "but I would have sat in class relaxed." She wouldn't have worried about her relationship with her teacher, which she felt was severely strained, despite all her diligence and good work, by her failure to comply with classroom expectations. And, most importantly, she would have enjoyed the material. "I know that school isn't always supposed to be enjoyable," she says, "but to hate the class *that much . . .*"

Lisbeth's report cards invariably reflected her failure to speak up. "It was kind of a running joke," she says: throughout elementary school her ratings were uniformly "Excellent," followed by that perennial refrain: "Needs to participate more." Eventually she and her teachers just got used to it; the teachers, appreciating Lisbeth's intelligence and diligence, would make the perfunctory report-card comment but stopped harping on it in person.

In high school, however, class participation resurfaced with a vengeance. Here it was no longer a distinct note on her report card, explicitly detached from her academic ratings, but was invisibly factored into what were now general letter grades. Its effects were most detrimental to Lisbeth's grades for senior-year English, for which it constituted 15 to 20 percent. Suddenly an A student who was still getting As on papers was now getting Bs and B-pluses for the course. Meanwhile confident, charismatic classmates who were no better than she was at analyzing and writing about literature were outdoing her with As, in yet another reenactment of the social hierarchy.

"It was kind of ironic because I actually ended up third in my class," observes Lisbeth. This was thanks mainly to math and science, in which she remained the best student throughout high school. But sitting in the English class, Lisbeth reports, "you never would have known it." Good public performance in this class was considered so strongly indicative of overall intelligence, and of who would end up at

the top, that Lisbeth was actually surprised to learn that she was number three.

And delighted. For she figured that this class rank, along with her
top grades in math and chemistry, and her high SAT scores—720 verbal, 700 math—would ensure her admission to her top choices for
college: Harvard or the University of Pennsylvania. But then came the
college interviews and, once again, the issue of sociability.

The actual interviewing seemed to Lisbeth to go well enough. The
setting—one-on-one with an adult and a well-defined agenda—is the
one with which she feels most at ease. The most awkward questions
were those about extracurricular activities. Not that Lisbeth didn't
have answers. She played on a competitive lacrosse team in the community, her head comfortably hidden under a goalie's helmet. She
designed and maintained various websites, sometimes sitting for "two
days in my room, bug-eyed at the computer," working out intricate
graphics. And she coached eight- to ten-year-olds on a community basketball team. But the interviewers kept asking her what extracurriculars she had done at her school, and seemed to reproach her for
spending so much time on outside ventures. Most salient in Lisbeth's
memory is her exchange with the Harvard alumnus:

"What leadership stuff have you done?"

"Well, nothing."

"What extracurriculars are you involved in at your school?"

"Well, I don't do extracurricular activities at my school."

Her lack of school-based leadership roles, Lisbeth now thinks, is
what clinched it: why she was accepted only to Haverford, while the
class president-cum-valedictorian got into Yale, Harvard, and Prince-
ton. Colleges are notoriously secretive about their admissions procedures, so it's impossible to know how accurate Lisbeth's impressions
are, and how typical her experience was. But it squares with Malcolm
Gladwell's observations in "Getting In." Colleges that want to admit
as many future leaders as possible will choose students who exert leadership over same-aged peers over those who do solitary Web design at
home and coach younger children in basketball.

At Haverford, Lisbeth lasted one semester. She tried putting on
a social face and going to parties, but continued to struggle to strike

up conversations and converse in groups. When the instructor of her mandatory freshman writing seminar announced that he was basing part of the grade on class participation, all the nightmares of senior-year English class returned. Lisbeth went home and is now taking courses part time at a local college while she considers her options: perhaps an engineering school that will value her math skills and not pressure her to participate in class.

However much she has adapted, however, Lisbeth has never managed to actually break out of her mold of unsociability. This, despite all the pressure and academic incentives for participating in class, despite her frequent loneliness in high school, and despite her determined efforts while in college.

HELPING YOUR UNSOCIAL CHILD AT SCHOOL

"We've never seen another child like yours"—however alarming this remark might sound, it's one that is commonly directed at parents of unsocial children by teachers, principals, and admissions personnel. Frequently following it are comments such as these: "She never plays with the other children." "He'd rather do math in the corner of the yard than join the ball game." "She never participates during Circle Time." "He doesn't cooperate in group activities." "Please have your child evaluated."

We who understand our children best, and care about them the most, are in a unique position to help them. But this takes energy and perseverance, requiring us to keep our morale up in spite of the multifaceted criticism that sometimes makes us downright despondent.

The first thing to remember is that neither we nor our children are alone. While our particular school may never have seen a child like ours, its staff is unwittingly repeating, almost verbatim, remarks that many other parents of unsocial left-brainers report hearing all the time from their own schools.

The second thing to remember when we're suddenly hit with all those reports of antisocial behavior at the onset of kindergarten is what's special about this point in our child's school life. Kindergarten, especially in today's test-conscious education world, is the locus of an abrupt transition from the free time of preschool to the required tasks of grade school. And it is, increasingly, a daylong, early-morning to midafternoon affair, rather than the half-day program it was for all previous generations of Americans. Suddenly our children, used to spending much of their school days painting, writing, building, or playing whatever, whenever, and for however long they wanted to, now face an extensive succession of specific activities to engage in, specific tasks to accomplish, and specific time intervals in which to do so. Many, as we saw, involve expectations of group participation that intimidate and frustrate unsocial children—and that we saw students like Benjamin and Max rebelling against in the previous chapter. These expectations, as we've discussed, persist throughout most elementary, middle, and high schools.

The third thing for us to remember, whenever possible, is to feel indignant rather than despondent—especially when schools harp on our child's shyness or inability to work well in groups. Bad study habits or disruptive behavior are one thing, but core personality traits over which child and parents alike have scant control are quite another, and have no place in academic assessments. We should recall that in most other countries, and even in the U.S. as recently as our own school days, remarks about unsociability and failure to work in groups are and were unusual. Earlier and elsewhere, self-motivation and independence were (and are) the ideals, and doing math in the corner was (and is) considered the behavior of a model student. Only here and now do such traits raise the specter of social pathology or autism.

Thus, a left-brain personality is in many ways something to cherish rather than to pathologize. It's just that the right-brain bias makes this difficult. Beyond those negative reports from school, there are all those kids who embody the social ideal against which, as we've seen, we inevitably find ourselves comparing our children. We must repeatedly remind ourselves that a child who looks unresponsive may be just as active inside her head as one who expresses herself overtly and speaks aloud, and that teachers are wrong to presume that the only way she can engage in the classroom is by participating orally and socially.

We must remember, too, the drawbacks of extroversion. More sociability means more exposure to social pressures. A world of right-brainers easily devolves into a world of conformists and social climb-ers—the world lamented by David Riesman, half a century ago, in *The Lonely Crowd*. In a society so obsessed with sociability, and so biased against nerds, Riesman's concerns apply more than ever. For all the diversity among people, he notes, "They lose their social free-dom and their individual autonomy in seeking to become like each other." In ostracizing those who don't conform, they display another loss: of basic human decency. The disproportionately left-brain non-conformists, insulated from social pressure by their introversion, and typically more independent, free-spirited, and accepting of other non-conformists than are their more outgoing counterparts, are therefore vital to relieving social pressures and maintaining diversity.

We see inklings of this vitality in a series of famous experiments ini-tiated by the late psychologist Solomon Asch. Some of Asch's results lead to disturbing conclusions about the power of group pressures: most subjects conformed to a manifestly false statement (e.g., about the relative lengths of different line segments) so long as all others pres-ent appeared to believe it. Other results were more reassuring: for sub-jects to maintain their true beliefs, all it took was one fellow "dissident." Who is most likely to play this crucial role? While Asch's experiments did not explore the personality traits of the nonconformist minority, we might speculate that these include below-average concern about how others will react—a trait shared by many of our children.

Besides diversity of personality and opinion, our socially aloof or unaware child can also help foster the kind of diversity that challenges social stereotypes such as gender. Our girl may pass over pink frills and dance classes for soccer cleats; our boy's best friend may be the girl down the road.

What about all the benefits of sociability we keep hearing about? Claims about these are constantly bedeviling us parents of left-brainers. How can our children succeed if they don't open up more to others? As we saw earlier, so common are statements like "Students understand that the search for excellence is best achieved coopera-tively, rather than by individual effort" that if we react at all, it's by yawning at yet another boring truism in a principal's summer letter to parents. But think again. How much of our cultural excellence has resulted from cooperative rather than individual effort? Consider a sampling of the greatest cultural icons of our civilization: da Vinci, Shakespeare, Mozart, Darwin, Einstein. However sociable they may have been, they did their best work not in groups but on their own. Indeed, we have an expression for the downside of group work: imagine if *Macbeth*, or Beethoven's Fifth, had been written "by committee."

What are we to make, however, of the persistent claims—by educators, by pop psychologists, and by best-selling books like *Emotional Intelligence*—that today's world is different and that, individual geniuses aside, most jobs require social skills? Even mathematicians and scientists, teachers insist, now primarily work in groups. Those of us with ties to mathematicians and scientists know otherwise. There's an important difference, people forget, between cooperation and collaboration. Yes, many modern mathematical and scientific puzzles are large enough that multiple scholars attack them simultaneously. But they do so by divvying up the pieces, working independently, and only reconvening to present and tweak one another's solutions. They *collaborate*, but they mostly work separately, *not cooperatively*. Social skills hardly figure in at all: many of our most productive mathematicians and scientists are as famously socially eccentric and aloof as they ever were.

Other collaborations are similarly dominated by individual work. As one professional coauthor reports, "I've written my last three books as the second author. By definition these books are group projects in the sense of partnered projects. Even as the second author, I spend the vast portion of my time working alone."

We've argued earlier that our right-brain society excessively values social skills for everything from college admission to career promotion. In terms of how people actually spend their time, however, many of today's jobs—especially those our children are most likely to seek out—do not require constant sociability and long hours working directly with others. Social deficits may handicap our child's ability to get the job she wants—and in the next chapter we will discuss how to lessen these deficits—but her aversion to group work will not hamper her job performance nearly as much as the education world would like us to believe.

How about what matters ultimately: is our child content? More social parents may worry less about their parenting skills, and more about their child. How, we might wonder, can she possibly be happy spending so much time alone? But, as many of us unsocial adults will report, some of our happiest, most creative moments of childhood occurred during the time we spent by ourselves.

Emphasizing Learning Styles and Accommodation

Cherishing the virtues of our unsocial child is one thing. Harder is getting the school on board. Given the classroom practices we observed above, how do we convince educators to stop shortchanging our children?

As it turns out, we can exploit two contemporary educational principles—principles, ironically, that rival the schools' right-brain ideals in the degree to which educators tout them. One is the notion that different children have different *learning styles*. A corollary is that classroom activities must *accommodate* the learning style differences of everyone in the room. Thus, we can describe our child's lack of sociability as a "learning style," and ask the teacher or principal about what "accommodations"—it may help to use the jargon—can be made for one who feels insecure, anxious, and stigmatized when pressured to work in groups, share feelings, and participate orally in class discussions.

To this, we can add specific recommendations. One is that whenever the teacher assigns a group task, she give our child the option to work by herself. Another is that our child be allowed to write about something other than his personal life and feelings. As obvious as these suggestions are, however, they may clash with our teacher's most cherished beliefs. Many are convinced that working in groups, practicing social skills, and expressing emotions all prepare students for life. "Aren't these precisely what your unsocial child needs practice with?" our teacher may therefore counter.

And, indeed, aren't they? Because educators care so much about social skills, it's important to stress that we do, too. But, we should point out, gently, working in classroom groups and being asked to share personal feelings have so intimidated and confused our child that he's been withdrawing in annoyance or discomfort. Worse, his group mates have caught on to his weaknesses and are teasing and bullying him. Given all her vulnerabilities, she needs to learn her social skills explicitly and systematically in a safer environment—in ways that we will discuss in the following chapter—run by someone who specializes in helping unsocial children become more sociable.

The second thing to ask for is an alternate way, other than speaking up during classroom discussions, for our child to meet the participation requirement. Most unsocial children are more comfortable making formal presentations that they practice ahead of time and present using notes or scripts. If even this terrifies our child, we can request the option of *written* responses to the class discussion topics. We should add that simply eliminating the spontaneous oral-participation requirement—as Lisbeth's experience shows above—may vastly alter how much our child dreads versus enjoys attending class.

As we saw, another strike against some of our children is when teachers view them as willfully inconsiderate or unkind. To forestall this, we must explain, often repeatedly and at length, that when our child refuses to look her teacher in the eye, or to share with her partner, or to speak loudly enough for her classmates to hear her, or to cooperate in her group, it's not out of a deliberate lack of consideration but because of her shyness, social anxiety, and difficulty grasping group dynamics.

Throughout these discussions, diplomacy is key. We must emphasize, continually, that we aren't criticizing the teacher, but attempting to inform her about unusual hang-ups and learning differences of which she may not be fully aware. The more we can emphasize that our ultimate goal is not to tell her what to do but to help lessen our child's anxiety about school, the more willing most teachers will be to make accommodations—particularly in today's education environment, which places so much emphasis on the psychological well-being of children.

Indeed, most teachers do want to accommodate all students and need simply to be informed about the less obvious problems and their possible solutions. As soon as she became aware of the plight of her shy students, for example, a writing instructor at Bryn Mawr College told them they could e-mail her what they would have said in class had they felt comfortable—an option for which several have enthusiastically thanked her.

If our school isn't accommodating, an independent, psychiatric evaluation may help buttress our cause. This worked for Paula, mother of Alan, the boy who spent recess running around the edge of the playground by himself pretending to be a train. "You really need to get your son evaluated," the school psychologist kept telling her. Finally, she and her husband grew so tired of such remarks that they decided a second opinion might actually be helpful. Fortunately, the psychologist they found spent time getting to know Alan, seemed to take a liking to him, and became as much an advocate as an evaluator. She visited the school, observed Alan at recess, and concluded that he was far too young to be diagnosed with anything. With her doctorate in psychology outranking the school psychologist's MA, she succeeded in persuading those concerned to let Alan be.

Paula's experience suggests some guidelines for selecting psychotherapists. We should attempt to interview the person ahead of time. We should pick someone whose protocol involves spending enough time with our child, preferably alone, to get to know him or her. We should pick someone willing to visit the school and advocate for our child there. Psychologists generally spend more time out in the field than psychiatrists do. But we should make sure the person we select has credentials that rival or outrank those of the school's psychiatric support staff, for example, someone with an MA or doctorate in psychology. Finally we should gauge whether he or she is emotionally invested enough in our child to really go to bat for him or her.

If no amount of advocacy on our part or recommendations by psychological professionals end up securing for our child what he needs at school, we should consider pulling him out and exploring other options. More promising schools include more traditional ones that don't place so much emphasis on group work or spontaneous oral class participation, and that still use the call-and-response format we discussed earlier, which unsocial children find more comfortable. These include not only many parochial schools, but also the international schools—French, German, and others—that are found in large metropolitan areas across the country. Such schools contain more diverse student bodies, representing cultures that don't stress sociability nearly as much as ours does, and that show far greater tolerance for unsocial personalities. As for the best secular, English-language options, these are the Montessori programs, with their individualized education and attention to different learning styles.

Both the international and the Montessori programs, however, generally have long waiting lists, tuition fees, and admissions requirements, and so aren't available to everyone. Indeed, some are just as reluctant as other private schools to admit the more socially quirky left-brainers. The French and German schools, moreover, use French or German as their language of instruction. While this may work for the more linguistically minded of our children, it may not be the best choice for those who are especially shy about speaking up in a foreign language.

If one parent is at home, a more realistic option may be homeschooling. For all the burden it places on us as the teachers, this, more than any other alternative, lets us ensure that our child's lack of sociability doesn't interfere with her education. Some states require us to produce lesson plans and assessments that follow certain guidelines, but no one can control how we actually teach our child. If he is sufficiently unsocial, we should be prepared to hear that we're only exacerbating things by keeping him at home. Indeed, it is important to nurture our child's social skills: in the next chapter we will review promising strategies that are completely compatible with homeschooling.

Furthermore, as veteran parents can attest, homeschooling is far from the isolating experience that outsiders assume. Networks of homeschoolers abound, with homeschool sports teams, math clubs, and other extracurriculars. Many homeschoolers form informal cooperatives, with different parents teaching different subjects. Some of these arrangements may work for our child, and their informality allows us to handpick those kids and those parent-teachers we think will best suit our child.

Other home-based options are online charter schools, such as the Florida Virtual School and the Wisconsin Virtual Academy. These admit children from all over the country, and have students working primarily on their own and interacting with one another over the Internet rather than in the face-to-face groups that intimidate all too many of our children in their local public schools. For the most socially reclusive students, indeed, online course work may offer the most comfortable learning environment of all.

Improving Your Child's Chances of Admission to Selective High Schools and Colleges

As we saw earlier, the three obstacles that stand between our children and selective high schools and colleges are their awkward performance in interviews, their dearth of extracurricular leadership activities, and their often mediocre grades.

As far as grades go, all the work we do to improve our child's schooling—whether it's in securing alternatives to class participation and group work requirements, getting our child into a school that better suits her, or homeschooling her—will also improve her grades. Or, in the case of this last option, eliminate grades as a factor entirely—their place being taken, typically, by our portfolios of our child's work.

As far as the interview goes, one possibility is simply to opt out of it, assuming it is optional. Another is to help our child practice his interview skills ahead of time. Some school guidance counselors offer such services, but our child may be more comfortable practicing first with us. We might set up a series of practice sessions, each with someone with whom he is less familiar or comfortable than the one before. We might tape record the interviews, preferably including video, and go over them with our child, gently making suggestions. Above all, we should keep practicing, knowing that the skills we are working on will carry over to many other key areas of social interaction.

As far as extracurricular activities and leadership go, our top priority should be to ensure that our child stays true to herself. We should cherish the fact that she's opted out of the furious résumé stuffing that so many of today's aspiring students engage in. And we shouldn't discourage the solo pursuits she is most comfortable with. But we should try, nonetheless, to expand her horizons in directions that will fill her leadership void. Are there some not so socially fraught ways in which she could show initiative and exert influence? Perhaps she could quietly delve into local politics—writing opinion pieces for the community newspaper or reading prepared statements at local hearings. Perhaps he'd be comfortable leading younger children—tutoring groups of students at the elementary school, or organizing an afternoon club for neighborhood youngsters. These ventures might not impress admissions committees as much as does leadership over peers, but they still count for something.

As for peer leadership, in the absence of any school club our child is comfortable leading, or that would have him as its leader, we might invite him to start a new one. It need not attract a lot of members: for college applications, its mere existence will suffice. We can suggest something that both interests him and isn't too socially intimidating—perhaps a writing group, music group, chess club, cleanup crew, or bike club. Perhaps our child can invite a friend to be cofounder—ideally a student in a similar quandary. Founding a club, besides being the best way to match our child with an activity she is most comfortable leading, is something that particularly impresses selective colleges, many of whom grant special recognition to "founding presidents."

Finally, we should spend time considering which schools our child should apply to. We might talk to admissions staff ahead of time, and seek out schools that aren't hooked on leadership. In the case of colleges and universities, most promising may be smaller schools that aren't in the business of churning out large numbers of future leaders, or large state schools that often—even the more selective ones—use a more efficient, cut-and-dried admissions formula that pays more attention to grades and test scores than to more qualitative factors like extracurricular activities.

Having Your Child Evaluated

The short answer is that we should have our child evaluated if we think it will end up helping him or her. The more reassuring evaluations, as we saw above, give parents a professional ally who can trump a school's niggling concerns. But many evaluations, given the expanding diagnostic criteria and rising social standards, do result in a diagnosis. Even this outcome, as we'll see below, is something we can use to our advantage. But that does little to lessen its emotional impact.

How upset should we be if our child gets diagnosed? Whether it's with a social anxiety disorder such as social phobia or an autistic spectrum disorder such as Asperger's syndrome, we should remind ourselves that she might well have grown up label-free a generation ago, when these disorders didn't officially exist, or even today in the numerous other parts of the world, including many fully staffed with psychiatric diagnosticians, that are less concerned than America is with sociability.

Recall Max, the ten-year-old boy who ended up diagnosed with Asperger's. His mother, a German national, wonders what would have happened had they remained in continental Europe, where students still sit in rows facing the teacher and learn as individuals rather than in groups. Even here and now a more traditional school might make all the difference, for so often it's the school alone that triggers the referral that leads to the diagnosis.

Moreover, the official criteria—those laid out by the *Diagnostic and Statistical Manual,* or *DSM*—are fuzzy and open to interpretation. Key factors are criteria such as "appropriate peer relations." Appropriate according to whom? Even the better-defined secondary symptoms—in the case of Asperger's, behaviors such as head banging and obsessing over details—are symptoms shared by people who are unequivocally social. For neither set of disorders is there a clear-cut litmus test.

What, then, does our child's diagnosis really mean? A question to ask is one that professionals pose in drawing the line between two other fuzzy categories: normal drinking and alcoholism. Does the trait in question impede major life activities such as work, parenting, and school? In some sense, considering all the ways it is indeed handicapping our child at school, the answer is yes. But put her in a more traditional classroom, and she might be much more at ease and eager to learn and—bright, quiet, independent-minded, and self-motivated as she is—appreciated as a model student rather than branded with a social pathology.

In the end, all purported pathologies that center on sociability are functions of the highly variable social expectations of specific societies. But because social expectations are so pervasive, the handicaps facing our children are very real. With this in mind, perhaps the best way to think of a diagnosis is in pragmatic terms: what is its practical effect on our child's life, and how might we exploit it to improve things?

We might start by seeing if we can convince school staff to accommodate our child without disclosing her diagnosis. However, for intransigent schools, the diagnosis is our trump card. What makes it powerful are two federal laws: the Americans with Disabilities Act (ADA) and the Individuals with Disabilities Education Act (IDEA). The former legally obligates public schools to make "reasonable accommodations" for any child diagnosed with special needs. And the latter requires schools to agree with parents on an Individualized Education Plan, or IEP: a legally binding document that specifies appropriate educational goals for our child and how the school will meet them.

Thus, the more stubborn our school is, the more we may gain by disclosing a diagnosis. If the person evaluating our child actually seems reluctant, as was the case with Alan, to label our child with anything, we should explain that the school won't meet our child's needs unless he has a diagnosis that warrants an IEP. Many evaluators are sympathetic to such pragmatic needs—so much so that, as epidemiologists have observed, the rates of various psychological diagnoses around the country reflect what kinds of educational and therapeutic services are available and what it takes to qualify for them.

For extremely shy children who never talk in class, the most appropriate of the official labels is "selective mutism." For children who do talk but are still very shy or socially anxious, a more likely possibility is "social phobia." For socially aloof children who don't seem overly shy or anxious, there's Asperger's syndrome. In all three cases, fuzzy diagnostic criteria mean professionals who disagree on where exactly to draw the line. But as long as at least one psychotherapist makes an official diagnosis that appears, as all three of the above do, in the *DSM*, we can use it to secure "reasonable accommodations" for our child's "disability."

Yes, disability: and that's why we need to consider the labeling option carefully, for it also has its downsides. The Individuals with Disabilities Education Act does not oblige ordinary private schools (schools not specifically designed for children with special needs) to admit or retain children with IEPs. Divulging a diagnosis to such a school may merely give it an excuse to turn down or dismiss our child. Indeed, even just getting an evaluation can work against us. School application forms invariably include questions about whether the applicant has ever been evaluated. So much the worse if this resulted in a diagnosis. Whether we publicize the diagnosis, therefore, will depend in part on whether our child is currently in the public school system, and whether we are committed to his or her remaining there.

Other disadvantages to diagnostic labels include how they may recast our child in the eyes of her teachers. Inaccurate generalizations abound, particularly about Asperger's syndrome, which the popular media has so prominently showcased. While the experts have remarked that children with Asperger's are more striking for their mutual differences than for their similarities, laypeople may assume that our child is a mindless calculator and an encyclopedia of inane facts, like Dustin Hoffman in *Rain Man*; or an overly literal-minded naïf, like Christopher Boone in *The Curious Incident of the Dog in the Night-Time*; or a "little professor" who carries on obsessively about his favorite topic without noticing people's eyes glaze over. More than anything else, it's important that our child's diagnosis remain as private as possible within the school, and that teachers not prejudge her or inappropriately lower their expectations.

In light of all this, what options have different parents chosen? Marc and Jessica have a fourteen-year-old son whom they suspect meets the criteria for Asperger's syndrome. Since kindergarten, he has attended various private grade schools that include children with mild learning disabilities, surrounded by sociable classmates who serve as good social role models, benefiting as well from a low staff-to-student ratio and an attention to individual learning styles. At no point have Marc and Jessica shared the Asperger's label with any teachers or other school personnel. Now choosing among private high schools, they are especially happy with their decision, since they believe it has kept open options that would otherwise have eluded them. Their conundrum is a relatively common one: the tension between what we, as parents, think are the best options for our child given his or her suspected diagnosis, and how that diagnosis, given how others perceive it, might limit those very options were it disclosed.

Katrina, mother of Max, the boy whom we saw earlier in this chapter acting up in kindergarten and later diagnosed with Asperger's syndrome, made a different decision. Max has been attending public school since kindergarten, when Katrina first had him evaluated. The evaluation, which she later realized was far too sketchy to be conclusive, deemed him normal. First grade went much better than kindergarten—perhaps only because the teacher kept his distance and let Max work independently. Then in second grade things fell apart again and Max was back to disrupting the class, spending time in the principal's office, and getting himself suspended from school. Katrina, meanwhile, was back to leaving her office at Microsoft early to drive across greater Seattle to pick him up. It was this year that she decided to put Max through a much more comprehensive, multi-hour evaluation at the Autism Center at the University of Washington.

"I don't think I would have had Max tested at the Autism Center if he hadn't started acting up so much at school," Katrina notes. "It is pretty clear that he is unhappy in school, that he doesn't get along with anybody and feels like a misfit and a failure."

But she hesitated before sharing the diagnosis with the school:

"As for the diagnosis, I am partly upset about it and partly see it as an opportunity for negotiating with Max's school. As an Asperger's kid he is entitled to certain accommodations. But I may be wrong here and I am worried that it is a wrong move to let the school district know. But then again, it doesn't make my life any easier if they continue to send him home from school early and suspend him (which they did the other week for three days). That isn't a good experience for him, and Bill Gates sure doesn't like me quitting early every week so that I can pick up my 'renegade' child."

In the end, Katrina is glad to have disclosed the diagnosis. Max now has an IEP, receives one-on-one tutoring, and is no longer acting up and getting suspended. Perhaps most importantly, he qualifies for a school-based social skills group, which, run by a trained speech therapist, is slowly but surely helping him open up to his classmates.

Halfway across the country in Minneapolis, an eccentric five-year-old girl inspired a similar dilemma. Throughout preschool, Rose had been socially delayed, odd, and disconnected. She'd concoct elaborate fantasy games and assume that the other children were joining in. She'd walk up and whisper strange, disjointed phrases in their faces. Whenever anyone tried talking with her at any length, she'd lose focus and start squirming. Two weeks before kindergarten began, a preliminary evaluation concurred with what Rose's mother, Beth, had feared all along: Asperger's syndrome.

"Let's not share any labels with the school just yet," the psychiatrist advised. "Let's see how the first few weeks of kindergarten go and then meet again."

Wary of labels, and unready to shed the cocoon of denial she'd maintained over so many years — the Asperger's was bearable if it didn't become public — Beth complied. After all, Rose had made it through preschool without incident; surely kindergarten would be similar.

Then kindergarten began, and so did the first reports of trouble. Rose wouldn't sit still and kept wandering around the classroom; worse, she kept covering her eyes and ears when spoken to; worse, she kept making clicking and hissing noises during Carpet Time and kicking her chair legs at Desk Time; worse, she only got louder when asked to stop; worse, she was spoiling show-and-tell by sticking her head in classmates' faces and making weird noises; worse, she was mimicking her teacher in the same mocking manner in which, for the last month or so, she had been mimicking Beth.

The worst of this, Beth notes, didn't seem like Asperger's syndrome. It seemed, instead, like a pathologically defiant, malicious child who was, quoting Beth, "more in need of an exorcist than an IEP." Though the teacher, Ms. G., kept urging her to visit the classroom and witness things firsthand, Beth kept hesitating, certain that her presence would only make everything worse. But she desperately wanted a second opinion. When would the school psychologist observe the class? Perhaps — indeed, this was now the best Beth could hope for — it still, somehow, was all about Asperger's syndrome, in which case, surely *someone* at school would recognize it as such.

But at this point, with Rose being repeatedly sent out of the classroom to the principal's office, the vice principal's office, or whatever other classroom would take her, and being threatened with exclusion from field trips, Beth was not about to divulge the suspected diagnosis unless it was clearly the answer. Kindergarten isn't mandatory in Minnesota: perhaps the school would end up expelling her. To let on that Rose had Asperger's on top of everything else, Beth feared, would only worsen her prospects for staying in a classroom where, she still dared to hope, things might ultimately work out for the best.

But something had to change, and soon. Ms. G. was increasingly distraught. Never in twenty-five years of teaching had she seen such defiant behavior, and she was stumped. Stumped by Rose's "unkindness," stumped by her "horrible" school days. Then there was Beth, beyond distraught, racking her brain from dawn to dusk and dusk to dawn. "Unkind . . . horrible . . . never in twenty-five years of teaching." How on earth, she kept asking herself, could she have brought into the world a child capable of eliciting such words, and the overwhelming emotional upset they conveyed, from this veteran, and—as she learned shortly after school began—*award-winning* teacher?

Rose's occasional good days, raising false hopes, only made matters worse. Teasing people further, she embarked, out of nowhere, on a three-day spree of good days, briefly convincing everyone that she'd rounded the corner. Then, with no rhyme and no reason, she was back to clicking, hissing, and otherwise disrupting. It didn't matter how much Beth talked to her—"I don't know," she'd say whenever Beth asked why she acted up; "OK," she'd say whenever Beth explained why she should stop—and no matter how much Beth rewarded her on good days and punished her on bad, nothing in the universe seemed to make the slightest difference.

Finally Beth forced herself to enter the classroom and observe her daughter, and all became clear. Every fidget, every click, every mouthing of Ms. G.'s words that Beth saw her daughter perform as she sat sprawled among classmates on the carpet while Ms. G. tried to read them a story—everything was about a highly distractible and fidgety child trying, with all her might, to hold herself together for a longer stretch of quiet time than she'd ever before been faced with. Beth glued her eyes to Rose's, trying to will her to sit still, to will her probing fingers away from the wall hangings behind her, to will her face to turn back toward Ms. G. "If Carpet Time goes on for even twenty more seconds," Beth thought to herself, "she is going to squirm one too many times and get in trouble." Sure enough, Rose rustled once more against the poster she'd been asked several times to keep away from, and Ms. G. told her to leave the group and return to her desk. Slowly but surely, she did. She was learning how to comply, Beth saw, but she saw, too, from the vague look on Rose's face, that she had little sense of what she'd done wrong.

Even as Beth glued her eyes to Rose's, she saw one more thing. Ms. G. was a phenomenal teacher, with an expressive voice, clear explanations, and engaging questions. It was all working beautifully for everyone else in the room—and, Beth was tremendously relieved and delighted to see as she watched her perennially squirmy girl holding herself more still than ever before, for many minutes longer than she ever did at home, and trying so hard to pay attention, it was *almost* working for Rose. In fact, it was just what Rose needed. If Beth and Ms. G. could simply spell out to her in painstakingly *literal* detail (for this is what Asperger's kids need) all the rules and expectations—of which there were, Beth now saw, so many more than in preschool—and if they could give her a few extra prompts and materials to help focus her attention, they could, Beth felt certain, get her to settle down, attend, and participate.

For it was all about Asperger's syndrome after all. At hand was not a horrible child, but a horrendous misunderstanding—a horrendous consequence of Beth's having withheld a truth that she'd been too determined for too long to keep safely confined to herself.

A few days later the school psychologist finally scheduled a meeting. Beth swallowed hard, seized the floor, and "outed" her daughter as a child with Asperger's syndrome. Everyone—the principal, the psychologist, and Ms. G.—was indeed surprised. And they surprised her right back. There were other kids with Asperger's at the school, it turned out, smoothly mainstreamed into regular classrooms. Why on earth, they kept asking, hadn't Beth told them sooner?

Beyond any remarks about Asperger's syndrome, or about Rose, or about how to manage Rose's behavior, the greatest accomplishment of this meeting, Beth suspects, was peace of mind and a sense of mission for Ms. G. This, more than anything else, seems to have been what has empowered her to accommodate Rose's quirks and guide her through a succession of increasingly good weeks at school.

The moral of the story for Beth, meanwhile, is that disclosing the diagnosis is sometimes the best move. If our child is lucky enough to have a teacher who is so devoted to her students as to be deeply concerned about a troubled child, and even more profoundly concerned if her tried-and-true teaching methods fail to reach this child, then this teacher needs to know the diagnosis. We should never underestimate the importance of open communication with a talented and dedicated teacher.

2

Playdates, Friends, and Family Life
The Unsocial Child at Home

Shelley, Jeff, and five-year-old Brian step out of their house to join the neighborhood block party. The street teems with people they haven't yet met. From across the street, out of a crowd of kids who are shrieking and blowing bubbles, a small boy emerges and runs over, waving both arms.

"Are you the new neighbors?" he calls. His voice, though hoarse, still sings out in a melodic falsetto. "My name's Zack."

"He must be somewhere between four and five years old, just about Brian's age," Shelley thinks, as the boy stops short, directly beside Brian, and looks up. Shelley can't help noticing his erect, open-armed posture, and how his wide, eager eyes meet hers, then dart over to Brian, then up again to Jeff, and then, the moment she starts answering him, right back straight at her.

"Yes, we've just moved in," Shelley says. She turns to Brian, who, clutching his bucket of sidewalk chalk, is already turning away. Putting her hands on his shoulders, she rotates him back. "Brian, say hi to Zack."

Brian slouches into Shelley's thighs, arcs his neck downward, and mumbles "Hello."

"Hi, Brian," says Zack. "Do you want to play bubbles?" He gestures back toward the bubble fest.

Brian shakes his downturned head, pivots, and, bucket to chest, shuffles sideways back to the stoop. Angling himself away from the street, he sits, sets down the bucket, and fumbles for chalk.

Shelley turns to Zack, who is watching Brian. "I think Brian's feeling a little shy right now," she says. "Maybe he'll join you later."

Zack is once again looking straight up into her eyes. Shrugging his shoulders with a cheery "OK," he zips back to the other kids.

While Jeff wanders off to the food, Shelley pauses to observe Zack. She watches as he cavorts with two little girls, clapping bubbles in their faces, laughing and whooping with them. In some ways this child could be Shelley's very own: his features—strong chin, snub nose, and large, brown, broadly set almond eyes—like Brian's, vaguely evoke her father. But in other ways, he couldn't be more different—from Brian, at least. Apparently the same age, he somehow seems older, smarter, more plugged in to the universe. Is it simply that confident, straight-backed poise? Those clearly articulated, fully audible, melodically intoned syllables ("Are you the new neighbors")? Or is it those eyes—"Yes," she thinks, "it's these more than anything else"—so similar to Brian's in shape and color, and yet so much more focused and active, seeming to take in far more of what's actually going on than Brian does.

She turns back to Brian, slouched over a sidewalk panel now full of rainbow sharks and jellyfish, gazing blank-faced out into the middle distance. Sometimes that gaze seems a window into a colorful, private imagination. But at other times Shelly can't help comparing it to the sharper, more reactive look of the many, many Zacks out there, and can't help wondering, with just a tinge of jealousy, whether something important—however commonplace—is missing.

One thing is certain: never in a million years would Brian, tables turned, ever have walked up to three strangers, looked into their eyes, and started talking.

———

It's the first warm afternoon of spring after a long, cold winter, and all the mothers and children are back at the playground. Alice longs to catch up with these casual acquaintances she hasn't seen since November. But her daughter, Miranda, three years old, has no interest in hanging around the climbing structure, where all the other moms are congregating, and all the other daughters are playing house. Instead,

Miranda keeps skipping along the ledge at the edge of the playground, jumping off from time to time to chase after sparrows and pigeons, her chestnut-brown ponytail bouncing in sync.

"Of course, I was the same way," Alice thinks to herself, remembering how her mother always said she'd shy away from groups when she was little. But now in the doldrums of her stay-at-home years, she's often lonely for adults.

She looks over her shoulder at the lively mothers, catching their peals of laughter, and feels a hint of how she felt when, nine or ten years old, she first started trying to join in. Everyone else always seemed to know one another already, and know how to be with one another, and seemed to have so many ready things to chat about.

But it's no wonder, Alice reminds herself, that she feels disconnected from the other mothers on the playground. All that previous fall, and even earlier, the same pattern would unfold. Before Alice could say much beyond hello, Miranda would be retreating to the edges of the playground, or into the park beyond, and Alice would have to look away, then step away, to keep her three-year-old daughter within sight.

Watching Miranda approach the latest dog walker to ask, "Can I pet your dog?" Alice wonders whether, once Miranda is finally interested in other children, she'll struggle as much to connect with them as Alice once did. All those increasingly painful years from fifth grade on—how will her daughter get through them? How much is Miranda, now tossing twigs to a husky while others play house, compromising at this very moment her future social skills?

"How much did my own young self compromise my own social future?" This is something Alice had wondered about well into her young adulthood. Since having had Miranda, she's revisited those early years with a vengeance. But nowhere do they lurk closer than here at the playground, with her daughter off with dogs in the distance, and herself once again cut off—way off—from a peer group of her own.

In the last chapter we explored the challenges left-brain children face in today's schools, as well as how to support and advocate for them there. In this chapter we'll look at the challenges they face outside of school and how best to address these challenges in the context of family and community life.

Most unsocial children fare better at home than at school. For shy children especially, home is a refuge — often the one place where they feel truly comfortable speaking out and being themselves. And most of us parents don't expect our kids to be as socially "on" and to perform at such a high social level as today's classroom teachers do.

But plenty of challenges still confront us at home. Those persistent negative reports from school, for instance, even if we don't see why they're justified, are still alarming in and of themselves — the phone calls, behavior slips, report cards, referrals to the school psychologist, suspensions. However much we dismiss these, and even if there's no official diagnosis to back them up, they may cast our children in a whole new light, and make us question things about them that we never before thought to worry about. All those solo projects, all that imaginative play with imaginary friends — all of which once seemed to show such refreshing independence and creativity — may suddenly start to alarm us. So much the worse, of course, if it has led to an actual diagnosis.

Diagnosis or no diagnosis, school or no school, there's a good chance our child's solitary habits would have already given us pause. In today's socially charged society, with its constant celebration of extroversion and its nonstop coverage of autism epidemics, our worries may have begun well before kindergarten. They may continue on even after school lets out for the summer. They persist as we watch our child spend the whole time at the playground building imaginary campfires with his imaginary friend, the whole time at the pool reading stacks of science fiction, the whole time at a block party examining grubs under bricks. They persist whenever we notice how few friends our child has, and how she rarely gets invited to playdates or birthday parties. Birthday parties, especially, can carry a lasting sting: some parents report that finding out about a party to which every other child in the class was invited except theirs can hurt them as much as if they themselves had been personally rejected. How much more hurt might our own child feel were she to find out?

When playdates and birthday parties do include our kids, our worries don't let up. Some unsocial children will readily ignore anyone with whom they aren't intimately familiar. One mother reports spending weeks arranging a playdate with a neighborhood boy she'd hoped would become "the best friend across the street," only to hear her son announce, as the boys headed upstairs, that he was going to count up to a thousand. Ten minutes later, they were back downstairs, her son pacing from room to room, intoning "Two hundred ninety-seven, two hundred ninety-eight, two hundred ninety-nine, three hundred," while the other boy trailed after him, trying to interest him in a board game. Unable to halt her son's counting, she ended up playing Candy Land in the kitchen with his would-be playmate, who never came back.

Other parents find their children, in a different sort of social cluelessness, doing all the talking and deciding, bossing others around or perseverating on subjects that start boring the other child. Perhaps she is loudly telling the other girls about the script she's written for the play they're going to perform, explaining which props they're going to use and who gets to play which part. Perhaps he is relentlessly arguing with his playmate about whether Pluto is a planet, or lecturing him about stick insects. Or perhaps she is nervously telling knock-knock jokes, laughing at them herself when the other kids don't respond.

And perhaps because of all this, or because of any number of other, more subtle symptoms of social ineptitude, we find our child being teased, ganged up on, or excluded—however subtly—by other kids in the neighborhood. The more of them there are, the worse it gets.

We look on in distress as our child inadvertently alienates one potential friend after another, or sets himself or herself up for bullying or exclusion. Do we step in and try to make him interact more meaningfully and stop lecturing and bossing? Do we ask her potential friends to stop being mean? Or does intervention only make matters worse and prevent our child from learning?

The more time we spend with our unsocial children, the more exposed we are to daylong montages of unsocial behavior, with long tracts of unstructured time in which to brood about them. As we brood, we might find ourselves caught up in making connections between our child's social life and our own. As noted in the Introduction, we ourselves may be left-brain, like many parents of left-brain children, and so may have struggled socially for much of our own early years. Many years later, we find our child's lack of sociability rippling through the social fabric of our family. It affects, in particular, our social lives as parents, as we saw with Alice and her unsocial daughter, Miranda. Like many of our peers in parenthood, we have shifted our focus away from the worlds of work and adult-centered activities and toward the worlds of our children. If we are stay-at-homes, this shift is complete. And when the new world we face is that of an unsocial child, when it doesn't embrace other children and activities that groups of children so often engage in (soccer, Scouts, ballet, theater), the normal social bonds, not just between our children and their peers but also between us and other parents, simply don't form. The more so if this child is our only one, or if all our children are similarly unsocial.

Then, even casual conversation in public places such as playgrounds and school yards soon grows difficult, as other parents accumulate stocks of shared experiences—yesterday afternoon's backyard escapades, the ongoing drama between Anna and Lisa—while we stay stuck on homework and weather. Increasingly, others pass us over for those with whom they have more things to chat about. We often feel nearly invisible: as much on the outskirts as our children.

The distress all this causes varies from parent to parent. The more sociable we are, the more frustrating we may find the limitations imposed by our children's dispositions. The most sociable of us, however, may find ways to befriend other parents anyway, and thereby to help our children—by initiating playdates, for example. But if we are such parents, our child's aloofness, so different from how we are or ever were, may especially disturb us. Where is this coming from? How normal can this be? How can my child possibly be happy spending all day long under a tree by himself?

Less social parents may find it easier to put their child's disposition in perspective. "I was like that, I was perfectly content to be like that, and I turned out OK in the end," we might keep reminding ourselves. At the same time, our child's being "like that" may limit our own current social life in ways we can't overcome, and recall painful memories of our social ventures of long ago. Even if we know that our child is perfectly happy right now, and that everything will probably work out by adulthood, our memories may make us worry about her middle years, particularly her adolescence, where the same social challenges we faced—timeless as they are—still lie in wait.

As a less sociable parent, we may also feel an additional pain: of responsibility. Are my deficient social skills making me a poor role model? Am I failing to pick up on my son's social and emotional cues and properly engage with him? Might my daughter's dearth of playdates and birthday party invitations be as much a reflection of my own social skills as of hers? Our parenting-obsessed culture has forgotten about Judith Rich Harris's groundbreaking book *The Nurture Assumption*. Harris reviews studies comparing identical twins raised apart with adopted siblings raised together. These studies underscore the influence of genes on personality: our children simply take after us, as they would even if they were raised in different households.

"WHY DON'T I FEEL CLOSER TO MY OWN CHILD?"

Perhaps the greatest sources of pain, loneliness, and worry are the challenges we face bonding with our left-brain children. Though they may interact more with us than with others, they may still not engage in anything like the emotional back-and-forth that other children seem, so frequently, effortlessly, enthusiastically, to have with their parents. Our children may clam up when we ask them how they feel, turn away when we probe what's upsetting them, stiffen and squirm when we try to hug them. Doesn't she need more affection than what she's allowing us to give her, we might ask, thinking of how much intimacy we ourselves are craving, and not getting, from her. If he doesn't bond with us, how can he possibly form close relations with anyone else?

Seeing other people's children, or imagining them, snuggling back, gazing back, and smiling at their parents' affections, we find ourselves struck with envy. Some of these other children will even bond with us, reminding us of what's missing, of what might have been, and making us feel even more poignantly, bizarrely wistful. "How can it be that this new boy is giving me more eye contact right now than I get in an entire day from my son?" "Why do I feel more of an emotional connection during my brief and infrequent conversations with the girl across the street than I do when I talk with my daughter?"

Especially compared with what we imagine in other people's houses, our dinner tables may be silent and stiff. We rack our brains at how to get our kids talking. "Tell us something about school today. Just one thing. What's the most interesting thing that happened?" "I had lunch" might be all we get back, after a seemingly endless stretch of dead air, which promptly resumes. Or we have conversational monopolies run by a more gregarious sibling, who, taking advantage, holds court while her brother withdraws even further.

Siblings raise a whole new set of concerns. If she's more social, refreshing as that is, she too often wins more than her share of attention. "How can I keep turning Julie down when she makes so many more overtures than Sam does?" We might witness in sadness her sisterly overtures, and how, ignored one too many times, she finally gives up and moves on to her peers on the outside. As the years pass, she may grow increasingly embarrassed by her socially awkward brother and distance herself ever further, even from us parents.

Or perhaps she's an equally unsocial child, and our worries compound as we watch our two children playing relentlessly in parallel, and think of all those mutually missed opportunities for sibling companionship.

Then there's the extended family and community. What do we do with a child who barely mumbles more than "hello" to her grandparents, whether in person or on the phone? What do we say to our wounded mother-in-law, who finds it hard to believe that her granddaughter doesn't dislike her? Or to our gregarious sister, who's convinced that something is wrong? What do we do when our child cowers in the corner whenever neighbors or cousins come over, and whenever we visit them?

Neighbors, cousins, siblings, potential playmates—all these occasion another sort of regret: that which comes from comparing our unsocial child, hard as it is to avoid doing so, to his or her many more sociable peers. Perhaps what stands out in these comparisons, more than anything else, is how young our child seems compared with most of his peers. Not just in her social skills, but in her overall alertness, articulateness, emotional presence, poise, and self-control. His unfocused stare; her flat, inexpressive face; his stammering and mumbled speech; her short, simple sentences; his slouch; her idle fidgets; his clumsy, awkward gate. Most concerning in some children is how quickly and frequently they tear up or start having a tantrum—whether when socially overwhelmed or ostracized or when asked to transition to new activities—as we'll discuss later in connection with analytic children. Their reluctance to share their feelings verbally *before* these feelings take over only aggravates their emotional outbursts.

As if to confirm his apparently global immaturity, our child, on those occasions when he does engage socially, may gravitate toward kids who are one or more years his junior. One mom reports realizing, with dismay, that her older son was limiting himself to certain friends of his brother, younger than him by three years. If our child is already years behind at the age of, say, ten or eleven, what does this bode for his or her social future?

Aggravating all these concerns, of course, is the negative feedback we're getting from school. It's often this that raises, most forcefully, the challenge that underlies all our efforts: how can we make an unsocial child more social? Playdates, as we saw, only go so far. Nor can we recreate, at home, those social situations that challenge our child at school, or in the school yard, or amid unsupervised groups of peers—let alone work through these challenges to somehow eradicate our child's problems.

Popular parenting-advice books, geared as they are toward more typical, social children, may end up only making us feel more anxious. John Gottman's *The Heart of Parenting* is typical: Emotions are paramount, the key to our child's heart. We must do all we can to encourage our child to share them. "How do you feel about school?" we might ask. "You seem uncomfortable being with other children. Is that so? What makes you feel that way?" If our child does respond, she may simply say that she doesn't like being with other kids, period. As we saw, unsocial children are often almost as private with us parents as they are with others, and our attempts to help our child process her feelings may not only frustrate her into silence but compound our own sense of helplessness.

The more so as messages like Gottman's have so permeated the popular culture that we see nearly every other parent we know validating and processing emotions with their kids, and nearly every other kid we know responding positively in turn.

Aggravating our concerns is the growing emphasis by popular psychologists, child development books, and education experts on how cognitive growth depends on certain social and emotional abilities, and how children can't, or shouldn't, move on to greater cognitive challenges until they have reached a certain level of social and emotional maturity—a theme we will return to in later chapters. Even our child's intellectual development, it would appear, is hanging in the balance.

However skeptical we manage to be about all these theories, no amount of faith in our unsocial child will change the reality of how he or she comes across to others—including the many who influence his or her current well-being and future opportunities. Nevertheless, there is much we can and must do to help our unsocial children to thrive in our families and communities.

HELPING YOUR UNSOCIAL CHILD TO OPEN UP AND CONNECT WITH THE FAMILY

For the sake not just of our child but of ourselves, our other children, and members of our extended family, we want to find ways to open up our child as much as possible—all the while without overly pressuring him or intruding on his privacy.

We begin with ourselves. How can we bond more closely with our unsocial child? At stake is more than just the quality of our parent-child relationship; it's through this relationship that we can best get to know our child and, in knowing her, help her to process emotions and practice social skills. When direct conversation remains impersonal or one-sided, we must find other channels. Many of our children, if we look closely, turn out to be expressing emotions and enacting social dynamics in other ways.

Some do so in imaginative play with dolls, cars, animals, LEGOs, and other objects. We should try, therefore, to listen discretely to what our child is acting out, seeing what we can learn about his social and emotional fixations, and feeling out whether he'll let us join in. Here the Floortime approach developed by the child psychologist Stanley Greenspan may be helpful. Without taking over the scene our child has created, we should gently insert ourselves as one of the characters. Figure out which one she is personally identifying with and try playing someone who interacts with it—a surrogate "you" to her surrogate "me." See if our surrogates can bond in some way. Perhaps our child has all the other dolls making fun of the protagonist doll; perhaps our doll can encourage this doll to talk things through, and then offer some reassurance and useful advice.

Other children process emotions through drawing and painting. Here, too, we may find ways to join in. We might see if we can start a collaborative art project—perhaps a series of pictures with interacting characters, perhaps a cartoon with dialogue-filled balloons. Again, we can locate the surrogate "you" and "me" and find opportunities for role-play through drawing and dialogue.

Some children are writers. We should try, discretely, to learn about our child from her stories. We might invite her to create one with us. Perhaps we can coax him into cowriting, and then acting out, an extended conversation between our surrogates.

Other children are readers. We might pick out a book featuring someone she can relate to—Little Bear, Charlie Bucket (from *Charlie and the Chocolate Factory*), Harriet the Spy—and encourage our child to read aloud with us. We might invite him to divvy up the parts of different characters with us during stretches of dialogue. Or engage her in an ongoing commentary on the protagonist's feelings and interactions with others.

Some children are hikers. Hiking side by side, of all joint activities, may be most conducive to extended, unpressured, spontaneous discourse—one in which frequent silences are natural instead of awkward, where eye contact is naturally and comfortably avoided, and where conversational icebreakers far removed from personal feelings keep turning up. Hollow trees, tempting berries, rock formations, animal tracks—we can try gradually making these topics more personal, inviting our child to share interests. Perhaps we can eventually get him talking about science class at school, and then school in general, and classmates, and friendships.

All this can substitute for the direct, face-to-face emotional processing that our child may find too intimidating to engage in. It may also gradually put him at greater ease with us, and so shade into something more personal. It may improve both our mutual relationship and her nascent social skills, as well as teaching us more about what bugs, frightens, confuses, or delights her. It may help us accumulate a repertoire of subjects which we can return to and build upon each next time we converse with our child, or bring up in drawing others into conversations with him.

What about siblings? How can we encourage our child to interact with his brother or sister? Or, if both children are unsocial, how do we get them to bond with each other? The most promising beginnings, once again, may be indirect bonds through third-party characters. We might try out a three-way version of one of the fantasy role-play activities mentioned above, in which all three parties (us and them) become characters in the favorite medium (plastic objects, paint, or pen and paper). If this proves too challenging, other options exist.

But first, let's consider the extended family. For relatives who visit infrequently, what do we do about children who refuse to talk by phone? We should remember that text-based communication can be as meaningful as speech. For even the shyest left-brainer, writing or typing out a message in solitude is far less intimidating than conversing spontaneously, and receiving a letter or e-mail back is as delightful as it is for any kid.

What about when faraway relatives visit? Our child, less familiar with them in person, may cower in the corner and refuse to say a word, however volubly he or she may earlier have communicated by e-mail. Grandparents, aunts, uncles, and cousins may be far less assertive and successful than we are in joining our child's imaginative play, or art, or writing—if our child even lets them get near. It's in situations like these where we may want to turn, instead, to more structured venues such as board games, ball games, or cards.

These options, indeed, apply as much to the nuclear as to the extended family, as well as to any friends and neighbors who come over. The more portable, interactive games can follow us to social events outside the house where our child might otherwise retreat to the sidelines, serving as potential springboards for increasingly social exchanges over time. Well beyond games, there's a whole host of joint activities—puzzles, projects, experiments—that our child can engage in with others, providing occasions for him to share, if not his personal feelings, then at least his intellect.

At least indeed. In fact, this is where we should consider standing all the popular advice on its head. The more emotionally withdrawn a child is, the more we might use the brain, rather than the heart, as the starting point, and structured, intellectual activities, rather than free-form, social ones, as the vehicles for interpersonal connection. Construction projects, science experiments, questions to research on the Web, even lessons that we or others can teach her about topics of special interest or, possibly, that she herself can teach to us and others— all these are possibilities. Many unsocial children who shy away from casual conversation are comfortable playing well-defined, scripted roles such as that of teacher. Whenever and wherever emotional bonds elude us, we can turn to the intellectual bonds that these ventures promote.

One father bonds with his reclusive teenager over math proofs. Handing pen and paper back and forth, father and son take turns drawing diagrams and writing equations until they convince each other that they've reached the solution.

A mother once broke the ice with her teenage son by asking him to teach her about the periodic table of elements. Suddenly an otherwise quiet boy was zealously fielding questions about metals, minerals, and the outer electron ring. By the end of the first lesson he had shared more than he ever had before about science class, creating a springboard for subsequent conversations about school in general.

Two brothers bond over Ping-Pong games—the venue for some of their longest spontaneous talks. A grandfather writes twenty-page-long, dialogue-filled stories back and forth, line by line, with a grand-daughter so reticent that she writes far more than she speaks. An aunt spends hours in her backyard with her taciturn nephew, turning over loose bricks and examining snails, slugs, and pill bugs.

To many people, these activities may seem like odd, unsatisfying ways to connect. But who is to say that an intellectual, or collaborative, or competitive exchange is any less meaningful than the more emotional ways in which more typical people connect? Indeed, such bonds can open doors for more general, emotionally robust connections to form, incidentally, over time.

Hanging in the air amid us and our closest relatives are all our concerns about our child's social deficits. How much should we put these into words? Might doing so merely amplify the worries that others have already, turning the extended family into an echo chamber of unproductive panic? Many parents, in fact, find it refreshing to vent their concerns with those who care most about their children and love them unconditionally. Some find that the sooner they express their worries, before others get a chance to express theirs, the more naturally and readily others will assume the roles of consoler and optimist. And some of their reassurances can carry real force as people start talking openly about how we, our cousin, or our uncle started out just the same way—and look how well he or she (or even we ourselves) turned out in the end.

When concerns arise about how socially isolated our left-brain children are from their peers, it's important not to overlook how much more sociable our children can be with adults. Grown-ups, after all, are typically more responsive to the left-brainer's often precocious academic or otherwise "serious" interests than children are. This means that our child will likely grow increasingly sociable with peers after entering adulthood. It also affords us left-brainer parents a special relationship that eludes most other mothers and fathers—however difficult it is for us to bond with our child in traditional ways. For our child, we may discover, is much more eager to spend time with us, even as she grows older, than other children are with their parents. In particular, she may eagerly join our adult-oriented intellectual pursuits. As one parent puts it, "What other nine-year-old would happily spend the afternoon at an arboretum with his mother rather than play games with his friends?"

HELPING YOUR CHILD TO DEVELOP FRIENDSHIPS
WITH OTHER CHILDREN

The structured activities that enhance our child's relations with family members can also improve her playdates. Many unsocial children are even less social with peers than with relatives, and during the typical, unstructured get-togethers, too often withdraw into their private worlds. Not only do they thus alienate potential friends; they also miss out on opportunities to interact with other children in the safe, nurturing environment of the home.

While an open-ended, spontaneous rapport with peers may be our ultimate social goal, structured activities—as we saw above with relatives—may constitute a more realistic first step. We might, therefore, organize his first dozen playdates around specific activities—board games, ball games, construction projects, science experiments, cookie baking—that will keep the other child happy even when our child ignores her, and keep our child engaged, at least superficially, with the other child. One mother reports success centering an entire playdate on a classic home science experiment: "We're inviting Jessie to come over and drop eggs from the roof with Jonathan." Such organized, activity-centered approaches are also key to successful birthday parties. Over time, when our child seems ready, we might loosen up or reduce the preplanned activities and see what happens.

Prerequisite to this, of course, is finding playmates. And prerequisite to this, often, are our friendships with other parents. Sadly, our child may otherwise receive few or no invitations, or see few of his invitations accepted. Beyond this, she may be quite slow to warm up to people, such that her most promising playmate is one who's up for many frequent playdates. Without a loyal friend who readily offers this, she depends on us having loyal friends whose children are willing, however reluctantly, to play with her. Forging friendships with other parents as early on as possible can also help mitigate teasing and bullying. In the worst cases, we may have no recourse but to turn to the perpetrator's mom or dad, and the inevitably awkward conversation goes more smoothly if we already have, behind us, a long history of trust and friendship.

Our child's social challenges thus become, to some extent, our own. Must we therefore go out and befriend every parent in the school yard, even those to whom we have nothing to say? When it comes to regular playdates, strong, loyal friendships trump superficial ones. It's probably best, then, to follow our heart and befriend those we'd want to befriend anyway. To the extent that like attracts like, and that childhood eccentricities are partly hereditary, many parents discover that their best friends among parents are also the mothers and fathers of the children who click best with their own.

As for the teasing and bullying, we may also want to befriend, as best we can, parents of those alpha males and females who are most likely to hold sway over the perpetrators, if not to be perpetrators themselves. Assuming our child is up for it, we might even try to preempt the bullying by setting up playdates with alpha classmates.

In picking playmates, a more general factor to consider is age. Many unsocial children, as we've discussed, lag socially and emotionally far behind their peers, gravitating toward significantly younger children. Why not embrace this? Young children may play more nicely with our child than older children do. They may be less likely, and able, to tease and manipulate him, may grant him more respect than he gets from his peers, and may feel downright honored to be invited over. We may worry that we're holding our child behind, but we should remember that everyone catches up in the end. Even if she spends her whole life hanging out with people who are three years her junior, this will hardly matter by the time she's twenty-three.

Another option is older children. They may enjoy playing big brother or big sister, and some otherwise unsocial children will happily play along. If our child is one whose cognitive precociousness matches her social delays, she may bond intellectually with older children in ways she cannot with peers.

Another consideration is gender. As with age, differences may be a more promising basis for friendship than similarities. Some studies suggest that boys, overall, are less socially sophisticated and demanding than girls are—particularly in their play styles. Expecting less from their playmates' responses, they have more patience for underresponsiveness. This makes them good social companions for unso-cial girls—so long as they're willing to befriend girls in the first place. Girls, however social, may likewise expect less of boys, and some will readily play nurturer with those who seem socially lost.

Age and gender differences, furthermore, may distract the other children from, or make them more tolerant of, the deeper differences that set our children apart. Paradoxically, therefore, the most promis-ing playmates for our unsocial child may be the opposite of what most parents assume are the most promising first friends, namely, children of the same age and gender. Linguistic and cultural differences are also worth exploring: children from other cultures who aren't native English speakers may be particularly tolerant of barriers to social inter-action—even those that, whether they realize it or not, stem more from a playmate's unsociability than from his language or culture.

Another consideration is number. How many playmates at a time? Generally, unsocial children find one-on-one playdates less challeng-ing socially; they're also less conducive to teasing and bullying. Even-tually, however, we may want our child to practice, within the safety of his home, navigating the complexities of two or more playmates at once. The key here is choosing the children carefully so as to mini-mize chances of ganging up or exclusion—for example, we might start with two kids who don't already know each other.

A final consideration concerns playdate mishaps. How much should we intervene when our child is failing to interact properly, or when the other child or children are excluding, teasing, or otherwise ma-nipulating her? Should we step in as things are unfolding, or wait until the playmate goes home? On the one hand, we don't want to embarrass or stigmatize our child; on the other, our child may not grasp our comments if the social dynamics they address are no long-er current. So we should follow our instincts. If possible, we should wait until we can sit down with our child calmly, avoid making him feel bad in front of his playmate, and take the time to role-play reen-actments of the social mishap and brainstorm strategies to address or avoid it. But if feelings are being seriously hurt or friendships seriously jeopardized, or if we think our child simply won't get it later on in an out-of-context discussion, we should step in right away. We can still be relatively discreet, taking him aside and talking with him quietly, saving a more lengthy discussion for later.

Inevitably, we and our child may hit dry spells in which, try as we might, the social overtures vanish or go nowhere. Perhaps it's our child's first year at a new school. Perhaps his one loyal friend has moved away or moved on. Perhaps she's hit adolescence, when parents stop initiating get-togethers; kids pick their friends increasingly for personality, charisma, and social standing; and open-ended hanging out replaces activity-centered interaction. We might still find potential companions whose loyalty may trump all this—cousins, old family friends, even siblings. But we want to be careful not to take advantage of such kids, who, especially in adolescence, will have their own needs and insecurities, and who may find it socially costly to hang out with unsocial peers.

During the dry spells, our children's abiding venues for interaction and friendship are formal, structured ones, such as after-school clubs and summer camps—chess club, Scouts, a string quartet, archeology camp—whatever matches our child's strengths and interests. Lisbeth's main social activity, you might recall, was lacrosse, where she could hide her face safely behind her helmet. Perhaps there's even a magnet school out there whose focus suits our child and attracts like-minded peers.

However carefully we can tailor their playdates and handpick their schools, camps, and extracurricular activities, we must also prepare our children for the larger world they live in. In particular, we must ensure that they have the necessary social skills to negotiate through school yards, classrooms, cafeterias, informal social gatherings, interviews, and, ultimately, places of employment. Whatever skills they lack, of course, they will learn best through left-brain pedagogies— that is, not informal rap sessions and cooperative group activities but explicit rules and structured practice.

The goal, it's important to note, is not to pressure our child to go against his nature. This is where some of the books that purport to help unsocial children, indeed, go astray. In her *Raise Your Child's Social IQ*, for example, Cathi Cohen advocates teaching a child how to feign interest in other people even when he is genuinely disinterested, how to feign understanding and empathy even when he doesn't actually understand or empathize, and how to join a group and go with the flow even when he has no actual desire to join in.

Given all the reasons we have for cherishing our left-brain children, in no way do we want to pressure them to conform away from who they are, or to befriend people who don't interest them. We should remember, as well, that many are happy with just a few friends, as Lisbeth, for example, will assure us. But, Lisbeth adds, she's glad to have figured out some basic rules about how to engage in conversations.

What we want to do, therefore, is to teach our children a repertoire of rules, strategies, and information that will help them function in the social world that surrounds them, avoid alienating people, and connect well with others in those specific situations where it pays off (for example, college and job interviews). Our children may need explicit rules for engaging in conversations; exercises in inferring people's emotions; systematic exposure to those idiosyncrasies of American youth culture that they don't pick up, as most people do, from the social environment; and access to special venues in which they are likely to feel most comfortable interacting with others.

TEACHING RULES FOR CONVERSATIONS

One of the greatest challenges for unsocial children is the back-and-forth of spontaneous, casual conversation. Many have no problem listening, however long their interlocutor might keep talking, while others are quite comfortable carrying on at great length themselves. It's the more typical, interactive, and ultimately more socially satisfying conversations that elude them. Too often, as Lisbeth reports, things petered out after "Hi." Only after she learned a few explicit rules could Lisbeth consistently connect with people enough to fulfill her modest social needs. How she learned these rules, incidentally, illustrates one way in which a good therapist can assist left-brainers, for Lisbeth's therapist quickly assumed the role of social skills coach.

The most powerful principle that she illuminated for Lisbeth was that people love to talk about themselves. You can keep a dialogue going by *just asking questions*. And asking is one social skill that comes naturally to Lisbeth, as it does to many left-brainers. Guided by her analytical curiosity, she can formulate questions about anything. More importantly, she enjoys doing so. It's just that this hadn't occurred to her as a means of prolonging conversations while remaining true to herself. The people she most yearns to connect with, indeed, are those whose experiences inspire questions. Now, whenever she meets an obvious candidate—for example, a coffee shop customer who volunteers that she's just returned from the Brazilian rain forest—Lisbeth can readily strike up a conversation that satisfies her.

Different left-brainers need different levels of training in conversational rules, but all unsocial left-brainers can benefit from the sort of explicit instruction that Lisbeth received. Unfortunately, very little of the instructional material out there explicitly aims to teach rules about verbal interaction to unsocial children. Popular books such as *Teaching Your Child the Language of Social Success* and *Helping the Child Who Doesn't Fit In* focus, rather, on some of the more obvious nonverbal rules, like how close to stand to other people, what to touch or not touch, and appropriate gestures, posture, and style of dress. These are important, but they are not nearly as subtle, challenging, or essential as the complexities of conversational dynamics.

For adults, books on conversation abound. To most older left-brainers, they are quite accessible; parents of younger left-brainers can use them as a teaching resource. Tim Page, the music critic for *Time* magazine and the author of a recent *New Yorker* article about living with Asperger's syndrome, cites Emily Post's *Etiquette* as his most helpful guide. But etiquette books like Post's devote only a few pages to the kinds of informal exchanges that most stymie unsocial people. Myriad other books, for example, Alan Garner's *Conversationally Speaking* and Don Gabor's *How to Start a Conversation and Make Friends*, discuss more subtle, informal rules for initiating and sustaining conversations.

The more systematically these rules are broken down, the more fully the left-brainer can master them. Ironically, the materials that do this best are aimed at a different audience: students from overseas who are here learning English as a foreign language. Many English-language classes for foreign adults now focus on culture-specific conversation rules. With a few minor adjustments, parents can do what perhaps no professional educator has done before: teach this English pragmatics curriculum to unsocial, native English speakers. In fact, it may be useful to think of the more unsocial left-brainers as foreign language learners from overseas, and as foreigners in the broader culture that surrounds them, who require precisely the kinds of explicit guidelines offered by these materials.

One good text is Rhona B. Genzel and Martha Graves Cummings's *Culturally Speaking*. Combining the basically similar Canadian and American cultures, it offers lessons on Anglo-American rules for introducing people, engaging in small talk, using appropriate gestures, building friendships, complimenting and reassuring people, expressing concern, accepting or turning down dates, making jokes, sharing interests, and participating in social events. It also covers facial expressions, types of friendship, and appropriate and inappropriate topics for small talk. And it lists specific cues for students to attend to during hypothetical situations.

As we've seen, left-brainers often find live conversations difficult to follow and fully absorb. Perhaps most valuable, therefore, are *Culturally Speaking*'s dozens of written transcripts of sample conversations, and exercises in which the student writes an appropriate response to a particular utterance, fills in missing lines in a conversation, or analyzes why someone said something and what they meant by it. Some exercises call for group practice, assigning students specific situations to handle and goals to fulfill, for example when someone makes a pass at you. Unlike the open-ended, emotionally driven role-play exercises we saw in chapter 1, these exercises, with their narrow, prescribed objectives and their analytical questions, perfectly suit left-brain learners.

Another good book is Bruce Tillitt and Mary Newton Bruder's *Speaking Naturally*. Its first chapter covers the subtleties of conversational openings and closings, which are particularly difficult for the more socially aloof, lots of whom can converse reasonably well once a dialogue gets rolling. Later chapters discuss how to make and respond to invitations, apologies, and compliments. They also address anger: how it is expressed, and what makes Anglo-Americans angry, things like breaking a confidence, interfering in personal matters, or failing to speak when passing someone—the sorts of faux pas that the more socially awkward left-brainers are apt to commit. And they explain how to express disagreement, including specific phrases for indirect disagreement—essential vocabulary for the many left-brainers who tend to disagree too directly.

Throughout its various topics, *Speaking Naturally* situates phrases along formality scales extending from the most formal to the most casual. These explicit, systematic scales for different shades of social nuance are just what many unsocial children require. Just as importantly, it gives them a tool kit for controlling the flow of conversations. These include ways to get people's attention and join in, phrases for politely introducing a change of subject, ways to show the other person that you are listening and comprehending and, finally, ways to get information while avoiding taboo topics and personal questions—key advice for the many left-brainers who put satisfying curiosity ahead of social grace. For either breaking into conversations, or showing that you are listening, the book notes the importance of eye contact, which is something that the more unsocial left-brainers need to be constantly reminded of. As for shy people in particular, lessons such as these, by empowering them to assert conversational control and, in particular, to switch away from uncomfortable topics, may help them feel less intimidated by conversations in general.

As with *Culturally Speaking, Speaking Naturally* offers sample dialogue and written exercises in which students analyze conversations or fill in missing lines. Other exercises have them identify the indirect compliments in a particular dialogue, or construct a dialogue from a specific set of goals and messages. Again, the problems are highly structured and analytical and, as such, well-suited to left-brain learners.

A third book aimed at foreign students but helpful to unsocial children is *Teaching Pragmatics,* written by Kathleen Bardovi-Harlig and Rebecca Mahan-Taylor and put out by the Bureau of Educational and Cultural Affairs of the U.S. Department of State. This book specifically addresses teachers of foreign students, but most of its lessons can also be used by us left-brainer parents. Covering many of the same topics and exercises as *Culturally Speaking* and *Speaking Naturally,* it also includes lessons on how to greet people, make requests, and enliven and personalize a conversation with parenthetical comments. Other lessons discuss conversational mistakes and enumerate handy formulaic phrases appropriate for chitchat—another big challenge for unsocial children.

Many of the book's suggestions are refreshingly specific. These include how to show solidarity by rephrasing what the other person said; how to use "mm," "yeah," and "right" to show you are listening; how to use "actually" to show gentle disagreement; how to use "would it be OK if . . . " or "I was wondering if . . . " to soften requests; and how to use "well" to take turns in a conversation, shift or resume a topic, clarify something, or introduce a negative or unexpected response. Other specifics include a classification of different ways to respond to compliments ("downgrading," "questioning," "shifting credit," and "returning"), and advice about how to adjust for specific social contexts. The general theme of these lessons is how to avoid seeming aloof, which many left-brainers find particularly challenging.

Another source of conversational pragmatics is *Fluent American English,* a video series created by Susan Steinbach, a specialist in teaching English to foreign students. These videos focus on the dynamics of group conversations, and discuss how to jump into a conversation politely, maintain the floor, and get your point across.

What makes all of these teaching materials useful is that they showcase those issues that unsocial left-brainers find most challenging: conversational openings, closings, and flow; how to join group conversations; and how to be polite, show interest, and soften requests and criticism.

As we begin exposing our children to the rules of social interaction, we must remember our ultimate goal. It isn't to pressure our children to go against their nature; it is, rather, to teach them a repertoire of basic rules and strategies for getting along with others, and for reaching out and joining in whenever they want or need to.

TEACHING YOUR CHILD TO READ EMOTIONS

We have thus far neglected one skill that underpins all successful social interactions: the ability to infer the emotions of the people you interact with. The ability, specifically, to detect genuine interest vs. boredom, comprehension vs. confusion, and flattery vs. hurt. Since people typically don't make these emotions verbally explicit—indeed, what they say often conflicts with how they feel—quite often the only way to detect them is through facial expressions and tones of voice. But many left-brainers, as noted in the Introduction, find these nonverbal cues quite difficult to read.

Simon Baron-Cohen, the psychologist who developed the notion of Systemizers versus Empathizers, has documented the difficulty Systemizers (many of our left-brainers) have in reading nonverbal cues and has created a software program called *Mind Reading* to teach these skills. *Mind Reading* contains a library of 412 emotions, each one linked with photographs of corresponding facial expressions and sound bites of corresponding utterances, and organized thematically into twenty-four emotion groups. Drawing on this compendium, *Mind Reading* offers lessons, exercises, and quizzes in matching different facial expressions and tones of voice to different emotions. Level I begins with basic feelings, such as "happy," "sad," and "excited"; higher levels tackle subtler ones, such as "fond of" and "bullied," ultimately reaching sentiments as subtle as "complacent," "insouciant," and "listless" (all members of the "bored" category), and "ambivalent," "disoriented," and "subservient" (members of the "unsure" category).

While the effectiveness of Baron-Cohen's program awaits a proper clinical study, anecdotal reports suggest that many find it helpful.

More recently, Baron-Cohen has developed a television show for four- to ten-year-olds called *The Transporters*, which features vehicles—trolleys, cable cars, and trains—with human faces that display a variety of different emotions. The fifteen five-minute episodes are designed to teach these emotions in context, and thirty interactive quizzes help to reinforce the lessons.

ENROLLING YOUR CHILD IN SOCIAL SKILLS GROUPS

As a child starts learning particular conversational rules or emotional expressions, she needs actual practice in applying this knowledge. As Lisbeth notes, "In my head I can see big bold letters of what I need to do. But the next step is always hard."

Immersing unsocial children in unstructured group activities, as we saw in chapter 1, often only confuses and intimidates them further. What they need, instead, is structured practice of the sort offered by social skills classes like those that have helped Katrina's son, Max. Unlike the group interactions that predominate in school, these sessions are led by an adult, typically a psychologist or a speech therapist, and occur mostly in clinical settings such as children's hospitals or psychiatry clinics. The key ingredients are structured activities—for example, games, or specific role-playing exercises like those we saw above in the English pragmatics curricula—and an expert who intervenes frequently and attends to the specific social weaknesses of the different children.

Unsocial left-brainers also benefit when children with more right-brain dispositions attend—children who can act, to some extent, as social role models. Perhaps one reason why Max's group has served him so well is that it consists entirely of himself and two ADD kids, whose social weaknesses result from deficits in attention rather than in social awareness.

Venues for social skills groups include public schools; children's hospitals; and psychology, psychiatry, speech therapy, and play therapy clinics. Outside the school setting, a referral from a psychiatrist may convince insurers to cover all or part of the cost. If neither your local school nor your local hospital offers social skills groups, check with the American Speech-Language-Hearing Association (www.asha.org) or the Association for Play Therapy (www.a4pt.org). Both of these organizations list therapists by local area who teach social skills.

Outside the therapy world, theater clubs also provide opportunities for structured role-play. Both the more informal improvisation exercises and the more formal reading—and, at some clubs, writing—of scripted dialogue can be highly therapeutic for unsocial children. They may also benefit from being surrounded, in the process, by more social role models. Many of our children, of course, don't enjoy doing theater, and by no means should we force it on them; but those who do may find it more fun than social therapy. One mother estimates that a summer at theater camp benefited her daughter as much as a whole year of social skills classes.

TEACHING THE SOCIAL DYNAMICS OF YOUTH CULTURE

The virtue of social skills classes is also their downside: the structured, highly prescriptive environment they provide, while enabling children to practice specific social skills, can't possibly simulate the buzzing world of peer interactions that surrounds them in real life. On the other hand, as their social weaknesses make clear, simply immersing left-brainers in this world is insufficient, even detrimental. A more effective way to acculturate them is to provide windows through which they can first observe the social world from afar, taking it in at their own preferred rates.

Ironically, many of the most revealing windows into the world of youth social culture are framed by fiction—albeit realistic fiction, set in school yards, cafeterias, classrooms, and backyards. And, while many of the details of American youth culture have changed over the years, most of its essentials are timeless, and numerous literary classics in youth-culture realism are still helpful (and in print) today. These include Beverly Cleary's *Otis Spofford, Ellen Tebbits, The Luckiest Girl,* and *Fifteen;* and Judy Blume's *Are You There God? It's Me, Margaret, Tales of a Fourth Grade Nothing,* and *Blubber.* Their contemporary, if less literary, counterparts include Cynthia Voigt's *Bad Girls* series, Sarah Dessen's *Just Listen,* Ned Vizzini's *Be More Chill,* and Frank Portman's *King Dork.* These last two, with their socially outcast protagonists, may resonate especially with those of our children who feel the most marginalized.

Even more instructional, with their live dialogue, close-ups of facial expressions, and complex social narratives, are movies and TV shows about teenage social life. The classic movies, of course, are the John Hughes teen-angst films of the 1980s, such as *Sixteen Candles, Pretty in Pink*, and *The Breakfast Club*, as well as *Fast Times at Ridgemont High*, based on the undercover work of the writer Cameron Crowe, who posed as a student at an actual high school. A surge of teen movies in the late 1990s provide more up-to-date, if less nuanced, takes on social cliques and dating: *She's All That, Drive Me Crazy*, and especially *American Pie*. The more relevant TV shows—all dating from the late 1980s to the present, and available over the Internet—are *Boy Meets World, My So-Called Life, Life As We Know It, Life Goes On, Dawson's Creek, Degrassi*, and *Freaks and Geeks*.

Some parents report playing an active role in such video lessons—to the extent that their children allow it—and, in particular, frequently pushing the Pause button. Depending on what our child needs help with, we might stop the action to scrutinize a face, to review a fast-paced conversation and see how outsiders joined in, or to discuss why one person said something and how the other person reacted.

One parent reports pausing at every joke, noting that most informal socializing is grounded in humor and that much of mainstream humor is conversely grounded in social settings. Humor represents, indeed, a major barrier for the more socially aloof left-brainers. It's also so elusive that no social advice book satisfactorily addresses it. Far more effective is studying a large number of actual examples—conveniently provided by the more popular movies and TV shows. By explicating each joke that goes by, we can train our child, if not to become a more effective jokester, at least to recognize mainstream humor on his own, which, in turn, will make social situations considerably more accessible.

ONLINE VENUES FOR OLDER UNSOCIAL CHILDREN

Besides helping them cope with the social world that surrounds them, we can introduce older left-brainers to *virtual* social worlds that better suit their interests, strengths, and comfort needs—namely, some of the many Internet chat rooms. A chat room, for the uninitiated, is a website where people with similar interests can communicate by typing on their computer screens messages that then appear on the screens of everyone else who is currently logged in.

As an entirely text-based medium for live, informal discussion, chat rooms meet myriad left-brain needs. Those who have trouble reading tones of voice and facial expressions often excel in exchanges where these confounding cues are entirely absent. Those who struggle to keep up with fast-paced oral discussions often perform like their peers when conversing at the slower rate of text. Finally, those who are shy about talking are often comfortable with typing. Lisbeth, who spent time in chat rooms during her later school years, reports that, for the first time in her life, she was able to follow a group discussion and join in with the right thing at the right time without feeling too intimidated.

Chat rooms also benefit left-brainers by uniting people with similar interests or personality traits. The website www.shyunited.com hosts the premier chat room for shy people. Several sites cater to people with actual or suspected Asperger's syndrome, the most popular being www.wrongplanet.net. Even undiagnosed children who are simply unsocial may find someone to bond with in the Asperger's rooms: many participants have never been diagnosed, and merely suspect that they meet the clinical criteria by virtue of their self-assessed aloofness or obliviousness to social cues.

Finally, for all left-brainers, there are special-interest chats—on topics from music, science fiction, and computers to the much more arcane. While some of these rooms may attract as many right-brainers as left, they're still based in that left-brain-friendly medium of text. They offer, as well, the benefits of the focused, content-based discussion—more serious and less mired in social chitchat than much of real-life interaction.

Another option for online interaction is Second Life and its offshoot, Teen Second Life (restricted to users between the ages of thirteen and eighteen). Users interact via two-dimensional icons, or "avatars," and communicate via online chat or instant messaging. One mother reports that her son has been interacting in this fashion with teenagers from all over the world, practicing his social skills "without feeling threatened."

Of course, the Internet still presents threats, and parents should be careful to monitor a child's Internet time, especially since the less socially savvy a child is, the more vulnerable he or she is to online predators.

It's important for us parents to remember that, for most left-brain children, the hardest years are those of primary and secondary school, when they spend so many hours so inescapably surrounded by the teeming social life of their classmates. All this culminates in junior high and high school, when the gap between the social awareness and sophistication of left-brainers and that of their peers typically reaches its zenith.

At a sufficiently large or specialized college, most left-brainers can find like-minded peers. Beyond college, contrary to what the popular books on emotional intelligence claim, there are plenty of satisfying careers in which sociability matters little and people mainly interact not by working together continuously but by divvying things up and convening only occasionally—fostering the sort of rapport that, as with music groups and team sports, can satisfy many a left-brainer's need for social connection.

We parents can also take heart in the probability that our left-brain children will become ever more socially engaged as life goes on. On the one hand, many of their peers will grow increasingly interested, as they mature, in more serious, left-brain topics and activities. Left-brainers themselves, on the other hand, will continue throughout adulthood to develop, in their own systematic, left-brain fashion, their conversational skills, their emotional sensitivities, and their interests in engaging with others.

3

Hindered by Reform Math and Other Major Trends in K–12 Education

The Analytic Child at School

"I hate school," Josh announces. It's a Monday night in late September, the beginning of Josh's fourth week at one of the best middle schools the city has to offer, a math and science magnet that attracts the strongest teachers in the district, a school that his parents had set their sights on for years.

Ben, Josh's dad, looks up from the computer. "What do you mean?" They're both at the dining room table, which doubles as an after-dinner work space.

"I hate school," Josh repeats, raising his voice and thwacking a yellow folder against the table.

If Josh has said this before, it's never been with such vehemence.

"Please explain," Ben says.

"Take a look at the projects they just assigned us." Josh scoots the folder across the table.

Ben takes it and peers inside.

"There's a sheet for each subject," Josh says. "Take a look."

Ben pulls out several sheets and pages through: "Design a Playground," "Decorate a Tissue Box," "Construct a Diorama."

"That's a lot of art homework," remarks Ben. "What about your other subjects?"

"Dad, that's the point," yells Josh. "These are for my other subjects."

"Which ones?" Ben pages back through. Everywhere the same phrases keep popping up: "Be colorful." "Be creative."

"All of them. Math, English, German . . . The tissue box is for German."

Ben looks again: "Decorate a box of tissues with German words, drawings, etc. Pick the vocabulary from chapters 1 or 2, and use those words to decorate your box of tissues. Put the number of the chapter you've chosen on your box also."

"You've got to be kidding."

Ben turns to the next page: "Construct a diorama illustrating the climactic scene of your novel."

"That's for English," Josh says. "The playground's for math. That last sheet is for science." He reaches for the folder, pulls out one more page, and hands it to Ben: "Write a three-page paper that includes a description of a movie, television show, or a book that involves a scientific concept, a summary of the scientific concept, and an explanation of the relationship between the actual concept and how it is used in the movie, television show, or book."

Ben and his wife enrolled Josh at the math and science magnet not only because their son excels in math and science but because he's never been that motivated about writing, and is even less inspired by the arts-and-crafts activities that dominated his elementary school classes. This school, they thought, would finally give him a break. Instead, it turns out, Josh now gets to take this nonsense home as homework. Assaulted by a mental image of him bent over a shoebox, scowling and clenching his jaw as he glues in a cardboard cutout of a Billy Pilgrim stick figure, Ben wonders how they could have been so wrong about the school. And how could the faculty of this math and science magnet be so wrongheaded?

Melissa scans down the column of 3s in Hannah's first report card: 3 in language arts, 3 in social studies, 3 in science, and 3 in math. "Might 3 be the highest grade?" she wonders, as she recalls the near-perfect marks *she and her friends got back in elementary school, and tries to decipher this apparently novel grading system. It's only when Melissa discovers the fine print on the back of this first report card that she learns that the highest possible grade is actually not 3, but 4. Hannah's grades aren't "excellent," which is what Melissa expected, but "good"—which, what with all that grade inflation Melissa keeps reading about, presumably means they're actually not even "good," but "fair."*

What gives Melissa pause, in particular, is the 3 in math. Social studies, language arts, science—who knows what's going on in these classes? Maybe Hannah's distractibility and disorganization are somehow getting in the way there. But in math? Melissa has seen Hannah's math homework, and it's much easier than what she's having Hannah do at home as a supplement. In fact, the very reason she's taking time out of her own—and Hannah's—busy schedules for extra math is because Hannah keeps remarking on how easy the class work is. And, judging from the few first grade assignments Hannah's taken home, it is way too easy. "Circle the larger of two one-digit numbers." "How many black dots are there?" "Add 3 and 5." This seems like kindergarten math, and yet it's as far as they've gotten after three months of first grade.

Hannah's parents, her grandparents, her aunts and uncles—the family lore has all of them dazzling people from day one, especially their teachers, with their way-above-grade-level math skills. What's going on with Hannah, who, at home, accurately and effortlessly adds and subtracts two-digit numbers?

Two possibilities occur to Melissa: Either Hannah is so bored by classroom math that she's underperforming at school. Or there is something that she's being graded on—even in math class—other than her actual math skills.

————

Some left-brain children are math geniuses, some more verbally inclined. Some tend toward science, others toward foreign language, still others toward political or philosophical debate. Some are also unsocial; others merely analytic. For all their individual differences, our analytical left-brainers share many of the following characteristics:

- Linear in their thinking: absorbing things one at a time
- Easily distracted by sensory clutter
- Needing, and seeking, logical organization
- Detail-focused; difficulty organizing large amounts of material all at once
- Learning better from abstract symbols and concepts than hands-on activities
- Excelling in math, science, verbal argumentation, and foreign language grammar
- Good at calculating numbers in their heads
- Needing and striving for precision
- Weak in handwriting, graphic arts, and/or visual representations
- Work best independently
- Highly critical, skeptical, and argumentative
- Difficulty adjusting to novel situations
- Deep, all-absorbing interests or seemingly encyclopedic knowledge of certain subjects
- Sometimes suspected of having a Nonverbal Learning Disability (NLD) or Asperger's syndrome

The above labels—NLD and Asperger's syndrome—while most likely to be tagged on to the more unsocial of our analytic kids, capture much of what characterizes analytic children in general. Both NLD and Asperger's symptoms include not just social impairments but also detail focus, sensory sensitivities, difficulty adjusting to novel situations, and all-absorbing interests. Symptoms for NLD include, as well, problems with penmanship, spatial reasoning, and large-scale organization. For most analytic children, however, neither disorder truly applies. Asperger's describes those with more serious social impairments than what characterizes most of our kids; two of the core symptoms of NLD are poor numerical skills and difficulty with abstract reasoning—areas where our children excel. But, just as we saw with unsocial left-brainers in chapter 1, that doesn't stop certain professionals from leaping to diagnoses.

Even if our child remains label-free, as many analytic children do, the above-listed traits still present challenges, both to us parents and to our children. As far as our children are concerned, these challenges are nowhere more compelling than in their classrooms.

As with their unsocial counterparts, analytic children face new teaching trends that have them disliking school more than we did, earning lower grades, receiving fewer opportunities for academic enrichment, and facing worse prospects for admission to competitive high schools and colleges.

Accompanying the shift from lectures and solo work to class discussions and group work, addressed in chapter 1, are several additional pedagogical shifts, spurred on by popular new teaching principles bearing names such as Constructivism, Project-Based Learning, and Writing Across the Curriculum. These are shifts from explicit instruction to incidental learning, from abstract problem solving to hands-on activities, from analytical assignments to personal reflections, from subject-specific homework to interdisciplinary projects, and from calculations and science experiments to open-ended writing. As we'll discuss below, all of these trends leave our kids bored, confused, and underappreciated. And, tragically, they influence especially those subjects that once most engaged our analytical thinkers: math, science, and foreign language grammar.

"WHY DOES MY CHILD HATE SCHOOL MATH?"

One window into what's changed in school mathematics is offered by a recent front-page article in the *Philadelphia Inquirer* profiling a retiring New Jersey math teacher named Jayne King. King was one of ninety-three teachers nationwide selected for the 2007 Presidential Award for Excellence in Mathematics and Science Teaching, an award that includes a cash prize of $10,000 from the National Science Foundation.

The article enumerates the most important lessons King learned from her three decades of teaching: "Show, don't tell. Let the students 'discover' the answers by asking the right 'prompt' questions. Make it real. . . . Math wasn't theories and concepts, it was a life learning experience to be shared."

Exhibiting this philosophy is the fifth-grade lesson on area and perimeter for which King earned her award. Working in groups, students had to decide how to deploy 32 meters of fencing to construct a pen for Scruffy the dog. Their tasks included pricing the fencing materials, assessing the pros and cons of different pen dimensions (greater area vs. a longer dog run), interviewing their parents on how area and perimeter figure in everyday life, and writing poems about area and perimeter.

As revealing as the lesson itself and its prestigious award is the *Philadelphia Inquirer*'s enthusiastic bias: part of the lesson's "beauty," the *Inquirer* reports, "was that there was no right answer, just lots of options, all of which dealt with math in a practical way."

Traditionally, math has been the academic subject most attuned to left-brain learning styles, even for the many analytic children who end up in nonmathematical careers. In the last two decades, following the publication of the 1989 *Standards* by the National Council of Teachers of Mathematics, all that has changed. What was once the most linear, logical, analytical, and left-brain-friendly component of the core curriculum has undergone a more comprehensive right-brain shift than all other subjects combined. More and more schools, public and private, are jumping on board, and if our child is bringing home books called *Everyday Math, Today's Math, Investigations, MathLand, Trailblazers, Integrated Math, Connected Mathematics, Math in Context,* or the *Interactive Math Program;* or assignments involving household objects, arts and crafts, games, and surveys, complete with complex, multistep directions and "Dear Family" or "Family Connection" letters—then his or her school is among them.

Known collectively as Reform Math, the new curriculum diverges drastically from what most of us experienced when we ourselves were students. While our children's textbooks and homework assignments show us some of what's new, it's much harder, absent detailed memories of our own math classes, to notice the many things they *omit*. In fact, to fully appreciate what's new and what's absent, we have to spend time in classrooms.

Here, chances are, we won't see teachers at blackboards guiding students through mathematical explanations, or students doing solo pen-and-paper work at their desks. Teachers are much more likely to be walking around and supervising as students sit in groups and play math games, cut and paste shapes, assemble blocks and beans, or collaborate on interdisciplinary projects such as "Scruffy's pen." Such activities, once specific to kindergarten, now persist throughout the school years. When teachers do step in front and call on students, they don't stop when they hear the right answer, but solicit as many solutions as possible, encouraging students to talk directly to one another about their strategies and—as we saw in chapter 1—retreating as the discussion gets rolling.

Classrooms, textbooks, and homework assignments alike have undergone a multifaceted transformation. They've shifted away from explicit demonstrations (whether on blackboards or in textbooks) to student-centered discussions; they've shifted from solo, pen-and-paper calculations to hands-on, group activities and open-ended writing; they've shifted from general procedures such as borrowing, carrying, and cross-multiplying—applied repeatedly to multiple problems—to multiple, ad hoc shortcuts, applied specifically to single problems; they've shifted from pure math to "real life" applications; and finally, they've shifted from mathematically challenging assignments to ones that are time-consuming for nonmathematical reasons.

As we will discuss below, these changes, collectively, clash with most of the core characteristics of our analytic children.

How Reform Math Challenges Linear Thinkers Who Are Easily Distracted by Sensory Clutter

Today's math is no longer the linear, one-thing-at-a-time affair it once was: first single-digit addition and subtraction, then borrowing and carrying across multiple digits, then long multiplication, then long division, and so on. Instead of practicing a single procedure—say, for finding common denominators—on a large number of problems, an entire class may address just one problem—say, the best pen for Scruffy—with each student reporting on all the possible solutions she found, and all the different strategies she used to get there. The ad hoc specifics of most of these strategies clog the curriculum with uninspiring details—to add 48 and 52, you can first add 2 to the 48 and subtract 2 from the 52—obscuring the underlying logic.

Adding to the conceptual clutter of multiple, case-specific strategies considered all at once is the clutter and confusion within the problems themselves. Word problems—also known as "story problems"—predominate, and they now challenge students less by tapping into difficult math concepts than by distracting them with extraneous verbiage, for example, about how Jenna feels about the birthday party she's planning, about how the spots on the giraffes look just like the meatballs in the submarine sandwiches served by the school cafeteria, and so forth. Many of the preliminary directions—whether expressed in writing on the homework sheets or orally by the teacher before an in-class activity—involve multiple steps, given all at once, often in contorted, imprecise sentences: "Draw several groups of an item that comes in groups of some number between 2 and 12. Describe the picture in words. Then, on the back of the student sheet, use that information to make a riddle."

Within the assigned activities, the pure mathematics of pen-and-paper calculations is increasingly crowded out by multimedia procedures: all that cutting, pasting, pouring, and manipulating. Similarly impinging on the relative quiet of solo activities are the half-dozen simultaneous conversations of a half-dozen collaborating groups.

Still more clutter accompanies the influx of material from other disciplines—civics, cartography, design, events planning, personal finances, and even creative writing—into the large number of interdisciplinary, "applied" math projects: "Survey your community." "Draw a map of your neighborhood." "Design a playground." "Plan a party." "Assemble coupons." "Compose a number riddle."

Collectively, all the conceptual, multisensory, and multidisciplinary breadth, combined with the multistep directions, extraneous details, and auditory clutter, overwhelm to distraction the linear, one-thing-at-a-time learner, impairing her ability to keep track of the actual math—however inherently easy it might be—and complete her work to her teacher's satisfaction.

The software retailer Abby Eckhoff is the mother of two analytic children who languished under these aspects of Reform Math—in their case, the *Everyday Math* curriculum. As Abby explains it, the cluttering of mathematics with nonmathematical content and hands-on multimedia activities so interfered with her children's ability to focus on math, and so clogged the logical connections between math concepts, that neither her son, Richard (who has Asperger's syndrome), nor her daughter, Justine, were able to master the basics of elementary school math. Justine, who describes *Everyday Math* as "horrible," took remedial math in middle school in order, as Abby puts it, "to correct the effects of *Everyday Math*." Since then, Justine has discovered that she's actually quite gifted mathematically. Richard, whose experience we will discuss in chapter 5, has likewise blossomed—but only after entering a middle school classroom that uses traditional math.

How Reform Math Shortchanges Those Who Need (and Seek) Logical Organization

Today's math lacks much of the logical structure that once defined traditional school mathematics—both in its individual lessons and in its progression of topics. As far as the former go, as we've seen with the multiple, ad hoc solutions, the Reform approach is organized more around specific problems and trial-and-error tactics than around more general, mathematical concepts (e.g., the ones and tens digits), procedures (e.g., borrowing from the tens digit to the ones digit), and argumentation (why borrowing from the tens digit gets you the right answer). De-emphasizing the concepts, procedures, and argumentation, in turn, weakens the logical backbone of arithmetic that they cumulatively comprise.

Further warping this backbone is the way the curriculum spirals from topic to topic, rarely pausing long enough to provide our analytic children with the depth they need and crave. As James Milgram, a Stanford mathematics professor, reports in his review of *Connected Mathematics*, "Topics are introduced, usually in a single problem and almost always indirectly—topics which in traditional texts are basic and will have an entire chapter devoted to them—and then are dropped, never to be mentioned again."

But perhaps nothing impedes the logical organization of school math more than the Constructivist pedagogy practiced in today's classrooms. As we've discussed, neither today's teachers nor today's textbooks provide much in the way of direct instruction; rather, Reform Math Constructivism favors holistic, incidental learning by doing— alternately called "discovery learning," "experiential learning," or "investigations"—mostly in groups via those hands-on activities we discussed above. In the words of the *Connected Mathematics* curriculum, teachers should allow students to "bump into the answer." As *Investigations* puts it, students "move around the classroom as they explore the mathematics in their environment and talk with their peers." The organizing principle is no longer the logical accumulation of math concepts, but whatever the twenty-plus students happen to discover, in whatever order they happen to discover it.

The fact that most of these discoveries occur during group work and class discussions disorganizes things further. In chapter 1 we saw such collective activities intimidating and disengaging unsocial children. For the more social left-brainers, the problem, rather, is confusion: questions and concepts emerge from many different perspectives in rapid succession, ordered not by logic but by who happens to speak after whom—especially in Reform Math's ideal, in which the teacher takes a backseat. Other children may absorb these discussions holistically; our child struggles to keep up. To learn new material, he requires a linear, logical presentation, for which a good teacher or textbook is a much more promising source than are groups of fellow classmates. To practice new skills, she needs to work independently so she can take logical control, think without interruption, and approach problems from her perspective alone. As Abby Eckhoff says of her analytic children in their *Everyday Math* classrooms, "They both need a logical hierarchy in which to put information, and there *was* no logical hierarchy."

How Reform Math Shortchanges Those Better Suited to Abstract Symbols and Concepts than to Hands-On Activities

Today's Reform Math prefers objects and visual representations to symbols; concrete, "real life" problems to purely mathematical ones; and, as we discussed earlier, case-specific strategies to general problem-solving procedures.

Blocks, sand, and tally marks now extend far beyond kindergarten. *Investigations*, for example, has fifth-grade students compute multiples by skipping their fingers along number charts, and volume by pouring sand into containers. *Trailblazers* fifth-graders add fractions by taping together "fraction strips." *Connected Mathematics* sixth-graders determine the volume of specially tailored boxes by counting how many cubes fit into them.

Then there's the emphasis on "applied math," which we place in quotes to distinguish Reform Math's version—designing that playground, planning that party, assembling those coupons—from the more rigorous and mathematical applied math of, say, engineering, computer science, or economics. As the *Everyday Math* website asserts, "Mathematics is more meaningful when it is rooted in real life context and situations." To many students, perhaps; not to our analytic children.

Some Reform Math exercises allow "real life" to trump the actual math. A third-grade *Investigations* problem shows a picture of a computer, an apple, a balloon, a TV set, and a pizza; asks children which of these can be shared by being split into pieces; and solicits other, nonmathematical ways of jointly appreciating balloons and TV sets.

Also detracting from mathematical abstraction are the case-specific strategies we discussed earlier. The more advanced the math, the greater this detraction—as when *Connected Mathematics* eighth-graders, instead of being guided through an inductive proof about adding exponents, "verify" the formula by checking out a few specific examples; or compute a slope not by doing algebra (solving for y), but by doing arithmetic (plugging in specific numbers and plotting points).

All this mires our children in the concrete, and keeps at bay the abstract, logical analysis that they most enjoy and excel in.

How Reform Math Shortchanges Those Who Excel in Math

An *Investigations* problem has each student drawing or cutting out a hundred shapes for their "pictures of 100." A videotape of a model class in California, played during a math-methods course for prospective teachers, shows an entire class session devoted to a single word problem in which eleven envelopes contain four beans each: after solving the problem, students sit and listen as one classmate after another presents her way of multiplying four by eleven. A multi-week-long *Interactive Math Project* unit has students studying the nineteenth-century migration across the U.S., planning what to take on an imagined 2,400-mile trek, and "studying the rates of consumption and of travel."

With its progress through mathematics bogged down by the inefficiencies of hands-on, experiential learning, lengthy discussions of multiple solutions, and time spent writing about math and applying it to geography, civics, and home economics, today's mathematics is both easier and less mathematical than it ever used to be. Further slowing and diluting the curriculum are gimmicks intended to stoke student interest—for example, journals about favorite numbers; Wanted posters about suspicious integers; or, in an infamous assignment from *Everyday Math*, a series of sentence-completion tasks that begins with "If math were a color, it would be . . . " Perhaps most elaborate is a birthday-party graphing activity for *Investigations* third-graders that opens with the teacher pretending to hold a baby in her arms, asking the students to sing "Happy Birthday," encouraging nonnative English speakers to sing the song in their native languages, and asking the class as a whole to make a poster displaying the words "Happy Birthday" in all the different languages they speak.

All of this waters down the curriculum and marginalizes whole topics. In particular, Reform Math drastically de-emphasizes or omits those concepts that don't lend themselves to student discovery through concrete materials. One casualty: standard procedures, such as borrowing and carrying (regrouping), long multiplication, and long division. Another: the "unfriendly" fractions that "fraction strips" omit—those with denominators other than 3, 4, 5, 6, 8, 10, or 12. A third set of casualties: abstract principles (e.g., place value and the distributive law), formulas (e.g., for the volume of shapes more complex than cubes and rectangles), and proofs (e.g., about adding exponents). Finally, there are those ventures that are either irrelevant to the real-life applications Reform Math considers so important or obsolete because of pocket calculators: memorizing the multiplication tables, dividing fractions; converting between fractions and decimals, and calculating with negative numbers. By the time Reform Math students are in fifth grade, some mathematicians estimate, they are up to two years behind their peers in other developed countries.

Much of what Reform Math de-emphasizes is critical for algebra. Without facility with the distributive law and the multiplication tables, for example, you will struggle to factor polynomials and complete the square. And if you can't do these things, you won't understand key algebraic concepts such as the quadratic formula. Much of the new algebra curriculum is accordingly dumbed down, and increasingly has students memorizing formulas without understanding them, and plugging in specific numbers and doing arithmetic rather than manipulating variables to solve equations symbolically. As Professor Milgram notes, there is often "no requirement at all that the students do any symbolic manipulations." Not all analytic children are huge fans of arithmetic, but, in the past, many would go on to love algebra; for the most mathematically inclined, indeed, it was often in algebra that they discovered their mathematical calling. For them, especially, algebra's new memorize, plug in, and calculate incarnation—which some mathematicians call "cookbook math"—deprives them of that which once most engaged math buffs about mathematics.

How Reform Math Shortchanges Those Who Calculate Numbers in Their Heads

One key feature of Reform Math we haven't yet addressed is its expectation that students explain their answers. Simply showing your work is no longer sufficient; you must also demonstrate your thinking process, typically in words or pictures, in what are now called "math journals" or "problem-solving notebooks." But we know our children. Swiftly and automatically, they manipulate numbers in their minds, apparently, as many will tell us, without accompanying words or pictures—especially when it comes to the simple calculations that dominate Reform Math problems. When asked to explain their answers, they typically have nothing to say. Even if they can come up with something, writing it down, rather than enhancing their mathematical understanding, only further disengages them from classroom math: "5 + 6 = 11," "10 × 10 = 100"—what more is there to write or draw?

Worse, some problems implicitly require explanations that are both verbose and minimally mathematical, as when *Investigations* asks third-graders to write letters to second-graders explaining why 1 ⅓ is larger than 1 ¼. *Remember, a second-grader must understand what you write*. Most analytic children would find it far more engaging to justify their answers in mathematical terms—of the sort that would convince a math teacher or fellow math buff—than to write an informal explanation to a seven-year-old.

How Reform Math Shortchanges Those Who Need and Strive for Precision

The writing skills of Reform Math editors are no match for the complexity of their instructions and, as a result, these often contain gaps or poorly defined constraints. A first-grade *Investigations* problem shows a picture of four chips next to an overturned cup. "There are nine counters in all. Four of them are next to the cup. How many are under the cup?" It's unclear: all we know is that there are five additional chips, not where they are.

A third-grade *Investigations* problem shows a grid of dots, some of which are blocked out by checkered rectangles, with a rabbit in one corner and a carrot on the far side. "Draw the shortest path from the rabbit to the carrot. Go around each [checkered rectangle]. (REMEMBER: The dots are 10 steps apart.)" The shortest path follows the dots diagonally; are diagonal paths allowed? Are the dots diagonally 10 steps apart, or horizontally and vertically? (What is a "step"?)

A fifth-grade *Trailblazers* "lab" problem asks students to flip two coins one hundred times. "Before the lab, predict how many times each number of heads will show in your 100 trials." What does "each number of heads" mean? Per trial, or per hundred trials?

Analytic children are close, literal readers. Particularly when it comes to math problems, they expect precision and resist relying on context or common sense to fill in what's left unspecified. They are, therefore, often stumped—even when the actual math is child's play.

Or, if they take things too literally (e.g., take "shortest path" to mean the absolutely shortest path, i.e., a diagonal one), they may end up confronting a much harder problem that exceeds even their precocious skills (in this case, one involving the Pythagorean theorem). The result, either way, is additional frustration with classroom math.

How Reform Math Shortchanges Those Who Struggle with Handwriting, Graphic Arts, and/or Visual Representations

The many assignments that require verbal and pictographic explanations, as well as the journal entries, posters, and arts and crafts projects that comprise so much of today's "applied math"—all of these tap into specific areas of weakness for many of our analytic children. Besides these, Reform Math stresses visual representations of data: bar graphs, box and whiskers graphs, pie charts and flow charts.

Once, math was a haven for the penmanship-impaired math buff with shaky skills in graphic design and visual arts. Now his work, however mathematically correct, looks sloppy and uninspired—just as he felt while completing it.

How Reform Math Shortchanges Those Who Work Best Independently

Mathematically precocious but confused, as we saw, by the multiple perspectives of group conversations, our analytic child longs to work independently and at her own rate, especially in math class, where, unconstrained by others, she would soar far ahead. But Reform Math proponents insist that students work mostly in assigned groups, often of mixed ability, and teachers are tasked with walking around and making sure everyone cooperates. For many of our children, this leads to tremendous frustration, not only with the activity in question, but also with their many mathematically less capable classmates.

―――――

All these changes leave left-brain talents in logical analysis and abstract thinking unchallenged and underdeveloped. Even those left-brainers able to do interesting math outside of school will remain bored and disengaged in the Reform classroom. Meanwhile, those who lack such extracurricular opportunities may end up thoroughly turned off to the subject that once might have interested them most, and ill prepared for the more advanced classes that otherwise might have engrossed them in college.

"Mom, what's wrong with this country that everyone I know is bored in math?" asks Benjamin, whom we saw in chapter 1 bursting out in frustration at his math group. For more and more of America's mathematically inclined school students, this is a very basic boredom — not from confusion, not from mindless calculations, but from the disappearance of mathematical challenge.

Even long before Reform Math took hold, the elementary school math curriculum failed to fully engage many left-brain math buffs. Earlier, the problem was that it moved too slowly for these children — albeit not as slowly as Reform Math does — and asked them to repeat ad nauseam procedures that they had already mastered. But at least by the time they finished arithmetic, these children had all the tools they needed to begin algebra, where math finally got interesting. Now, as we saw, all that has changed. As one retired mathematician puts it, "While I found the grade-school arithmetic I did back in the 1940s and '50s mildly irritating, I would have been completely bored and disgusted by Reform Math."

"WHY DOES MY CHILD HATE SCIENCE?"

Spurred on by Project-Based Learning, Writing Across the Curriculum, and the new National Science Education *Standards*, ever more science classes are following in the footsteps of Reform Math. Increasingly they emphasize communicating about science, interdisciplinary science, and science appreciation, over actual science. "It's not like I have my kids go in and do an experiment, and then go in the next day and do another one, and so on," one science teacher reports. It's more important, he said, for students to make personal connections to science, and develop "higher level" skills, such as reflecting on and communicating about scientific ideas.

The result is a watered-down curriculum in which fourth-graders are writing about their favorite rocks and then sorting them by color and texture; fifth-graders are reading Dr. Seuss's *The Lorax* and choosing natural phenomena to speak for (just as the Lorax spoke for the trees); sixth-graders are reflecting on science articles in the popular press; and most assignments have students doing interdisciplinary projects, producing posters and presentations, and writing about science rather than mastering it.

The new textbooks reflect these priorities. Looking inside the middle school *Science Explorer* series, we see "Interdisciplinary Activities" in every chapter: for example, read Jules Verne's *Journey to the Center of the Earth* and write about your own imaginary journey to earth's center; write a news bulletin about an earthquake "following the five w's" (*what, where, who, when,* and *why*).

Drastically de-emphasized along the way are rigorous scientific standards. As one popular new physics textbook puts it, "There is no single scientific method. . . . Knowledge, skill, luck, imagination, trial and error, educated guesses, and great patience—all play a part." For example, it says, the two Swiss scientists who "discovered" the new superconductors said they "felt free to try something crazy." In seeps the romanticization of science that we discussed in the Introduction, in which scientists appear as intuition-driven, paradigm-busting artists rather than as diligent, detail-oriented researchers and analyzers. As for the scientific method, what is actually a rigorous, step-by-step protocol for hypothesis testing—the backbone of science—has softened into a fog of haphazard strategies, recalling Reform Math's ad hoc solutions.

As with Reform Math, all this watered-down science and disorganized clutter, both scientific and nonscientific, distracts and disengages our children.

LANGUAGE ARTS AND LITERATURE

Right-brain pedagogies have influenced both how teachers teach reading and how they assess comprehension. As far as the former goes, the quintessential pedagogy is Whole Language, which dates back to the 1980s. Its most vehement proponents argue that children should learn words not by attending to sequences of letters and translating them into sequences of phonemes but through context clues and a general immersion in written language. Most school systems now consider this orthodox version of Whole Language, which completely avoids phonics, an abysmal failure. A number of educators, however, have continued over the last two decades, in what's now called Balanced Literacy, to emphasize context clues over sound patterns.

Like the spontaneous, incidental, child-centered approach to math, Whole Language especially shortchanges those who struggle with haphazard, holistic, context-based strategies. For such students, context clues are minimally helpful, especially since so much of the context in today's school books is social and emotional. In contrast, the narrowly focused and systematic linear analysis of traditional phonics is ideally suited to their analytical minds.

A new cornerstone of reading comprehension, as we discussed in chapter 1, is what today's educators call "text-to-self." Both in class discussions and when teachers assess reading skills, students are supposed to draw connections between what they read and their personal lives. Earlier we saw how this requirement impinges on the privacy of the less social children. It also clashes with the talents and preferences of the detail-focused, analytic child, whose strengths lie in closely analyzing texts, and who is disengaged by digressions about his own and his classmates' personal lives.

Writing assignments have also turned personal, even in secondary school. Abby Eckhoff's daughter, Justine, had to keep a journal in which, alongside her essays about literature, she was to log her thoughts *about* these essays—a variation, of sorts, on Reform Math's "explain your answer." She had to discuss why she had chosen a particular topic, what feelings she had about the points she was making, and how all this related to her personal life. So fed up did Justine become with this "huge emphasis on journal writing" that she ended up switching schools.

Along with "text-to-self" is "text-to-world," which touts social and political connections. Together, both priorities have marginalized the close literary analysis that once was the centerpiece of college-prep English classes. As Francine Prose, a novelist and college English teacher, observes in a 1999 *Harper's* article, "I Know Why the Caged

Bird Cannot Read," students are now relating easier, more socially relevant works to their personal experiences. Surveying about eighty reading lists from English classes in public, private, and parochial high schools around the country, Prose finds a strong bias toward books that offer "simplistic prescriptions about how to live."

The new goal, Prose notes, is to teach values through literature, using the novel, and in some cases the race, ethnicity, gender, or political affiliation of its author, as a springboard for the sort of discussion that belongs more in social studies class than in English. Thus, as we saw with Lisbeth's experience in chapter 1, class discussions proceed from the book's themes to students' reflections about the world at large. Questions such as "What do you believe?" and "What do you think about the world?" were, as Lisbeth reports, "what it almost always came down to." Writing assignments have followed suit: instead of analyzing literary technique; identifying themes, symbolism, and structure; or placing books in their literary or historical context, students might be asked to treat *Star Girl*, *Slaughterhouse Five*, and *The Color Purple* as mere springboards for essays that focus more on their personal feelings about conformity, war, or racism in present-day America. The result, Prose argues, is that we no longer appreciate "felicitous or accurate language, images, rhythm [and] wit" and "no longer believe that books were written one word at a time, and deserve to be read that way."

All this reduces our children's opportunities, not only to engage in the kind of close textual analysis that most suits them but also to visit exotic worlds—whether of classical Greece, futuristic Mars, Wonderland, or the inner musings of a Raskolnikov or Stephen Daedalus from Joyce's *A Portrait of the Artist as a Young Man*. Even when teachers include works far removed from the here and now, such as *The Odyssey* or *Crime and Punishment*, constantly asking students to make personal connections to the text limits how much they can truly immerse themselves in other worlds. Literary wanderlust is not specifically a left-brain predilection, but left-brainers, more than others, would much rather lose themselves in settings far removed from their personal lives and social surroundings than connect everything they read to that which they prefer to keep private and often wish to escape.

Thus, we find many of them devouring volumes of unassigned books whose worlds they can inhabit entirely on their own terms, sometimes at the expense of their performance in English class.

Besides text-to-self and text-to-world, another notion popular with educators is that reading comprehension and literary appreciation are multisensory phenomena. Many of today's English and language arts classes, therefore, dilute the analytical not just with the personal and societal but also with the nonverbal. In first and second grade, teachers tell children that books "paint pictures in your head," and have them draw these pictures in their reading-response journals. In later grades, dioramas take over, often standing in for book reports. By secondary school, the assignments become more elaborate: compose a song (an assignment for Lisbeth's English class); perform a dance (an option for her literature presentation); construct an astrological chart (for the characters in *Catcher in the Rye*—an option at another school); design a *Lord of the Flies* T-shirt "that you would sell at a book fair."

All of these changes tap into our children's weaknesses in open-ended visual and creative tasks, and edge out the close literary analysis that once was their greatest source of enjoyment and achievement in English class.

FOREIGN LANGUAGE

While Reform Math is the apotheosis of right-brain trends in public school education, foreign language instruction clocks in a close second. Here, too, the focus has shifted from general, abstract rules to practical, real-life situations, together with a relentless emphasis on communication. According to both the 1996 National *Standards for Foreign Language Learning* and such popular new pedagogies as Input Processing and Total Physical Response, today's teachers are supposed to stress practical communication and culture over abstract grammar rules and linguistic structure. In the words of the 1996 *Standards*, what matters is "what students can do with language," not "what they know about language."

As far as practical communication goes, the most obvious requirements are vocabulary, and speaking and writing practice. So long as your vocabulary is sufficiently large and your pronunciation sufficiently clear, you can express and comprehend a fair amount, even with minimal grammar. "Content-based instruction" has thus replaced "form-based instruction." Meanwhile, the growing emphasis on culture has diluted language instruction in general with non-linguistic tidbits about Spanish meals, French friendships, and Berlin department stores.

All this is reflected in the new textbooks. In the popular French text *Bon Voyage*, for example, chapters like "Friends," "Family and Home," and "In a Café or Restaurant" spend many pages on vocabulary and culture and few on grammar. Verbs appear as individual vocabulary items in present tense, and not as part of an overall verb conjugation system. As with Reform Math, the spotlight is on the specific, here-and-now case rather than on the general pattern.

Recalling Reform Math's aversion to repetitive practice of standard procedures, today's foreign language textbooks lack the extensive grammar and translation drills of their predecessors. More frequent are open-ended, personalized writing assignments, with such topics as birthday invitations, "myself and my family," or "the house of my dreams." Eerily reminiscent of Reform Math exercises, the *Bon Voyage* workbook has students surveying their classmates' food preferences, answering geography questions, filling in their daily schedules, and working with charts. Then there's the journal, or *autobiographie,* that students work on throughout the course. What's important, throughout, is communication and vocabulary, not grammar.

Like their Reform Math counterparts, today's foreign language teachers are supposed to teach incidentally through multimedia presentations, field trips, and group interactions (conversations and skits), rather than explicitly through systematic, linguistically organized instruction. Students spend large chunks of class time speaking with classmates and sharing personal information. *Bon Voyage* activities include discussing "the qualities of an ideal friend" and describing a classmate's girlfriend or boyfriend while others try to guess who it is. This might be a way for the more right-brain students to develop their communication skills, but left-brainers, just as in math class, depend far more on explicit, systematic instruction, even when grammar is not the focus.

Let's return, for example, to Lisbeth's high school French class. She and her classmates would spend many classroom hours preparing skits based on passages in their textbooks. Consistent with the new teaching priorities, they were graded not on grammar but on how clearly they communicated the gist of the reading. In planning these skits, moreover, they were allowed to water down the French curriculum with procedures that had nothing to do with the language, or even the culture. Lisbeth's teacher let them discuss and write out their skits in English first, and spend significant time assembling costumes and props.

Homework assignments likewise require time on nonlinguistic activities, particularly arts and crafts and design: designing French restaurant menus, adorning tissue boxes with German pictures and vocabulary, filling miniature paper suitcases with slips labeled with Spanish clothing words, and pasting photographs on posters for a discussion in French about family relationships. All this frustrates the nonvisual thinker, whose goal is to learn the structure of a new language. As Lisbeth reports, much of her French class was "a complete waste of time." Comparing today's textbooks with those from a generation ago, we see that where second-year French and Spanish students were once translating entire paragraphs, parsing out syntax as well as recalling word meanings, they're now identifying individual vocabulary words on reprints of movie posters and advertisements.

For Lisbeth and many other left-brainers the aspect of foreign language that most strongly appeals is grammar. Indeed, it is through a systematic focus on this most systematic aspect of language—the general rules for word order, the declension systems, the consistent patterns of difference between English and the other language—that left-brainers learn best. However, as with pure mathematics in the Reform Math programs, so too with grammar in the modern language curriculum: the implicit instruction that predominates is a highly inefficient way of learning, as researchers in second-language acquisition have recently confirmed. Far better is explicit instruction and grammar-focused textbooks. Lisbeth's best French resource was a traditional text, left behind by a retired teacher, that she rescued before it was junked.

For many left-brainers, language is far more than an aspect of culture and a vehicle for communication. It is also an intricate system of rules that reveals much about human cognition. Languages differ from one another in systematic ways, such that in learning a second language you also learn more about your language of origin. You don't need to be a linguist to find these revelations interesting, but merely someone whose mind enjoys abstract systems and analyzing the human mind. The *National Standards for Foreign Language Learning* may view what matters most as "what students can do with language," not "what they know about language"; for our analytic children, it's often the exact opposite.

GENERAL TRENDS ACROSS DISCIPLINES

As we've seen, several right-brain teaching trends cut across all disciplines. The informal, open-ended discussion, for example, dominates more and more classrooms. There, whatever the specific subject, the content and concepts emerge much more chaotically and haphazardly than they would from lectures, textbooks, or online resources. The systematic, one-thing-at-a-time thinker struggles to follow and contribute. Several other trends in elementary, middle, and high school education are also problematic for analytic children.

Writing Across the Curriculum

Writing Across the Curriculum, an educational priority that dates back to the 1980s, has pushed language arts ever further into subjects that once involved little writing—which, as we've seen, is partly why math and science classes are frustrating our analytic children. Worse, most of the writing involved isn't focused analysis but open-ended discussions of personal feelings and experiences—for example, favorite numbers and rocks; opinions about science articles and social conformity; or *The Catcher in the Rye* and your personal philosophy of life. As Daniel Singal, a history professor at Hobart and William Smith Colleges discusses in a 1991 *Atlantic Monthly* article, writing in all subjects now involves "first-person narratives that describe what the student has seen, felt, or experienced," whereas the genres that might engage our analytic children, namely, "essays in which the writer marshals evidence to support a coherent, logical argument," are, in Singal's words, "all too rare."

Project-Based Learning

Another general trend is the shift from in-depth, self-contained, systematically organized topics toward broader, interdisciplinary units organized incidentally around field trips and hands-on projects. Promoting these has become such a high priority among the powers that be in education that they've taken to lobbying state governments to add them to high school graduation requirements—as Rhode Island and North Carolina, with much approving press coverage, have recently done.

Project-Based Learning stretches core subjects such as math, English, science, and foreign language in the direction of arts and crafts (the hands-on activities, visual representations, graphic design, and colorful decorations), drama (the skits), personal psychology (communicating about how you feel), and social studies (conducting community surveys; connecting the material to broader societal themes; playing identity politics with American literature). Perhaps no one core subject more exemplifies the project-oriented classroom than social studies itself. Consider, for example, how one model school characterizes its social studies program:

> Through an active, interdisciplinary curriculum, students learn about their community, from the local to the global, and from the present to the past. Classroom projects such as a student-produced play about Lewis and Clark and a clay model representing land formations help bring social studies alive.

Here we have Project-Based Learning in all its glory. But notice how, as with all the other core subjects, this incarnation of social studies is interdisciplinary in a very specific way. That is, it enthusiastically embraces drama and clay modeling, but shies away from more left-brain topics such as population statistics and the geological mechanics of mountain building.

Picture now our analytic child, whose linear mind works best with one or two concepts at a time. For her, interdisciplinary activities generate mental clutter that makes it hard to absorb content and make connections. She learns much more about the Pilgrims, for example, by immersing herself in a history book and writing an essay than by collaborating on a play, creating a diorama of the landing at Plymouth Rock, and writing and talking about how the First Thanksgiving compares and contrasts with her family's. The open-ended breadth of many of these projects, moreover, challenges her detail-focused take on things: without a series of specific steps to follow, she doesn't know where to begin.

Especially frustrating is the creative visual element that more and more projects require. Design a cover page, make a colorful game board, write a song or poem or riddle: "Be creative!" is typically the only guideline. Many left-brainers, already weak in penmanship, graphic design, and visual arts, are completely stymied by such open-ended calls for creativity. Even if they are as visually or literarily creative as their more right-brain classmates, they tend to require more specific parameters: design a cover page with icons that express the themes of your paper, arranged in the order in which those themes occur; write a poem in iambic pentameter, with the initial letters of its lines vertically spelling out its topic. When mapping out his own, freely chosen project, the child may readily concoct such parameters himself; projects assigned to him, particularly of the broad, interdisciplinary sort favored by today's schools, are another story. In general, it's hard to come up with specific parameters for a project that doesn't engage you. Furthermore, teachers will appreciate our child's left-brain, parameter-constrained creativity only if they happen to notice the parameters at hand—for example, the pattern of the initial letters of the lines of his poem—and accept that creativity can be analytical and parameter-constrained as well as artistically extravagant.

Multisensory Learning

An unintended by-product of today's group-centered, project-oriented, hands-on classroom is much more noise, clutter, and bustle than many of us experienced when we were in grade school. Students shuffling from activity to activity; blocks clunking, beads skittering, staplers crunching; a half-dozen groups talking simultaneously; twenty-plus bodies squirming side-by-side on a carpet. All this may be familiar from preschool. But most preschools let children choose what to do, and the one-thing-at-a-time thinker can absorb herself in a favorite activity and tune out everything else.

Not so in grade school. Although they face far more sensory stimulation than we did, today's grade-schoolers, as in our day, have schedules to follow and tasks to complete. Our child enters kindergarten, and no longer can he retreat into a corner with a book or paintbrush, shutting out the clutter and commotion. Instead, he is expected to take it all in, make sense of it, and participate in it. The result, for the more linear left-brainers who process only one or two things at a time, is sensory overload. At times, they may become so overwhelmed that they simply can't get their work done. Worse, they may retreat into their own worlds and refuse to participate. Or, alternatively, they may act up—either from frustration or to impose order on what strikes them as chaos. One kindergartner would rhythmically click her tongue and kick her desk during group assignments; another would sing his way through hands-on activities.

For such students, the most challenging time, indeed, is kindergarten—especially now that most kindergarten classes run from morning to afternoon. Not only is this grade the locus of that abrupt transition from the free time of preschool to the required tasks of grade school (including those expectations of group participation that we saw unsocial students like Benjamin and Max rebelling against in chapter 1); it also features, typically, the most chaotic of grade-school classrooms. The younger the children, the more disorderly their behavior. The kindergarten room is at once the place of maximal fidgeting, shuffling, cluttering, bumping, vocalizing, and inarticulate, pause-filled, hard-to-follow contributions to class discussions, and the first place where children must find order in chaos in order to meet expectations.

Thus a happy, motivated, well-behaved, left-brain preschooler may turn into a stressed-out, unfocused, disruptive kindergartner—raising red flags with teachers, with school psychologists, and, ultimately, with us parents. Ironically, as we will discuss later in this chapter, what such children need is the last thing that their distraught teachers think they're ready for: speedy advancement to first grade and beyond, where the sensory chaos declines and the academic challenges increase.

The Emotionally Affirming Classroom

In a teaching-instruction video for prospective elementary school math teachers, the model teacher stands before her fourth-grade classroom and, each time a student presents his or her solution to a math problem, responds with, "Questions or compliments?" Her response embodies not only today's student-centered classroom, where students reply to one another rather than to their teacher, but also another right-brain trend that has permeated classrooms in general, namely, the growing preference for emotional affirmation over critical judgment.

Avoiding criticism clashes with the very core of the analytic child. Analyzing things means adapting a critical stance, scrutinizing belief systems for thoroughness and consistency, assessing behavior for reasonableness and rationality, and constantly watching for errors and omissions. Analytical thinkers are forever finding counterexamples, counterarguments, logical gaps, inconsistencies, lack of evidence, and muddled thinking. Positive, uncritical acceptance of other people's opinions and decisions is difficult to fake. The ironic alternative, as we saw with Benjamin and his outburst in chapter 1, is to be criticized as "too negative" by your teachers and classmates. Combine this with the left-brainer's frequent social immaturity and tendency toward directness over diplomacy, and place him in situations—whether in class discussions or in collaborative group activities—where he is asked or tempted to comment on his classmates' ideas, and, as we saw in chapter 1, you set him and them up for hurt feelings and mutual antagonism.

Then there's all that the affirming classroom avoids or minimizes: criticism, high academic standards, differential ability-based class work, competition, and special honors. While eliminating these might raise some students' self-esteem, at least superficially, it lowers that of many left-brainers. Their scholastic achievements typically exceed their social standing, and their self-image and happiness, threatened in the school yard and in group activities, very much depend on challenging, solo assignments and academic distinctions that honor and stimulate their intellectual strengths. As Charles Sykes puts it in *Dumbing Down Our Kids*, "Students who were gifted or who worked exceptionally hard were increasingly attacked or ignored by the people who were supposed to be educating them and encouraging 'excellence.'" This happens especially when these people, as we'll discuss in the next section, are weak enough academically that our argumentative child is constantly taking them to task and pointing out their mistakes.

Yet another casualty of the affirming classroom, Maureen Stout argues in *The Feel-Good Curriculum*, is "one of the lost arts of the American public school," namely, student debate. The campaign against criticism, observes Stout, has prevented teachers and classmates from challenging kids "to defend a point or make an argument." Gone, then, are most opportunities for left-brain children to cultivate their special argumentative talents productively.

Student debate is following into oblivion all those other left-brain opportunities that we have reviewed throughout this chapter. The sad result of it all: a subsector of children bored with the very subjects they should most enjoy—math, science, and foreign language. Meanwhile, where class discussions and interdisciplinary group projects predominate, we see these once-model students floundering—straining to absorb the material and engage themselves in the classroom.

"WHY IS MY CHILD GETTING LOW GRADES?"

Before we become aware of what is going on in their classrooms, the last thing we parents expect of our analytic children is low grades, particularly in the more analytical subjects such as math, science, and foreign language. However, the new classroom practices we discussed above, combined with the new grading practices we discussed in chapter 1, have conspired to brand our children with grades as mediocre as those earned by their more unsocial counterparts. If they're both unsocial and analytical, so much the worse.

The new grading, recall, replaces "summative assessment," or grades based on such end products as papers and tests, with "formative assessment," which focuses on effort, attitude, and performance in classroom activities. Today's new report card guidelines do allow testing, but discourage short-answer tests, and warn that tests in general should not be the primary basis for grades. Once, high test scores could trump classroom attitude, and teachers, however reluctantly, had to grant high grades to top achievers; now in-class attitude and behavior trump everything else.

The kind of attitude that top grades require, recall from chapter 1, includes such qualities as cooperativeness, enthusiasm, effort, discipline, and, to quote one report card's guidelines, "independent exploration of ideas and concepts." But the less engaged you are by the material, the harder it is to summon up the necessary motivation. And the more overwhelmed you are by clutter and lack of structure, the harder it is to display the focused effort that teachers expect. Many of our children are seen staring off into space, kicking their desk legs, humming to themselves, or exhibiting other tics, fidgets, or blank looks, which often are their best means of coping but which make their teachers think them lazy, unfocused, and unable to do the work.

The oral responses targeted by formative assessment have as their most common venue, as we discussed in chapter 1, the informal class discussion, which many left-brainers have so much trouble following that they either say the wrong thing at the wrong time or give up and say nothing at all. Similarly challenging are all the group assignments, which prompt poor ratings for performance in classroom activities.

Formative assessment's strongest emphasis, samples of finished work, first of all tends to inflate the importance of neatness, visual clarity, and color—particularly when the actual content is as unchallenging as is now typical. Heightening this are the types of assignments that predominate: all those presentations with posters and other visual aids; all those extensive written explanations and reflections required even for math and science; the emphasis in these subjects on visual representations of data. Math tests in particular, according to some report card guidelines, should include things like graphing, drawing, and labeling. No longer do students get separate grades for penmanship: indeed, few of today's teachers even teach this skill, further impeding the handwriting-impaired. Rather penmanship, graphic arts, and overall neatness are invisibly factored into academic assignments.

Two other left-brain weaknesses, big-picture thinking and visual creativity, are tapped into by what often comprises the largest chunk of finished work—namely, those weeks-long interdisciplinary, multimedia projects. Their open-ended breadth, their vague exhortations to "be creative," and their lack of analytical challenge, both trip up and disengage our children, preventing them from going the extra mile that top grades require. A middle school math buff, for example, found himself downgraded for "insufficient coloring." Many of us parents, meanwhile, receive little or no direct information from teachers about the specific requirements—guidelines, due dates, and so on—and before we realize it, our children may be turning in work that barely, or hardly, meets the requirements or deadline. Adding insult to injury, the sheer size of the assignments makes them a major component of our children's overall grades.

Further lowering these grades are the many shorter assignments that replace analytical rigor with personal connections, for example, discussing your "favorite mountain" rather than analyzing its geologic properties. Even if the more rigorous, analytical assignment remains an option, teachers, in allowing students to opt out of it, end up reducing our child's chances for academic distinction.

Nor can left-brainers leverage their strengths in compensation, doing extra credit, extra-hard math assignments, and the like. Report card guidelines increasingly reflect the state-mandated, No Child Left Behind testing standards, which many states have set at a low enough level to pass as many students as they can get away with. Teachers are advised to assess "what students know in relation to the standards," not what they might know above and beyond them. Even though some report cards designate top grades for those who "consistently extend mathematical concepts and make new connections beyond grade level expectations," students are stuck with the concepts deemed appropriate for their particular grade level. Going that extra mile, in other words, is only about effort, output, conceptual extensions, and "creativity" within the confines of what, for our analytic children, are uninspiringly low academic standards.

What seals their mediocre report cards, however, is another component of the new grading guidelines that school districts increasingly are adopting, along with the new 1–4 scale—namely, an unprecedented restriction on how many students get top grades of 4. Flying in the face of all we keep hearing about rampant grade inflation (which now is rampant only at the college level), this "grade compression" is the upshot of two new circumstances. First is the growing pressure put on teachers by progress-obsessed principals who want fall and winter grades to be lower than spring grades. This means that students to whom teachers would otherwise give 4s are supposed to start out with 3s.

Second is an ever more forceful antielitist attitude emanating from America's education schools and permeating our primary and secondary schools, one that seeks to minimize academic distinctions among students. Many teachers are instructed to give 4s sparingly, if at all. Parents in a wealthy New York district report being told that only an "extraordinary performance" will earn a 4. A Connecticut parent reports that a 4 indicates work that is "better than an A-plus" and would "normally be unobtainable." In general, the gulf between a 3 ("meets expectations") and a 4 ("vastly exceeds expectations") is almost unbridgeable, and the overwhelming majority of students receive 3s. As one parent notes, "Students who turn in math homework on time with all problems done correctly are being given 3s, apparently because an on-time, perfect assignment was what the teacher expected."

Combine this grade compression with the right-brain priorities of formative assessment, and it's virtually impossible for analytical students to obtain the academic distinction that traditional schools once bestowed on them.

The most insidious effect of formative assessment, for all children, is how it rules out alternative routes to learning. Once, so long as a student somehow learned the material and aced the tests and homework, it didn't matter *how* he got there. In particular, it didn't matter if he spent all of class time staring out the window or reading *Popular Mechanics* behind his textbook.

Not that teachers ever especially liked such students. It's hard to like someone who acts bored and disengaged in your class, or constantly corrects and criticizes you, particularly if you suspect that he or she doesn't respect your intelligence and in many ways may truly outsmart you. But new trends in education have only aggravated this antagonism. Compared with earlier generations, teachers today have significantly lower academic credentials and test scores relative to those who choose not to teach. They tend, particularly, to be weak in math and science. Their analytical students may unsettle them as never before. The material they teach, meanwhile, disengages and frustrates these students more than ever.

The cycle grows particularly vicious when combined with those subjective assessments of student work and students at work. Here a teacher can pick and choose what to observe, when to observe it, and how to judge it, and focus not on short, right-or-wrong answers, but on personal reflections and opinions, and on fuzzy internal traits like motivation, attentiveness, effort, conceptual extensions, and "creativity." All of these are impossible to measure objectively. So much the worse for the kind of child who might remind the teacher of those who outrivaled her back when she was a student and more traditional practices held sway: the skeptical, argumentative, underchallenged left-brainer.

Math

Besides all this, there are specific challenges in specific subjects, as defined by the new curricula, that further lower the grades of our analytic children relative to their peers. In math, we have the cluttered, logically disorganized, nonlinear curriculum, and the poorly written, difficult-to-follow multistep directions—all things that lower the grades of analytic children for reasons that have nothing to do with math. Also in this category is the requirement that they explain their answers. Communicating about math, asserts the *Standards* of the National Council of Teachers of Mathematics, is one of the primary goals for math achievement. Deferring to this, growing numbers of No Child Left Behind–mandated state math tests grant only partial credit to unexplained answers, however correct. Test-score-obsessed schools, in their own grading practices, have been quick to follow suit. But, as we saw, analytic children readily do math in their heads, and often have nothing to say about how they got their answers, especially when it comes to the easy calculations that dominate Reform Math.

Even when they do have work to show, analytic children don't impress their teachers as much as their peers do. Some strategies are better than others. Consistent with formative assessment, a good result is not good enough; *how* you got it is paramount. Today's teachers are biased toward the nonstandard, concrete, ad hoc strategies—which they frequently praise as "creative" or "risk-taking"—that left-brainers are least likely to deploy, such as calculating 5 + 6 with reference to an egg carton, or 13 × 4 via a deck of cards. Analytic children gravitate, instead, toward more abstract and systematic procedures such as regrouping and long multiplication. Reform Math has today's teachers not only marginalizing these strategies but also second-guessing any child who uses them. Perhaps her parents have been helping her out; in any case, she probably doesn't understand what she's doing. Particularly if she's unable to explain in words how her method works.

The more sophisticated a math strategy, though, the more difficult it is to verbalize it. It's a lot easier to write "I know that a deck of cards has four suits that each have thirteen cards, and that there are fifty-two cards in all" than "I multiplied the two ones digits together and carried the tens digit from the result over to the tens place" and so on. This means that verbally justifying an answer may, paradoxically, end up being most challenging for the most mathematically advanced children. On top of this we have the prototypical profile of the math prodigy: some of our children are so highly skewed toward abstract analysis that their math skills far surpass their communication skills.

The downgrading of unexplained answers runs deep among educators. Our education schools have convinced many that explaining an answer is inherently connected with understanding it. As one teacher writes on her blog, "Simply put, writing is evidence of thinking." Unexplained answers mean "mere calculation," which is discounted by current education theory as "procedural" or "instrumental" understanding. Deeper than this, they claim, is "relational understanding," or "higher-level thinking," wherein a child applies math to real-life situations using concrete materials, and demonstrates his strategies in words and pictures. A child who doesn't thus apply or demonstrate her math is one who, however accurately she calculates, purportedly doesn't understand underlying concepts. Conversely, a child who does explain her thinking shows conceptual understanding, even, purportedly, if she gets the wrong answer. Thus, some teachers not only award only partial credit to our children but award full credit to others who neatly and verbosely explain why they *weren't* able to solve particular problems. The upshot is a complete reversal in who gets good grades in math. As our blogging teacher writes:

> We have found that sometimes this [demonstrating strategies] is difficult for our high achieving students who may "get" the correct answer to a problem, but who either can't explain how or don't really want to think deeply about how they got it. On the other hand, we will have lower achieving students who are creative thinkers or risk-takers who will find a different way to solve a problem.

Worst off are those to whom math comes so easily—particularly in its watered-down, standards-based incarnation—that they can ace the actual math without doing the extra work. These students not only see no virtue in the explanations, the journals, the group assignments, the discussions, and much of the homework, but are so bored by these activities that they often opt out or tune out, which lowers their grades even further.

Science

As with math, one of the most notable changes in science grades is in the renunciation of objective grading standards. On this, the *Standards* of the National Science Teachers Association are quite explicit. They advocate a multidimensional shift in assessment from "what is easily measured" to "what is most highly valued"; from "discrete knowledge" to "rich, well-structured knowledge"; from what students "know" to what they "understand"; from pure "achievement" to "achievement and opportunity to learn." And, in all this, from "end-of-term assessments by teachers" and from standardized, external measurements to "students engaged in assessing their own work and that of others." In short, along every dimension, a shift from objective and easily measurable to subjective and ill defined.

Factor in the notoriously poor science background of most science teachers, and the emphasis by the National Science Teachers Association on "the ability to inquire," "the ability to use science to make personal decisions and to take positions on societal issues," and "the ability to communicate effectively about science," and you have a recipe for grades that have less to do with a student's scientific achievement than with how well he communicates, gets along with classmates, "takes positions" that his teacher agrees with, and demonstrates curiosity during activities that all too often contain little of scientific interest. Underperforming on all of these counts relative to his or her classmates is our skeptical, argumentative, analytic child.

Writing

Subjective standards applied by nonexperts also skew the grades our children earn in elementary school writing. While secondary school English teachers are supposed to have taken courses that are supposed, in turn, to teach good prose, primary-school teachers need not do so. A generation ago this didn't matter. Most of us, when we were in elementary school, were graded only on spelling, grammar, and punctuation. But now a whole host of subjective factors have taken center stage. Quoting one set of report card guidelines, these include "effective introduction and closing," "smooth transitions," "appropriate sentence variety," "concrete details," and "vivid word choice." Factor in the excessive verbiage, purple prose, and bombastic diction that naive judges of writing often favor, and you get a very specific, unreasonable sort of bias. Many analytic children, meanwhile, don't think in concrete details and vivid pictures, favoring instead a direct, concise, abstract style that, however effective a professional writer might judge it on its own terms, will strike today's typical elementary school teacher as sorely lacking.

Foreign Language

As we've discussed, the area of foreign language instruction in which analytic children most excel is grammar, and the teaching method that most suits them is explicit instruction. The shift from explicit teaching to incidental learning, and the upstaging of grammar and composition by creative menus and tissue boxes, severely lowers the achievement and grades of our children, many of whom would have thrived in traditional classrooms.

In General

In the most general terms, what stands between our children and the high grades we might expect of them are the dual forces of grade compression, which limits top grades to a very few students, and of subjective, anti-left-brain criteria, which keep analytic children out of this privileged minority. On the inside are those who aren't bored by low academic standards, and who show the highest perceived levels of effort and creativity on sprawling but analytically underchallenging projects, and the greatest willingness and ability to participate in groups: the diametric opposites, in other words, of our analytic children.

The upshot is that we should take their grades with many grains of salt, and focus on what to do next—a question we will tackle later in this chapter.

"WHY DOESN'T MY CHILD QUALIFY FOR ENRICHMENT?"

The obvious antidote to the boredom that dogs so many analytic children in today's classes, particularly in math and science, is challenging, independent work. Even if his teachers consider him an average math and science student—what with the mediocre grades they so often assign him—can't they at least accommodate him in those specific areas in which he clearly excels? Even if they discount calculation skills, for example, as relatively unimportant, can't they let her do multidigit arithmetic whenever her classmates are doing the single-digit calculations that she invariably breezes right through?

Several educational trends keep such enrichment out of our children's reach. No Child Left Behind has schools focusing on those in danger of failing. Growing antielitism in the education establishment makes schools balk at singling out, and catering to, high-performing children. Today's teacher-training classes focus on average and weaker students: a math-methods class instructor, for example, tells students to steer clear of math buffs when interviewing children for their classroom research projects. The upshot is that ever fewer schools are offering enrichment programs, and ever fewer teachers have spent much time thinking about the needs of analytic children.

Even where enrichment programs exist, our children often fail to qualify. The formal admissions criteria are frequently crude, consisting of general test-score and grade-point-average cutoffs rather than cutoffs for specific skills. As we've discussed, many analytic children fall shy of top grades. Even if the number of classmates who outperform them is small, that number often exceeds the "gifted" quota.

Also problematic are their test scores. Gifted programs assess candidates either using standard IQ tests or via the official state math and English achievement tests mandated by No Child Left Behind. State math tests, as we've mentioned, set too low a mathematical bar to measure above-average math skill, and sometimes include verbal explanations as a criterion for full credit, which many analytic children are loathe to provide. Our children, therefore, can end up with state test scores as mediocre as their grades.

The IQ cutoff, meanwhile, can stymie the skewed math whiz we discussed earlier. No matter how high his math score, he may not perform well enough on the test's other components—say, those that measure general knowledge or social reasoning—to score above the "gifted" minimum. As for the bulk of our analytic children—those with high IQ scores and mediocre grades—they tend to strike gifted-program admissions committees more as underachieving than as underchallenged.

Still more problematic are the new tests that some schools are using. Concerned that traditional IQ tests measure only a narrow subset of intelligence, namely memory and analytical skills, educators have been replacing them with other assessments that purport to give greater weight to creativity. One example is the Aurora Battery, designed at Yale and specifically intended to identify gifted students. Questions include "Number 7 and Number 4 are playing at school, but then they get in a fight. Why aren't 7 and 4 getting along?"—a question that would send many of our children into paroxysms of paralyzing irritation.

The trend toward broadening "intelligence" has schools discounting other formal indicators of academic talent, such as winning a math competition or earning a high score on the Wechsler Achievement Test, a standardized test of verbal and mathematical achievement. Such measures, educators argue, are even narrower than traditional IQ tests, gauging "mere calculation" rather than higher-level thinking. Thirteen-year-old Frank, for example, failed to impress his seventh-grade teachers with his scores on the ACT (a standard college admissions exam like the SAT, used most commonly in the Midwest and South). His math score was 23, high enough to qualify him to take courses at Northwestern University. "He can't be that good at math," his teachers insisted, because on the school's algebra placement test he filled out a chart incorrectly, exhibiting "weak inferential thinking."

Then there's the developmental component of "gifted." Buying into the notions, popular with child psychologists, that intellectual development depends on social and emotional growth, and that schools shouldn't push children ahead of their developmental timetables, many programs increasingly consider the "whole child," that is, his social and emotional maturity, attention span, responsibility, organization skills, and, in some cases, even his physical development. Here again, the skewed developmental profile of many of our children becomes a liability.

Joseph, for example, is an incoming eighth-grader at a Quaker middle school who received the school's second highest score on the American Mathematics Competition, a test sponsored by the Mathematical Association of America. Joseph's boredom with seventh-grade math drastically lowered his apparent maturity level. Disengaged and unmotivated, he didn't pay attention, let alone participate, and failed to organize his work and complete it on time. This convinced teachers that, however strong his numerical skills, Joseph would flounder in the eighth-grade advanced algebra class, and they instead placed him in regular algebra. Or consider Chris, a gifted third-grade math buff deemed, among other things, too short to be placed with older classmates.

Without objective measures for qualities such as social and emotional maturity, responsibility, and creativity, schools resort to student essays, teacher recommendations, and closed meetings between teachers and administrators. This allows staff, consciously or not, to favor the same kind of eager beaver they distinguish with top grades. Thus, the very boredom and disengagement that makes enrichment so urgent for our child may preclude his teachers from recommending him for it. Told only that they deemed him insufficiently creative, responsible, mature, or even, as one parent reports, "amiable," we have little recourse for contesting a rejection. Complaints merely antagonize our relations with the school and worsen teachers' attitudes toward our children.

Some parents have responded by taking their school districts to court. One mother chose this option after the school refused to let her first-grade math whiz, Daniel, do math with the second-graders. On standardized tests of mathematical aptitude, Daniel performed extremely well. On the Wechsler Achievement Test, he scored above the 99.9th percentile, at a 7.7th grade–level equivalent—the highest score ever seen, in thirty years of practice, by the psychologist who administered the exam. Similarly impressive were his scores on the Woodcock-Johnson Test of Mathematical Achievement, a well-respected measure of mathematical understanding.

The school's math and science coordinator, however, considered these scores an insufficient measure of the kind of mathematical understanding that, as she testified in court, is "consistent with the *Everyday Math* curriculum's emphasis on problem solving, understanding, and explanation, rather than rote practice of math facts." Computation, she noted, "is one small portion of our math programs," adding that "we have had students that are remedial students who score well on the Woodcock-Johnson." Given that, outside the education establishment, the Woodcock-Johnson is a highly respected test, this remark speaks volumes not only about the deficiencies of *Everyday Math* but about the education establishment's antagonism toward traditional measures of aptitude.

Far more important to the math and science coordinator was her own assessment of Daniel's math skills, in which she required the seven-year-old to explain his answers in words, marking him down for referring to a three-dimensional rectilinear container as a "box" rather than a "rectangle," testifying that "his explanation lacked logical reasoning," and dismissing the idea that precocious math students sometimes lag behind in writing. While acknowledging that Daniel would have done well in the computation component of second-grade math, she concluded that "in other areas of mathematics, he would have had difficulty." As final justification for her position, she cited Daniel's overall maturity level: Beyond academics and "knowing the math," she testified, Daniel would have "developmental issues" working in a second-grade classroom. In particular, he would need "to be able . . . to be collaborative in groups" and "to have some organizational skills."

Beyond the many biases of the admissions criteria, there are the deficiencies of the enrichment curricula, particularly in math. As it turns out, even those children considered sufficiently mature and mathematically capable often don't get what they need. This stems, in part, from the Reform Math protocol of "spiraling," or of repeatedly cycling back through topics already covered. The underlying assumption is that students can apprehend a given type of problem, however simple it might appear, at an ever deeper level as they advance through math. Thus, Reform Math enrichment often means doing much of the same math as the rest of your classmates, with some additional work on top. Daniel's teachers simply added one more digit— invariably a 1—to each problem. While his classmates were adding 12 and 6, he was adding 112 and 16.

But even enrichment programs that depart from the standard curriculum often lack analytical rigor. Many educators consider interdisciplinary projects the ultimate challenge for higher-level thinking. Thus, even in math and science enrichment, assignments may consist entirely of applied projects—science and science fiction; mathematics and the seven architectural wonders of the world—that offer little in the way of novel, advanced math or science, and lots of work with nonmathematical or nonscientific material that hardly addresses the needs or talents of our analytic children.

"WHAT ARE MY CHILD'S PROSPECTS FOR COMPETITIVE HIGH SCHOOLS AND COLLEGE?"

Mediocre grades and a lack of high-level course work can impede access to competitive high schools and colleges. The most convincing alternative indicators of academic talent are high test scores on the SATs or ISEEs (Independent School Entrance Exams). Ironically, however, such scores often work against our children. Many admissions committees view the combination of low grades and high test scores as the classic symptoms of the underachiever—someone to whom they might once have granted the benefit of the doubt but who now, with today's glut of applicants, they can comfortably reject. It does not occur to them that the problem may lie not with our child but with the school we are trying to get him out of. Furthermore, as we discussed above, a subset of the standardized tests can be as biased against analytic children as grades are, namely, the state math tests, mandated by No Child Left Behind, which public magnet schools often consider as part of their selection process.

Nor have most of the selective schools caught on to the phenomenon of public-school grade compression—especially how it disfavors analytic children. They will interpret 3s as Bs, even though nearly all students receive them, and will assume that the courses are easy enough, and their grades inflated enough, that all bright students can easily get 4s.

Then there's the interview that many schools require. While the more social of our children don't have the problems with interviews that their shy counterparts do, they may still tend toward the kind of lecturing, argumentativeness, and directness that alienates many interviewers.

But the biggest barrier between our children and the competitive high schools and colleges that might best meet their needs is the widespread preference for artistic, literary, social, and leadership skills over analytical ones. This holds even in some schools that claim to stress science or engineering but that, true to current trends, focus largely on team leadership and public speaking.

Particularly enamored of leaders are colleges and universities, as we saw in chapter 1. During his term on the Yale admissions committee, a physics professor reports, the committee as a whole was so suspicious of science and math whizzes as insufficiently well rounded that it admitted only a tiny fraction of the graduates of highly competitive science magnets like Stuyvesant and Bronx Science.

Recall, too, how much more interested Lisbeth's college interviewers were in her leadership roles and social life than in her academic strengths, asking her not one question about her math and science skills. "I don't think colleges were interested in that. At least that's not the impression I got," Lisbeth observes, surmising that colleges view high scores in math and science as something that any smart student who applies himself or herself can achieve, while holding up high scores in English as signs of one who is truly creative.

Granted, it may well be much harder for anyone to predict—whether from high school grades, SAT scores, awards, extracurricular activities, application essays, or answers to interview questions—who the future stars in math and science will be, as compared with those in literature, politics, and the arts. Predictions are even more difficult when schools downgrade math buffs and deny them any chances for distinction. For all these reasons, America's most selective colleges end up passing over many budding mathematical and scientific geniuses.

Recently, some colleges and universities are taking a second look at their mathematically and scientifically skilled applicants, as they wise up to the declining quantitative skills of their student bodies. But this wisdom comes at a time when increasing numbers of overseas students are competing for admission. These students, overall, are much better equipped mathematically and scientifically than are even our most analytic children. However much they might have exercised their math and science skills outside of school, it's still extremely difficult for our kids to compete with those who have had twelve years of significantly more rigorous math and science instruction.

Even those of our children lucky enough to gain admission to top colleges face stiffening competition from their international peers, who comprise approximately 10 percent of recent undergraduate classes at Ivy League schools. For all our country's wishful thinking that our best and brightest math and science students can ultimately transcend the deficiencies of our primary and secondary schools and compete successfully in the world at large, a recent MIT graduate reports on the Kitchen Table Math Blog blog that:

> The kids with natural math talent who are not utter prodigies DO NOT come from behind at a school like Harvard, MIT, Caltech in the math or sciences. They are completely outclassed by the Russians, Czechs, Estonians, Koreans, Japanese, Singaporeans, etc. In physics at MIT, the Russian kids were an order of magnitude ahead of the brightest American math kid in physics. In math, it was the same.

The competition for graduate school stiffens even further, with approximately two-thirds of America's top mathematics doctoral candidates coming from overseas. As our blogger reports:

> In grad school, it's almost a lost cause. There are virtually no Americans in the top programs. . . . They have to have been the real prodigy (skipped high school, or college at 15, etc., and never fell off the train of perfection) to get there.

Faced with this, many American-educated math and science students end up in investment banking and other business careers that attract less competition from foreigners. But this leaves in the lurch the most hard-core of our children, who are far more suited to rigorous, abstract, and scientific fields such as math, chemistry, and physics than they are to banking, management, or venture capital and who, in addition, may lack the social skills to be admitted to MBA programs or hired and promoted by businesses.

Thus, our schools threaten yet another phase of our child's life— her future career. Even years after she extricates herself from their antianalytical grip, they continue to limit her options.

HELPING THE ANALYTIC CHILD AT SCHOOL

"His grades are mostly mediocre; some may even be low." "Like an electronic calculator, she can mindlessly manipulate numbers, but lacks meaningful understanding and 'higher-level thinking' skills." "He flounders when asked to apply concepts." "Her work is sloppy and lacks creativity." "His narrow interests and disorganized projects show a persistent inability to see the big picture and pull it all together." "She's got all the symptoms of a Nonverbal Learning Disability."

However much we question our school's assessments, it can sometimes be difficult to formulate a different and more positive view of our children. Is there another way to look at them that counterbalances the negative feedback we receive from teachers and school counselors? Given the challenges they face at school, our children depend on us to appreciate and celebrate their unique strengths and talents—and to advocate for them and help them through a system that too often under-serves them.

Appreciating Analytical Thinkers and Learners

Let's begin with the school's repeated marginalization of our child's math skills as "mere calculation" and mindless reliance on formal procedures. All this "instrumental understanding" purportedly contrasts with the "deeper, richer" relational understanding, with its integration of concrete materials and its higher-level thinking. Now, especially if we ourselves are mathematically inclined, we may long have assumed that our child's ability to perform fancy calculations quickly and accurately using the standard algorithms of arithmetic *does* indicate something meaningful about his aptitude for math. The schools, though, may have us second-guessing ourselves. And, indeed, how can we know for sure that someone who diligently borrows and carries from one place value to another, or who fastidiously follows the divide-multiply-subtract algorithm of long division, really knows what she is doing—especially if she does it mostly in her head?

The thing too few of today's educators consider is what it means to calculate correct answers consistently. When a child seamlessly borrows, carries, inverts, and multiplies her way to the correct solution, no matter how difficult or unusual the problem, what are the chances that she *doesn't* understand what she's doing? When the only mistakes he makes are such careless ones as multiplying 6 and 8 and getting 42, as opposed to more fundamental errors, such as borrowing instead of carrying, adding instead of multiplying, or subtracting the tens digit of one number from the ones digit of another, what are the chances that he *doesn't* understand how the standard procedures work?

Indeed, she not only understands what she's doing but also may be exhibiting and developing her mathematical insight and potential for higher mathematics. In applying the standard procedures consistently and correctly, as such mathematicians as Roger Howe, David Klein, and James Milgram have argued, students develop their understanding of the fundamentals of arithmetic, many of them preparatory for algebra.

Almost as suspicious to teachers as calculating via general procedures is calculating things rapidly in your head. To many of today's educators, this skill, recalling electronic calculators, seems like yet another symptom of mindlessness, but mental math and speedy calculation in fact require real numerical proficiency. The brain is not a calculator, pre-wired for math. Rapid mental math means finding new patterns and shortcuts and performing clever applications of such axioms as the distributive law of arithmetic, all of which entail insights far more meaningful than most schoolteachers acknowledge.

In other words, our child's conceptually accurate, rapid calculation skills are symptoms not of mindless, rote brain activity, but of *higher-level mathematical thinking* in the truest sense of the term.

What about her supposed lack of creativity? To put this criticism into perspective, we must appreciate how narrowly most of today's teachers define creativity. As suggested by the "be colorful" exhortation that typically accompanies so many "be creative" guidelines, we're talking, first and foremost, about a particular kind of superficial, showy, visual creativity. Similarly narrow is the "paint pictures in your head" criterion for creative writing. The only nonvisual creativity that today's schools harp on is "creative problem solving," generally measured by how far a child deviates from standard problem-solving strategies. Its apotheosis is the concrete, ad hoc, "risk-taking" math solution that uses nonstandard manipulatives such as card decks and egg cartons.

None of this captures the kinds of creativity in which our analytic children excel: abstract ideas and strategies, abstract representations, abstract connections between ideas, and reworking of abstract paradigms. These are the kinds of creativity it took, in the extreme, for Darwin to formulate his principles of evolution, or Einstein his general relativity—the sort of creativity, in other words, that finds little inspiration or opportunity in today's concrete, conceptually easy assignments, and that few of today's teachers are either trained to appreciate or encouraged to reward.

What about our child's difficulty with all those big projects that might seem like ultimate measures of higher-level, putting-it-all-together thinking? It is this difficulty, in particular, that some people are eager to blame on Nonverbal Learning Disabilities. The typical culprit, though, is somewhat less sinister: namely, underdeveloped skills in global organization. Without these, putting together a large, interdisciplinary, or multimedia project can be truly prohibitive.

The underlying brain mechanism, recent research in cognitive science suggests, is something called "executive function." EF is what allows us to switch from one subtask to another, see the big picture without getting distracted by details, and plan out and organize things. EF, furthermore, is a developmental mechanism that grows at different rates in different children; it is not one that people can learn or teach. Many students, particularly boys and detail-focused girls, seem to lag behind their peers and are unready for the EF demands that interdisciplinary projects impose, even well into high school. We parents of such children can rest assured that, by adulthood, the vast majority will develop the EF skills they need in order to cope with the organizational demands of college and beyond.

All this means that we should take neither the negative reports nor our child's mediocre-to-low grades as any indication of actual cognitive and academic deficits. In fact, such assessments often suggest—unwittingly, of course—the exact opposite.

Utilizing the Concept of Learning Styles

As with unsocial children, we can improve the schooling of our analytic children with appeals to the education establishment's purported mission to accommodate all learning styles. Using the establishment's own lingo, we must convey to teachers the subtleties of our child's analytical mind-set. Let's consider, therefore, the learning-style theory most popular with educators: Howard Gardner's theory of multiple intelligences. Gardner argues that different people have different strengths and weaknesses along seven intellectual dimensions: logical-mathematical, linguistic, musical, spatial, bodily-kinesthetic, interpersonal, and intrapersonal. Most emphasized by contemporary educators, of course, are those intelligences that traditional classrooms neglected—interpersonal, musical, and bodily-kinesthetic. Among the others, two of them, the linguistic (or verbal) and the logical-mathematical, coincide neatly with left-brain strengths.

We should explore, therefore, whether our child's teacher buys into Gardner's multiple-intelligences theory. If so, we describe him as strong in the logical-mathematical and linguistic areas. Otherwise we simply characterize him as having a linear, analytical, and verbal learning style. If applicable, we should include some caveats about her delay in executive function (EF), perhaps backing this up with a formal or informal evaluation from a sympathetic developmental psychologist, and her resulting difficulties with organization, big-picture thinking, and sensory clutter. The key point to get across is that our child's abstract, analytical way of solving problems; his difficulties with free-form discussions, "creative" assignments, and large-scale interdisciplinary projects; and his dependence on explicit, systematic instruction are nothing more nor less than a particular "learning style."

To this, we add specific recommendations. As with unsocial children, we can suggest that teachers let our child do independently what others are doing in groups. We can request that, for those subjects in which she feels confused, disengaged, or held back by the rest of the class, she be allowed to work not only independently but also at her own rate. We can assure teachers that, if appropriately challenged, he will make progress with minimal supervision, and that an appropriate textbook may be all he needs to master the material on his own.

As for the interdisciplinary projects, where our kids so often flounder, we can inform teachers that our child's difficulty with EF and big-picture thinking makes her dependent on more specific directions broken down into more discrete steps than other students require. We might request that teachers communicate ahead of time, directly with us, all the directions and expectations so that we can assist in providing this supplementary guidance and specification of subtasks.

We should explain that her difficulty with open-ended assignments also hampers her fulfillment of the creativity requirements, and that she needs more detailed guidelines than "be colorful" and "be creative." We should add that, in fact, he is perfectly creative, but that his creativity resides less—using Gardner's lingo—in the spatial, bodily-kinesthetic, and interpersonal zones (visual arts, dance, and theater), and more in the linguistic and logical-mathematical (questioning, arguing, and solving analytical problems). We might suggest, therefore, that whenever the teacher gives an open-ended, creative assignment, she provides, at least to our child, a more prescriptive, analytical alternative: writing an essay instead of a song; translating some German paragraphs instead of decorating a tissue box with German vocabulary and pictures; conducting an experiment about the three phases of matter instead of designing a colorful poster that depicts them.

What about the most problematic of school subjects, discussed at length earlier: Reform Math? Where do we even begin? One starting point is the 2000 *Standards* of the National Council of Teachers of Mathematics, which touts, among other things, the "equity principle." This, says the *Standards*, "demands that reasonable and appropriate accommodations be made as needed to promote access and attainment for all students." In particular, the *Standards* continues, "Students with special interests or exceptional talent in mathematics may need enrichment programs or additional resources to challenge and engage them." In requesting mathematical enrichment for our children, this line can become our abiding slogan.

Admittedly, as we saw earlier, securing appropriate enrichment for left-brainers is surprisingly difficult. Some parents have succeeded only by having their children's math skills confirmed by independent testing—an option we'll elaborate upon in the next section. But even this, as we've observed, won't convince many schools. Most of us must take on the "whole child" developmental bias that has teachers refusing to advance academically any child who seems socially, emotionally, or physically immature. To this end, we might argue that our child only seems immature because he is academically underchallenged and disengaged. Or we might inform teachers that she gets on much better with older classmates. Or we might insist that, at school, academics are more important to us and our child than his social life is.

Beyond how easy Reform Math is for our child, there are all the additional problems it presents to him. One of these, namely the emphasis on multiple solutions, particularly lends itself to appeals to the equity principle. As we saw earlier, many Reform Math activities have students solving math problems several times over, using different strategies or listening to a series of classmates present a whole gamut of strategies. Reform proponents reason that students with different learning styles have different ways of doing math, and that no one should favor any one way over others. But how well are we accommodating an individual child's *particular* learning style by forcing him to focus on alternative solutions that are often more suited to—if not actually devised by—those with *different* learning styles? Wouldn't the principle of equity be better served if teachers simply allowed each child to use whichever strategy works best for him, without requiring him to attend to myriad cognitive takes on the problem at hand? For those who do math automatically in their heads, incidentally, this means exempting them from explaining their answers.

As for Reform Math's interdisciplinary clutter, hands-on activities, and complex, multistep directions, we must keep reminding teachers of our child's abstract, one-thing-at-a-time, explicit-teaching-dependent learning style. And when they insist that kids only know what they're doing if they can explain their answers in words or pictures, we should explain that our child's abstract learning style means that she thinks neither in words nor in pictures, but instead does symbolic mental calculations that don't lend themselves to explanation or depiction.

Like parents of unsocial children, we must take care to set the right tone. Concerned as we are about how unchallenged our child is, we not only must avoid criticizing the teacher, but also must avoid being pigeonholed as "helicopter parents"—the latest term, especially popular with educators, for the pushy, micromanaging, "my child is a genius and I know better than you do what's best for him" subspecies of adult. We should, therefore, keep our discussion focused on our child and on how best to accommodate his specific needs and frustrations, avoiding such phrases as "push ahead," as well as general criticisms of classroom conventions (saving these, the focus of chapter 6, for venues like the Home and School Association and school board meetings).

Once our child is in high school and can pick and choose courses, we might present some of our suggestions directly to him. At some schools the math and science offerings, for all their shortcomings, may suit her better than their counterparts in social studies and literature. We might, for example, suggest physics over comparative cultures. More subtly, we can investigate which teachers run more traditional classrooms. In selecting among the foreign language offerings, in particular, our child might be able to ensure that he's assigned to the classroom that suits him best. Latin—for those schools that still offer it—is by far the most promising language, with its reputation for systematic grammatical rules; its feature (as a dead language, that is) of not lending itself to group conversations and skits; and its tendency to attract teachers who are especially drawn to the more analytical aspects of language.

Changing Schools

If, after all this advocacy and careful course selection, things still don't work out for our child at our local public school, we might seek out special schools that follow more traditional, left-brain conventions. Among these are some of the public magnet schools that have sprung up in various metropolitan areas that specialize in highly left-brain fields such as math, science, and engineering. We should beware, though, that some of these magnets, despite bearing names like "science academy" and "technology institute," manage to be quite right-brain. They may emphasize "scientific leadership skills" over scientific rigor, and open-ended projects over analytical enrichment. Some school districts may require them to adhere to the same Reform Math curriculum that all the other schools use. So, while seeking out the math and science magnets, we should be sure to visit their websites and classrooms and review their curricula.

Other left-brain-friendly schools are mostly private. The best options are those that follow the traditional, left-brain European model, with its rigorous math and science curricula—the German, French, and international schools found in many large metropolitan areas. Particularly suitable to left-brainers is the continental European approach to math, called Unified Math, which introduces the abstract principles of arithmetic as early as kindergarten. Unified Math is also used in Montessori schools. The latter, with their sequential organization of topics and an individualized instruction that lets children progress at their own rates, constitute another major category of left-brain-friendly schools.

Not all left-brainers are up for the linguistic challenges of the international schools. In addition, international schools and Montessori programs often have long waiting lists, tuition fees, and highly selective admissions standards that don't take into account public-school grade compression and anti-left-brain grading practices. In the next section, we'll discuss how to cope with this last obstacle. But we should be prepared for the possibility that, at least in the short run, the private-school option may not pan out.

For those of us who don't mind the religious alternative, parochial schools are often less selective than their private counterparts, while still offering a similarly traditional, academically rigorous approach. Particularly promising are the Jewish day schools, the Lutheran schools, and the Catholic schools, especially those run by Jesuits. Some of these enjoy such good reputations for academic excellence that numerous non-Jews, non-Protestants, and non-Catholics have enrolled in them. As for concerns about time spent on religious education, as one parent who enrolled her son in a Jesuit school reports, the higher academic standards more than compensate. In her words:

> If it weren't for the Catholics, we'd be in a fix. There simply aren't enough private schools to go around; competition for seats is more intense than for the Ivies . . . [My husband], who is Jewish, would have had nothing to do with applying to Catholic high schools on his own, though he is now extremely happy that [our son] can attend one!

Then there are the options of homeschooling and online schools. The latter offer a wide range of courses, including numerous foreign languages, ideal for the more linguistically inclined left-brainers. As distance-learning operations, they also let students work independently and learn at their own rates.

Modifying Homework

If none of these options are feasible, and we're stuck with inflexible practices at our local public school, even then we can improve our child's education. For all the warnings some schools give us parents about not doing things that interfere with classroom practices, we rightfully control what happens after hours at home. No school can actually force us to make our child do the homework. When confronted with assignments that especially disengage him, then, we might consider altering them or supplanting them with ones we pick ourselves. We might even explore whether his teacher, however reluctant she may be to change what she does in the classroom, might sign off on adjustments we make to the homework. One mother reports that all of her son's teachers have accepted the advanced-math problems she gives him in place of the usual worksheets.

The most problematic of our children's homework assignments, namely, the large-scale projects, are also the most easily modified to suit our children, assuming we have the time to do so. Precisely because of their open-endedness, we can not only break them into smaller, more manageable pieces, but we can also insert additional requirements that make them more challenging and educational. If it's "invent a game using everything you know about math," we might ask our child to incorporate solutions to a specific set of challenging problems in fractions and geometry. If it's "invent a culture," we might have him research three specific, esoteric cultures and combine their most exotic features into a new one.

Using Singapore Math

Whether we are homeschooling or simply handpicking the home-work, an excellent remedy for Reform Math is Singapore Math. Of all the foreign, left-brain math programs, it is the most readily and cheaply available to American customers. The refreshingly slim but pithy textbooks and workbooks, written in English, cost less than fifteen dollars apiece and can be purchased online at www.singapore math.com. More importantly, the curriculum may well be the best there is, at least for math whizzes. It far surpasses even the most left-brain-friendly of America's non–Reform Math texts, such as those of McGraw-Hill and Saxon Publishers. The math is rigorous but clearly explained; the exercises are challenging and interesting; the word problems are clearly written and to the point, without the excess verbiage and distracting nonmathematical details that bedevil many left-brainers doing Reform Math. A handful of carefully chosen exercises, each with an interesting twist, substitutes for the large number of repetitive problems for which America's traditional math texts are notorious. And, by the time they reach the fourth-grade textbook, students are doing problems that mystify most American eighth-graders.

We might hear people criticize Singapore Math as unsuitable to American students because it's the product of an infamously rigid and punitive society. In fact, it was developed by a team of mathematicians and educators convened by Singapore's Ministry of Education, and its most culturally charged elements are the names of the Singaporean characters and tropical fruits that appear in the word problems. Mathematically speaking, the most notable thing about Singapore is that in international comparisons of primary and secondary math achievement, its students consistently outperform those in most other developed countries.

Including Tutoring and Extracurricular Academics

If we can afford it, there's also extracurricular tutoring, another option many parents report pursuing. In fact this can be quite cost-effective, particularly if we hire a college student: a reasonably good tutor can accomplish in an hour, working one-on-one, what it takes even the best classroom teacher many hours to achieve.

Also far less expensive than private and online schools are individual online courses. Most useful are those covering material—for example, in math and science—that parents and tutors would struggle to teach without special training. The most reputable of these are offered by the Johns Hopkins University Center for Talented Youth, and the Stanford University Educational Program for Gifted Youth. They include online tutors and graders (who regularly communicate with students via e-mail) in addition to online lectures and exercises.

An increasingly available third option is Kumon, a chain of after-school learning centers that have spread around the continent—now fourteen hundred strong—in response to perceived gaps in school-based math and reading instruction. With a math curriculum that ranges from basic through calculus, these centers serve both remedial and enrichment needs. Their individualized, step-by-step, worksheet-based approach, developed fifty years ago by a Japanese math teacher, especially suits left-brain learners. At $80 to $110 a month per subject, with two sessions on-site per week, Kumon is comparable in cost to one-on-one tutoring.

Other after-school opportunities for analytical enrichment include math teams, chess clubs, and math and science enrichment camps—to be discussed in the following section. The Russian School of Mathematics, with branches in Boston and San Jose, offers both options. For the linguistically inclined, the French and German societies found in many of our big cities offer evening and weekend courses for schoolchildren. Finally, some science and engineering labs will take on older students as interns. One left-brain adult reports learning more during an internship at Bristol-Myers, where she designed and ran her own experiments, than in an entire year of high school.

For children who crave more entertaining options, there are a number of decent educational software games in mathematics and logic (see the appendix for details).

The more we're able to provide in extracurricular academic enrichment, the more comfortably we can accept what our school is actually doing for our child. No longer the primary source of academic training, it's still an opportunity, however imperfect, for hands-on activities, for social interaction, and for learning how to cope with the cluttered, chaotic, right-brain world.

Improving Your Child's Prospects for Competitive High Schools, Colleges, and Graduate Programs

As we saw earlier, the barriers between our children and appropriately challenging high schools and colleges are their often mediocre grades, their lack of distinguishing credentials, and their poor training relative to counterparts from overseas.

As far as grades go, the better we succeed in securing accommodations at our child's current school, or in placing him at a more appropriate one, the more his transcript will impress subsequent schools. Beyond this, she needs as much official recognition as possible for her analytical talents—the more so if we end up putting an end to official grading by resorting to homeschooling. Such distinctions buttress not only her future prospects but also her current sense of self.

If our child's school offers a math team, we should encourage him to join it. If it doesn't, we might consider setting one up. Once our child is in secondary school, her school might allow her to start one herself, which will enhance her leadership credentials to boot. If a school-affiliated math team doesn't pan out, we might seek out the various independent math competitions. These include the USA Mathematical Talent Search (in which students share solutions online), and the Problems of the Week program, coming out of the Math Forum at Drexel University. For other contests, such as the Math Olympiad for Elementary and Middle Schools, MATHCOUNTS, and AMC (American Mathematics Competitions), our child must be part of a "homeschool team," for which we might recruit other interested math buffs in our community. The website http://homeschoolmathcontests .com provides a long list of additional math competitions.

Consistent high rankings on math competitions, trumping her mediocre math grades, will boost her mathematical credentials. The same goes for other teams and competitions—for example, science, chess, and debate. One concerned parent has her child submitting projects to every science fair in their region. Parents whose children enjoy challenging tests—as many analytic children do—can further certify their analytical credentials through such standardized tests as the Wechsler Achievement, the Johns Hopkins Spatial Test Battery, the SAT-9 and PSAT, and the various Advanced Placement tests, which are available even to students whose high schools don't offer AP courses (see the appendix for more details).

As we've discussed, however, the combination of mediocre grades and high test scores, along with all those competition prizes, can mark our child as an underachiever. To address this concern while further boosting his academic credentials, we should seek out more extensive programming. During the school year, if we can't get him into an appropriately challenging enrichment program at his school, we should seek out those on the outside. We might consider, for example, enrolling him in one or more of the online math, science, computer science, or foreign language courses, discussed above, that are offered through Johns Hopkins and Stanford. If she's in high school, we might enroll her in online AP courses, or in a math or science course at the local college or, alternatively, hire a college student to work with her one-on-one. Even with a full load of regular school classes, complete with interdisciplinary projects, she may happily make time for the much more engaging material that these other venues offer.

During the summer, we should consider a math, science, engineering, or computer science camp. Math camps include the highly competitive Hampshire College Summer Studies in Math, PROMYS at Boston University, and Ross at Ohio State; more are listed at www .ams.org/employment/mathcamps.html. Extensive regional listings of other academic camps are found at http://kidscamps.com. We might also look into opportunities for internships in nearby science labs or in the software divisions of local companies, or research assistant positions at local universities.

All this will not only help convince the schools our child is applying to that he isn't, in fact, the classic underachiever they are so reluctant to admit, but will also give him essential training, way beyond what most American schools offer, for competing for college, and later for graduate school, with all those students from overseas.

To further enhance our child's prospects, we might keep a portfolio of all her independent, self-initiated projects, including blueprints and photographs of her elaborate machines and other constructions, printouts of her Web pages and computer programs, and recordings of her musical performances and compositions.

A key component of the application process is the teacher recommendation. As we've seen, many teachers are, at best, not especially fond of our kids. We must therefore take care in deciding whom to ask for recommendations, and include at least one teaching authority from outside of school, for example, a math camp teacher or a science fair judge. Even if our application requires recommendations from schoolteachers, their impact may be lessened by additional letters from those who better appreciate our child's talents, effort, and output.

Finally, there is the interview. To reduce the propensity of some of our children to argue, lecture, or nitpick during such interactions, we might want to run them through the same sort of practice interviews that we discussed in chapter 1 in connection with unsocial children.

The best way, however, to enhance our child's prospects for competitive high schools and colleges is also the best way to enrich his analytical experiences and enhance his self-worth—namely, making the most of all those extracurricular opportunities in math, science, and other left-brain fields.

4

All-Absorbing Interests and Other Quirks
The Analytic Child at Home

Like unsocial children, analytic children generally fare better at home than at school. We parents can often appreciate their quirks and talents in ways that their teachers may not be able to. However, a number of challenges still arise at home, including how to help our children cope with homework assignments that don't fit their left-brain learning styles; how to handle their argumentative dispositions; what to make of their narrow, obsessive interests; how to respond to their difficulties being flexible and coping with disruptions to their routine; and more.

THE CHALLENGES OF MANAGING SCHOOLWORK AT HOME

One of the major home-life challenges for analytic children is the fact that today's right-brain curricula and teaching methods follow them home each day. The work they bring in from school often explicitly enlists us parents as surrogate teachers, whether through interactive games, family surveys, or tracking down household objects for math assignments. We are more implicitly drawn to the far more demanding large-scale projects—with their dioramas and posters and Power Point presentations—as we know from experience how our linear thinker will flounder in all that amorphous, interdisciplinary sprawl. So much the worse if the assignments in question are so terribly ill suited to our kids that we know ahead of time that they'll get little or nothing out of them.

Worst of all are the summer projects that more and more schools are assigning and that, taking advantage of those many weeks off, are especially open-ended and all-encompassing. "Design a board game using everything you know about math," "Plan a festive meal and create a colorful booklet or poster showing recipes, purchases, guest lists, and photographs," "Invent a culture"—and everywhere: "Be creative." What if our kid is spending six weeks at math camp, finally being challenged academically, and when he's home we want to let him relax and do his own thing? We're already upset enough about what goes on in the classroom; do we really want it to continue in the home, the place that should be his abiding refuge from it all? In fact, there's no easy answer.

If we require our child to do the assignments, we may be setting ourselves up for endless strife. How do we defend, to such a rational, logical, argumentative a child as ours is, what we ourselves think is silly or pointless? Also, the more we make him do his work, the more we may heighten his antagonism toward school, which, if he doesn't get enough of a break from it, he may eventually completely give up on. If, on the other hand, we step back and leave it all up to her, she may do a half-baked job, or no job at all, and further jeopardize her grades. Finally, if we take the middle road and help him get through it quickly, we may teach him two things that he may misapply later in college: to depend on others, and that assignments are not to be taken seriously but rather to be gotten over with as quickly as possible.

Nonetheless, some sort of middle ground, one that sacrifices neither our child's grades nor his intellectual engagement, is probably our best bet. We might validate his frustrations by sharing what we ourselves don't like about the homework, while still encouraging him to get it done. In discussing the dilemma, we might invite her to elaborate her own thoughts. How much time does she think she should spend on the assignment at hand? What's the best way to get what there is to be gotten out of it, and satisfy the teacher, without wasting time? We might start a more general conversation about the issues that arise: well-intended but misguided fads (we might compare education trends to those in health and fashion); what it takes to get good grades and why they matter; the gap between actual ability and how others judge you; and the many gaps between practical reality and an ideal world. In other words, we might make the nightly homework dilemma into an ongoing life lesson on how students and teachers alike sometimes need to get the job done, do it well, and do it in good faith—so long as doing so doesn't actually harm others—even if parts of it seem silly, boring, or pointless. "Putting this lesson into practice now," we might tell our child, "will help prepare you for life as a grown-up later on."

At the same time, we can reduce our child's boredom, and satisfy her intellectual needs, by supplementing the homework with more challenging material. This, however, raises additional concerns, to be discussed in the following section.

As for the open-ended assignments and large-scale projects in particular, we've seen how many analytic children flounder without specific parameters and a structure of smaller, discrete tasks. If our child's teacher hasn't made such accommodations, we must make them ourselves. Since much of what may intimidate him is how sprawling and amorphous the projects seem, we can substantially raise his morale by going through them ahead of time, organizing them into subtasks, and supplementing the directions and guidelines, before we sit down with our child. We can then feed her one step at a time— each step, as much as possible, as a discrete, self-contained task. We might supplement this with a linear flowchart, which some of our kids may enjoy drafting along with us, to help him keep track of what he's done, what's next, and how it all fits together. For the more open-ended assignments, we may need to propose a much more specific starting point than what the teacher has provided. When broaching an "invent a culture" assignment, for example, one mother advised her son to imagine a civilization on another planet and to begin by describing this planet's geography—thus supplying her son with the inspiration he needed to get going.

DILEMMAS ABOUT SUPPLEMENTING LESSONS

Another dilemma we face is whether we should be teaching at home what our child is missing at school—especially all those standard arithmetic procedures that today's schools are so loathe to embrace. Besides the demands this places on both our own and our child's time, there's an additional concern. Many schools actively discourage parents from teaching things that conflict with what's taught in school. As *A Teacher's Guide to Homework Tips for Parents*, put out by the U.S. Department of Education, advises teachers to tell parents, "Try to be aware of how your child is being taught math, and don't teach strategies and shortcuts that conflict with the approach the teacher is using." This, of course, is precisely what happens when we show our children the traditional way to add and subtract numbers.

Should we take such warnings seriously? Are we somehow confusing our child or otherwise jeopardizing his ability to learn things in school? Even if we're comfortable rejecting the official objections, we may worry that we're dispensing with one problem (how bored she is in math) only to give rise to another (how even more bored she'll be in school). The more we challenge him, the more disengaged and annoyed he may be in the classroom, particularly when required to explain his answers to what, for him, are increasingly easy problems, or to use more time-consuming strategies than those he has learned at home. Is worsening her attitude toward school, especially given how this may lower her grades, a reasonable price to pay for enriching her education?

Related to this is the barrage of exhortations, not just from schools and teachers, but also from the parenting-advice industry, that we shouldn't be pushing our children too hard academically. "Helicopter parents" is the popular label with which all purportedly pushy parents are branded. We think that our children are geniuses and that, to challenge them appropriately, we must push them far ahead of their peers.

Big-name advice gurus insist that this is wrong. Kathy Hirsh-Pasek and Roberta Michnick Golinkoff, in their popular book *Einstein Never Used Flashcards*, warn parents against propelling children prematurely into academics. Stanley Greenspan adds that social and emotional benchmarks necessarily precede key cognitive milestones. Unstructured playtime is key: when we do get involved, we should follow the child's lead and keep him in charge.

But here we are with our left-brain child in all his or her developmentally skewed glory, with an array of cognitive skills and interests that far outpace his or her social and emotional growth. A child who, even well before he starts grade school, may crave intellectual and academic challenges. Who, even as young as three or four years old, may yearn for chances to learn the phonetic patterns of written language; to solve carefully contrived, methodically arranged math and logic problems; or to acquire, systematically, the names and properties of all the planets, dinosaurs, or U.S. presidents. Who may continue to crave such things even at the end of a long school day, particularly one dominated by the kinds of classrooms we've discussed above. Such activities, for such a child, may be as absorbing and joyful as open-ended play is to others—even though they require the sort of direct instruction and imposition of parental authority that makes so many parenting gurus squirm. True, she may also thrive in the unstructured play that the experts urge, but homes that completely eschew structured learning may leave her unfulfilled. Are we really to ignore our child's cravings? All that current wisdom about developmental timetables and not pushing our children may leave us thinking that it's a choice between this and inflicting psychic damage of unknown long-term consequences.

As far as developmental readiness goes, there's actually little evidence to suggest that academic skills such as adding and subtracting, as opposed to more naturally developing skills such as walking and talking, are "developmental"—that is, that they require a certain level of brain maturation. Pushing a child ahead in math, reading, or science, in other words, does not seem to entail pushing him ahead of his developmental timetable. Nor does academic acceleration appear to cause psychological damage. Indeed, in classrooms across Europe and East Asia students are taught math at a significantly faster rate than ours are, without any obvious harm to their overall mental health. If there are psychological risks in academic acceleration, it's when kids are forced to do things they dislike, are overwhelmed with too much work, or are excessively pressured to perform beyond their capabilities—all things we can be sure to avoid.

In particular, we should take care not to overwhelm a child who may already have lots of time-consuming, if easy, regular homework. In the previous section we discussed how to motivate our child to get this homework done. While supplementary enrichment activities (see chapter 3 and the appendix for specifics) may be far more inherently engaging, our child still may dismiss them as extra work that other kids aren't doing. One way around this is to choose material that seems more gamelike than scholastic, for example, a book of logic puzzles, a chemistry kit, or, most convincingly, a math curriculum masquerading as a computer game—complete with characters, adventures, and sound effects—such as Math Blaster or Zoombinis (see the appendix for more).

Enrichment in the form of an after-school club may likewise seem more like fun than like work; it also prevents our child from feeling singled out. Finding no after-school math club, two mothers ended up starting one themselves, teaching to all the second- and third-grade participants the material they wanted their daughters to learn. Whenever her daughter complained about the extra work, one of the mothers would point out that all the other kids in the club were doing it, too, and that being in this club was a privilege.

As long as we can find at least one other child who is working through the same extra material, we can also harness our child's competitive drive. For competition to work its magic, the competitor need not even be physically present. Two parents, both using Singapore Math at home after school, regularly update their respective children about what page the other child is working on, thus inspiring both kids, each of whom was initially undermotivated, to progress through the workbooks as fast as he and she can. If we don't know another child who's doing supplementary work at home, we might seek out the parent of a similarly analytic child, make the case for after-school enrichment, and brainstorm about how to coordinate it for maximal communal and competitive benefit.

More generally, we should keep reminding our child of the reasons why we consider the extra work valuable: that he himself finds his schoolwork too easy, that we know he can handle harder stuff, and that this harder stuff will help him advance to even more interesting material in the subjects that especially engage him.

ARGUMENTATIVENESS

In addition to the challenges of managing homework assignments and academic enrichment, we may also face struggles with certain aspects of our child's analytical temperament. Many analytic children are consummate arguers and rationalizers—the types of people who constantly hear, from others if not from us, "You should be a lawyer." And, indeed, living with an analytic child can be like living with a lawyer. She may argue or nitpick about everything—from our choice of words ("Not *less; fewer*") to the casual generalizations we make ("You say that fruit is better for us than sweets, but fruit contains sugar") to the things we ask him to do ("Do you really want me to clean up *everything* in my room?"). He's constantly finding exceptions (however arcane), raising objections (however contorted), and playing the devil's advocate. Making matters worse, she's usually right. Or at least, her logic is usually flawless.

If we share our child's analytical mind-set, we may enjoy this kind of lawyerly argumentation, up to a point, so long as it doesn't paralyze us, for example, when we're just trying to get our child to brush his teeth and go to bed. If we don't like such intellectual wrestling matches, we may have trouble keeping our cool. Either way, getting our child to just drop it and accept what we say may be quite a challenge.

As much as our child's argumentative character might annoy us, particularly when it works as a stalling mechanism, we should appreciate how refreshing it is that he questions authority in intelligent ways and diligently practices his argumentative skills—pursuits that are increasingly rare and valuable in a society that so prefers compliments to criticism, personal reflections to argumentation, and political echo chambers and political correctness to political debate.

If we find that living with our child is like living with a lawyer, perhaps she will go on to *become* a great lawyer—or logician, or op-ed columnist. In other words, we can decide to embrace, rather than bemoan, our child's lawyerly approach. Perhaps we can redirect his forensic skills toward more interesting and less disruptive topics. Instead of debating whether it's reasonable to call the grapes you've just served her "dessert," or whether she should be allowed to stay up until midnight on weekends, challenge her to defend her views on seat belt laws or whether the chicken came before the egg. If she's not sure which side to take, pick one side and have her play devil's advocate.

Many of our child's playmates might have less patience than we do for his arguments—as well as for his lecturing, his always being right, and his bossy tendencies. We might seek out like-minded children, similarly confident and strong-willed, who can hold their own when our child criticizes them, boss back when she bosses them around, or defeat his arguments when he tries to defeat theirs. Besides reducing the chances of our child hurting another's feelings, we give him an instructive taste of his own medicine. Also promising are playmates with shared talents and interests with whom she can more easily agree on what to do and how long to spend on it. On both counts, particularly when it comes to the more precocious, analytic children, older, more serious peers may make the best playmates.

But playdate mishaps, when our child acts overly pedantic or critical or controlling, may still be inevitable, even with playmates whom we've carefully handpicked. Given how direct and confident our child is in that which he cares about most (all those logical, analytical topics), we can often be quite direct, without seriously hurting his feelings, about social issues. His argumentative temperament, indeed, often makes the challenge not one of how to be sufficiently tactful, but rather how to be direct enough.

LECTURING

Let's focus in for a moment on our child's tendency to lecture others. Many analytic children will carry on and on about a favorite topic, seemingly oblivious to whether or not their addressee is engaged or even listening. One mother struggles to conceal her boredom when her eight-year-old son lectures her about their local public transportation system, including the many subtle differences between the buses that serve the 96 and the 77 bus routes (including the various mechanical sounds, seating, and signage). Should we indulge this urge to enlighten others, or is it better just to tell our child that we don't share his passion for the topic? Should we encourage a narrow but healthy interest, buttressing our child's self-esteem where others might roll their eyes, or should we discourage him from holding forth on topics that turn off most other people?

Ideally we want to listen and support our child as much as possible and, simultaneously, to discourage her from perseverating on topics that people find boring. We might therefore allow her to carry on about certain things with us, but not with others: "As your parents, we like to hear what you have to say, but that much detail about bus systems doesn't interest other people." If our child has trouble appreciating this, we might ask him how much he'd enjoy it if someone spent half an hour recounting all there is to know about sales contracts—unless, of course, he enjoys listening to lectures on other people's narrow topics as much as he enjoys delivering his own lectures.

When it comes to pet subjects on which our child particularly perseverates, we probably want to discourage her from lecturing anyone, ourselves included. To minimize hurt feelings, we might let her give one final performance and then reply, "Thanks. You've taught me all about the 96 and 77 buses, so you don't need to tell me any more." The next time our child reopens the topic, we simply remind him of what we said earlier.

We also want to make those lectures we do allow as interactive as possible, helping our child grow more sensitive to the needs and preferences of her audience. We can accomplish this, and simultaneously minimize our own inclination to tune out, by interrupting her with as many questions and comments as we can dream up. Such interruptions can also increase his flexibility and expand his focus, by influencing the order in which he presents the material, and by extending it to other areas. "Why do you think the 96 bus makes fewer stops," we might ask. "And what buses cover the south side of town?"

DIFFICULTY WITH EVERYDAY TASKS

Even with all their knowledge and analytical skill, analytic children often lack the more global common sense that comes from looking around, paying attention, and seeing the big picture. Sometimes this can nearly send us parents over the edge.

One mother recounts what she had to go through to get her son to hand her a cotton ball soaked with peroxide while she held down their dog, who was writhing in pain over an open wound on his back. To begin with, there was the endless back-and-forth it took to guide her son, first over to the cotton balls and then to the hydrogen peroxide container. "No, the cabinet, not the drawer." "No, the middle cabinet. Look on the top shelf." "No, the top shelf . . . ." Then there was the matter of soaking the cotton ball with peroxide. "Put the cotton ball on the container." "The peroxide container." "No, take the lid off first." "OK, now turn it over." "No, not the cotton swab, the container." "No, stop; turn the container over while you're holding the cotton swab on top of it." "Wow, Mom," her son finally exclaimed with full sincerity, "that's a really clever idea." This thirteen-year-old is two grade levels ahead in math and, at the time, was finishing his fifth Kurt Vonnegut novel.

The worst of this sometimes seems not like a cognitive deficit or immaturity in big-picture thinking but a willful obtuseness, or a failure to be sufficiently emotionally invested in the task at hand, and it can be difficult for us not to start snapping at our children. We must constantly remind ourselves that our child's sluggishness in properly busing his plate, cup, and silverware ("Put the small plate on top of the big one, hold it all with two hands . . .") is akin to his sluggishness in designing that game board for math class: many analytic children need specific, clear, step-by-step instructions in order to complete a multistep task.

Even when we do accept them as a cognitive limitation, these kinds of difficulties with seemingly simple, everyday tasks might still bother us, perhaps because we see them as debilitating deficits in common sense or as a disturbingly limited way of apprehending the world. Yet it's important to realize that much of this results from delayed EF, or executive function (the cognitive mechanism that helps us switch from one subtask to another, look past the details to see the big picture, and plan out and organize things). We may wonder how, if he can't figure out how to soak a cotton ball with peroxide at the age of thirteen, he can possibly cope with life later on. But we can take heart in the likelihood that over time our child's EF will improve significantly, along with all those skills that depend on it.

NARROW, OBSESSIVE INTERESTS

Analytic children tend to have very focused and obsessive interests. On the one hand, we may delight in their stupendous Sudoku skills, or the encyclopedic knowledge they've amassed about black holes and quasars. On the other hand, we may find these hobbies to severely limit their ventures out of the house or even away from their computers or out of their bedrooms. All the other kids may be making snow forts out front, or playing dodgeball in the alley, while our child, oblivious to the falling flakes, the fresh breeze, or the outdoor cries of the neighbor kids, is memorizing arcane chess skewers. How much, in the interests of broadening his horizons, do we intervene in what might, on balance, be a productive fixation? Perhaps our attempts will backfire. If he resists, how insistent should we be?

These are not easy questions to answer, but why not cast our child's interests and fixations in a more positive light? When pursuing their passions, analytic children display tremendous focus and drive. Drive, after all, is what distinguishes the truly accomplished from the merely impressive. Intelligence alone is never sufficient. Furthermore, evidence from cognitive science suggests a feedback loop between drive and intellect, in which focused drive enhances cognitive skills. When contrasting our child with others, we might notice how many have the opposite problem: laziness or lack of direction. Finally, we should bear in mind that, no matter how narrow and meaningless her obsessions may appear to us, chances are she will gravitate toward increasingly meaningful, productive activities as she and her executive function mature.

ALOOF AND OFTEN HARD ON OTHERS

Like unsocial children, many analytic children have trouble with personal relationships. While they may know how to be sociable, they often let analytical interests trump social niceties. During playdates, we may hear our child relentlessly lecturing his friend, or arguing with him until he thinks he's proved himself right, or sharply criticizing him for any perceived lapse in logic or evidence. Her love of systems and predictability, and her difficulty making transitions, may turn her into a control freak who bosses her friends around about what to do, how, and when. He may snap at those who seem slow or make mistakes, and openly denounce classmates as idiots. All this can impede his or her social life as much as an unsocial child's disposition can impede his or hers.

Once again, how much should we parents intervene; how do we know what is productive and what might backfire? As suggested in chapter 2, it's probably best to save our advice and analysis for later, interrupting the playdate only if feelings or friendship are in jeopardy.

Beyond playdates in particular, our child's analytical orientation may make her less emotional, and/or less responsive to others' emotions. The range of emotions she displays may be skewed toward the cerebral: annoyance with mistakes; impatience with answers that emerge slowly; amusement at the absurd; delight in new information and ideas and when her ideas prove correct. The warmer, more social emotions—affection, sympathy, mirthful teasing—she may display infrequently, or with far less intensity. He may make it clear, furthermore, that he finds it boring, pointless, or stupid to talk about feelings.

We must keep reminding ourselves that, just like our child's difficulty with big-picture thinking, all this may be more a matter of intellect than emotion—a rational disposition rather than an emotional deficiency, emotional repression, or a deficit in affection for us or others.

We might start to suspect, indeed, that engaging with our left-brain child intellectually may be the most productive route to good behavior and a happy, healthy parent-child relationship. Indeed, as we saw earlier, it is often the chessboard, or the periodic table of elements, or a table strewn with gears and pulleys that occasion the most powerful bonding between a caring adult and a left-brain child. Sometimes these bonds can be quite moving to witness, especially when they occur between the special people in our child's life who share the same interests, or when they transcend vast differences, say, in age or background. Consider the eccentric seventy-year-old who spends hours down in his basement with his equally eccentric, analytical four-year-old grandson, where they joyfully take apart antique clocks and reconstruct the gear systems.

INFLEXIBILITY

Many analytic children like to follow a predictable routine, and adapt poorly when someone or something interferes with their plans or expectations. They might steadfastly refuse to move on to the next activity until they've completed the one they're on; or flip out when the regular, systematic, daily routines they thrive on are broken or interrupted.

Rule-driven as these children are, they can best handle disruptions that are maximally predictable. We should try, therefore, to antici-pate what we can and warn him ahead of time. We might display pending disruptions prominently in a clearly organized format, say, an annotated flowchart or calendar, or a personal graphic organizer in which we have her write down each important, upcoming event as we become aware of it. The idea is to make as systematic and predictable as possible what might otherwise strike her as distressingly disruptive, and to give her some sense of "ownership" over it all. Posting disrup-tions ahead of time also gives her time to get used to them, instead of having to rise up to them the moment they occur. If our child is a fret-ter, early warnings may backfire, but in general removing the abrupt edge makes change less upsetting.

Of course, unpredictable interruptions are inevitable, in our home life as well as in life in general; the hope is that the more we can help our child accept the predictable ones calmly, the less even the unpredictable ones will upset him. We might further tame the unpre-dictable by organizing these events, too, into some sort of systematic format, for example, diagrams that divide them by type and rate them by urgency (medical emergencies, power outages, unexpected visits, sudden opportunities), and by how quickly people must drop what they're doing to address them.

For younger children, "crisis story books" can help prepare them for new experiences or out-of-the-ordinary events. A brainchild of Susan Senator, the author of *Making Peace with Autism*, these are individualized picture books, accompanied by simple text, that you create for your child and in which your child plays a starring role. Though Senator developed these books for her severely autistic son, many parents have found them useful for more typically developing children who have difficulty adapting to new situations and people.

Here's an example of how a crisis story book could prepare a child for a move to a new house. The first page might read, "In May, John's family is moving to a new house," and this could be accompanied by a photo of the new house, perhaps with a photo of John and his family superimposed in front of it. Subsequent pages would systematically list and illustrate all the stages of the move: "In April the family will begin putting all their clothes, books, and toys into boxes." Or, "On moving day, a big truck will arrive. The moving men will take all the boxes and furniture out of the house and put them on the truck to move them to the new house."

Parents have used these kinds of custom-made books to prepare their children for large family gatherings, vacations, the birth of a sibling, starting at a new school, and more. Some parents also include statements about how their child might feel ("It might feel strange to sleep in a new house at first . . ."), and also some reassurances ("but in time John will feel as comfortable as he did in his old house"). Some parents add guidelines about appropriate behavior and tips on social etiquette. ("When our guests arrive for Thanksgiving dinner, we'll look them in the eye and say their name: 'Hello, Aunt Sally.'") Crisis story books can greatly reduce the trauma of the new and unexpected, helping an analytic child know what's coming and how to behave.

RESISTANCE TO OUTINGS

Many analytic children, as we've discussed, gravitate toward all-absorbing activities that keep them holed up in their bedrooms for hours, days, or weeks on end. Some may balk at leaving home for outings such as trips to the park, the museum, or the theater. How should we handle this?

Step one is to understand where this comes from. Often it's all about control. The more control he has, the more systematically and predictably he can run his life. The more dependent she is on other people's whims, the less in control she feels. Family outings mean maximal dependence on the whims of parents.

Step two, therefore, is to give our child some sense of control, and some sort of organizing principle that makes the outing feel less chaotically open-ended than it otherwise would. We might give her a map to follow and invite her to help us navigate. Once at the destination, we might get maps of the park, or museum, or botanical garden, and let him help decide the route. If there is no map, we can have her create one as she goes. Other options are detailed brochures and guidebooks, or lists of things to look for—checklists for plants, or famous painters, or state license plates.

We should seek out anything that can keep her engaged while the rest of the family enjoys, in perhaps a more typical, open-ended way, the beach, canoe trip, or outdoor cookout. If we're visiting an art museum, we might check out the interactive audio tours that some museums offer. Their detailed, prepackaged information about the works on exhibit, satisfying our child's hunger for structured knowledge, may keep him happily engaged while the rest of us wander around at our leisure. For outings that lend themselves neither to maps, nor to in-depth literature, nor to checklists or audio tours, we should consider letting him retreat, at least temporarily, to something more engaging that's portable—a novel or puzzle book or Rubik's Cube.

Wherever possible, however, we want to distract him from his obsessions. The goal of an outing, after all, is not just to enjoy a family adventure but also to broaden the horizons of our analytic child. We might therefore begin with outings that she's most likely to end up enjoying in spite of herself. For one family, this was a lecture series at the local science museum. Their son, highly resistant at first, enjoyed the opening talk and soon enough allowed regular museum trips into his routine. Better yet, though few activities engage him as much as the science lectures do, he no longer reflexively resists novel outings.

Outings that don't engage our child can inspire a second concern: misbehavior. Sometimes we may not realize what's causing our child to act up. Why is he suddenly kicking the seat in front of him, or harping on his sister's ignorance about air molecules, or whining nonstop about how tired he is? He wants our attention, the parenting books insist. He's feeling left out or neglected. But he doesn't relent when we try to connect with him. So readily do the popular purveyors of parenting advice read emotional needs into every act of misbehavior that we may forget that for analytic children unmet intellectual needs are the more likely culprit. When the things that interest other kids don't interest him, and he desperately wishes he were back at home with his Erector Set, he may grow increasingly restless. And there is, perhaps, no cause of misbehavior that is more underappreciated than restless boredom. All the more reason to rack our brains for supplementary materials to keep our child productively engaged.

The more we coax her out of the house, the more we address concerns about her narrow interests and time-consuming preoccupations. But what about those long stretches when she's at home and we have nothing to offer that attracts her away? Forcing her to quit may merely heighten the obsession. A better option may be the "when you can't beat 'em, join 'em" approach. We might see if our child will let us help connect the circuits or construct the bridge. But not all enthusiasms allow joint participation, and the more obsessive children prefer to do everything themselves. Another option, then, is to invite them, from time to time, to explain what they're up to. If our child is a lecturer, we must then brace ourselves for what's to come, and strike a balance between encouraging him to share and discouraging him from going on for too long and in too much detail.

Another option is to try to stop worrying. So long as our child attends school and enjoys occasional playdates and adventures out of the house, spending the rest of his time on his enthusiasms may not severely limit him. Indeed it may take her to places that few people attain. As we've discussed earlier, obsessive drive can be highly productive. Even if our child's current preoccupations don't seem like they're leading anywhere exciting, he may eventually switch enthusiasms, or shift into more sophisticated, productive versions of his current ones. After all, few children stay wedded to the same exact obsessions all their lives. Thus one father, a clinical psychologist, has found it's best just to ride out whichever enthusiasm is current, and to take advantage of any that happen to invite input from parents and peers, as does his son's current obsession with baseball statistics.

A final way to coax our child out of the house, broaden her interests, and encourage her to interact more with others—all the while respecting her preference for structure and routine—is to get her involved in extracurricular activities. Specifically, all those analytical venues we discussed earlier: math teams; debate teams; chess clubs; and math, science, and engineering camps. They may not match our child's current enthusiasm, but their analytical slant will still draw him in. For some kids, one of the most suitable extracurriculars of all, one that harnesses not just their analytical interests but also their pedantic side, is tutoring. The most suitable tutees are often younger versions of themselves—children who are understimulated in school and crave mathematical and scientific enrichment, and whose learning styles and intellectual needs our children understand better than anyone else does.

5

Helping Our Most Extreme Left-Brainers

Understanding and Supporting
the Mildly Autistic Child

In the previous chapters we explored the characteristics of two types of left-brain children: the unsocial child and the analytic child. This chapter discusses a third type of left-brainer, the child with mild autism. As I mentioned in the Introduction, some research indicates that certain subtypes of autism may be understood as an extreme form of the left-brain personality type. The connections and commonalities between being left-brain and being autistic may make some parents wonder whether in fact their child is mildly autistic and whether to have him or her evaluated.

Let's begin answering these questions by taking a look at the standard criteria for autistic spectrum disorders. (The term *autistic spectrum* refers to the varying levels of severity seen in people with autism—some people are minimally affected by the disorder while others are quite severely impaired.) The standard criteria, as laid out by the official handbook of psychiatry, the *Diagnostic and Statistical Manual of Mental Disorders*, include delays and impairments in social interaction and communication, and restricted or repetitive behaviors or interests.

Starting with social interaction, the *DSM* outlines that a diagnosis of an autistic spectrum disorder involves at least two of the following:

a. Marked impairments in the use of multiple nonverbal behaviors such as eye-to-eye gaze, facial expression, body posture, and gestures to regulate social interaction [e.g., pointing at something to call attention to it, and then looking at your companion's eyes to see if he or she is looking where you're pointing]

b. Failure to develop peer relationships appropriate to developmental level

c. A lack of spontaneous seeking to share enjoyment, interests, or achievements with other people (e.g., by a lack of showing, bringing, or pointing out objects of interest to other people)

d. Lack of social or emotional reciprocity (e.g., not actively engaging in basic social interactions)

As for communication problems, one distinct form of mild autism, Asperger's syndrome, involves "no clinically significant delay in language." Other forms of autism involve at least one of the following:

a. Delay in, or total lack of, the development of spoken language (not accompanied by an attempt to compensate through alternative modes of communication such as gesture or mime)

b. In individuals with adequate speech, marked impairment in the ability to initiate or sustain a conversation with others

c. Stereotyped and repetitive use of language or idiosyncratic language

d. Lack of varied, spontaneous make-believe play or social imitative play appropriate to developmental level

Finally, as for "restricted or repetitive behaviors or interests," a diagnosis of autism involves at least one of the following:

a. Encompassing preoccupation with one or more stereotyped and restricted patterns of interest that is abnormal either in intensity or focus

b. Apparently inflexible adherence to specific, nonfunctional routines or rituals

c. Stereotyped and repetitive motor mannerisms (e.g., hand or finger flapping or twisting, or complex whole-body movements)

d. Persistent preoccupation with parts of objects

Overall, a diagnosis of autism requires a total of at least six of the above criteria, and Asperger's requires unimpaired language—though, as we'll discuss below, impairments in conversational skills are common to both disorders. Related conditions that don't meet all the criteria for autism or Asperger's syndrome but do involve impairments in social interaction, communication, and restricted or repetitive behaviors and interests are labeled with the umbrella term Pervasive Developmental Disorder Not Otherwise Specified (PDD-NOS, or what I'll call PDD for short).

As we discussed in previous chapters, some of these criteria are fuzzy and open to interpretation—particularly impairments in eye contact, body language, "appropriate" peer relationships, and "social functioning." Thus, whether or not our child gets a diagnosis, and whether it is for autism, Asperger's syndrome, or PDD, may depend, to some degree, on the particular professional who ends up evaluating him or her.

If we suspect that our child may meet the official criteria, should we go ahead and get him diagnosed? As we discussed in chapter 1, even being evaluated, let alone receiving a diagnosis, can sometimes work against him—handicapping, in particular, his chances for admission to selective schools. If enough of the above traits seem likely to apply, however, the benefits probably outweigh the costs. An official diagnosis will help him qualify for services such as social skills groups, which, as we saw in chapter 2, can help unsocial children tremendously. As we'll discuss below, it also qualifies our child for an IEP, a legally binding document that specifies educational goals and how schools should meet them, which we can use to combat some of the many educational practices that shortchange our children.

———

Rebecca is attending a math-placement meeting for her six-year-old son, Ethan, diagnosed with HFA, or high-functioning autism. Though many subjects stump him, he excels in math and does multidigit arithmetic in his head.

"Just because he can do the calculations doesn't mean that he understands the underlying concepts," the principal says, widening her eyes at Rebecca.

"Actually, he does understand the underlying concepts," Rebecca says. She explains how Ethan uses math at home, doubling the cookie recipe with all the right proportions, calculating how to set the bread-machine timer to have bread ready at 7:15 the next morning.

"But remember his performance on the word problems," the principal says, retrieving a test booklet from her stack of documents and handing it across the table. "He hardly got any of these right, and he never shows his work."

Rebecca knows the problems; she's tried to work through them with Ethan: "Mary and John share the apples. How many does each one get?" Or: "John pays a dollar for a pretzel that costs 50 cents. How much money does the cashier give him back?" For an autistic child, it's not the math that's hard; it's the social concepts of sharing, paying, and giving back.

"Today's math is much more than doing calculations," says the principal. "Sharing and giving back are an integral part of math. So is working in groups and writing in math journals."

It is concluded that Ethan is not ready for multidigit arithmetic. At least not the way it's now taught in school, Rebecca thinks, as she exits the conference room and begins considering her alternatives.

———

Meetings like Rebecca's are not unusual. It's one of the most maddening paradoxes of autism and education. At a time when ever higher numbers of children are being diagnosed with autism, and an ever higher proportion of such children are being mainstreamed into regular classrooms, the pedagogy of these classrooms is less and less conducive to their learning styles.

Within the autistic population, those high-functioning enough to end up in regular classrooms either have Asperger's syndrome, high-functioning autism, or PDD. While not an official category in the *Diagnostic and Statistical Manual, high-functioning autism* (HFA) is a term used typically to describe those within the autistic population who have at least basic verbal skills and average non-verbal IQ scores. For the purposes of this chapter, however, I'll be using the term slightly differently. In order to single out the left-brain contingent of the autistic spectrum, I'll use *HFA* to denote the many high-functioning autistic children, including those with PDD, who, like most people with Asperger's syndrome, not only have weak social skills but also excel in left-brain subjects such as math, science, computer programming, or engineering.

What distinguishes my HFA children, whom I'll call HFAs, from children with Asperger's syndrome, whom I'll call Aspies, then, is that, while the former may have small vocabularies and struggle with the basic mechanics of language, the latter tend to use large vocabularies and to speak much more fluently and grammatically. Both groups, however, struggle with more subtle linguistic tasks, such as reading between the lines, interpreting nonliteral speech, and following informal conversations. Socially, both are disconnected, underaware, and awkward. In terms of gender, for every HFA or Aspie female there are somewhere between four and seven males—and thus I will mostly use *he* when referring to the hypothetical child.

Like their nonautistic, left-brain peers, Aspies and HFAs prefer learning things linearly and one at a time. But even more than other left-brainers, they struggle in situations where many things occur simultaneously and haphazardly, and when assignments are open-ended and unstructured. Heightening their need for structure, some have impairments in executive function, the cognitive mechanism that controls attention. Many are easily distracted by extraneous details and visual and auditory clutter. Others have auditory processing disorders that impair, in particular, their ability to comprehend spoken language in noisy environments.

As for their strengths, both groups excel in what the autism specialist Simon Baron-Cohen calls systemizing, or what we have been classifying here as left-brain, analytical skills. As the most extreme left-brainers, our Aspies and HFAs present many of the same challenges, at home and at school, as their more moderate counterparts, but with doubled or tripled intensity.

POOR BEHAVIOR AND DISENGAGEMENT IN MAINSTREAM CLASSROOMS

"Why does my child dislike his classes when he enjoys academics outside of school?" "Why am I getting all these reports of bad behavior at school when he behaves OK at home, especially when academically engaged?" No sooner are our children mainstreamed into regular classrooms than questions like these start relentlessly harassing us.

Because our Aspies and HFAs are left-brain in the extreme, the new educational practices that shortchange their merely unsocial and analytical counterparts—group-centered learning, Reform Math, the marginalization of analytical skills, and determinations about who qualifies for enrichment—are all the more troubling for them. Further problems specific to Aspies and HFAs are posed by other practices, especially those involving elaborate or indirect language. At the same time, since they typically communicate even less about their feelings than other left-brainers do, we may be especially unaware of what's frustrating our Aspies and HFAs at school.

THE CHALLENGES OF GROUP-CENTERED LEARNING

Most unsocial left-brainers, however reluctantly, will participate in group activities; Aspies and HFAs are another story. Let's consider what various parents have heard from their schools, or witnessed themselves during classroom visits. Some children, such as Jessica, ignore their group mates and stare blankly into space. Others, such as Timothy, pull out a book and start reading. Still others, such as Scott, disrupt things by throwing fits or wandering off. Even when they do try to cooperate, they may ultimately fail. Mark, for example, always insists on leading his group and controlling everything. The other group mates, meanwhile, grow so annoyed by their socially awkward classmate that they start excluding him, often in subtle ways that the teacher doesn't notice.

Key to successful cooperation, of course, is keeping up with and contributing to informal group conversations, something that we've already seen posing problems for other left-brainers. For a child with impaired language skills, this is harder yet. Auditory-processing difficulties only make things worse: the cacophony of a classroom full of talking groups may muddle the child's perception of what's being said in his immediate vicinity.

As soon as he begins to lose track of the conversation, a vicious cycle begins. The harder he has to work to follow what's being said, and the more confused he becomes, the more likely he is to lose focus and get distracted. The less he attends to the conversation, of course, the harder it is for him to keep up with it. Once sufficiently disengaged, he starts getting bored. And boredom, as any autism parent knows, is a recipe for misbehavior. As one mom reports, "My son gets fidgety and sometimes gets up to do his own thing. Teachers think he is being rude and disrespectful. Really, he has trouble maintaining his attention, has more trouble in large groups paying attention and tunes out or gets bored."

In general, the larger the group, the worse the problems. The biggest bugaboo of Aspies and HFAs and their parents, and always a popular topic for autism discussion groups, is Circle Time. Once specific to kindergarten but, as we discussed in chapter 1, increasingly prevalent throughout today's elementary schools, it involves the entire class sitting on a rug and engaging in what is frequently a rather informal discussion. For the Aspie or HFA, some of its biggest challenges are the noise of several students talking at once, the dead air of no one saying anything, and the red herring of a student going off on a long, confusing, or contorted tangent. The mother of one Aspie girl reports visiting Circle Time and finding *herself* starting to squirm in exasperation during a kindergartner's minute-long, pause-filled digression, certain that her daughter would soon lose all focus and start fidgeting out of control.

To many Aspies and HFAs, Circle Time brings additional distractions that only aggravate their difficulties sitting still and concentrating. Besides noise, there is all the bodily movement and physical contact that occur when you are sprawled on the floor among classmates, not even the best-behaved of whom are holding themselves motionless. For their part, many Aspies and HFAs have what's called "low muscle tone," which can make it extremely difficult to sit still without the support of a chair. Some have a poor sense of personal space, and frequently brush up against their classmates. Indeed, so numerous and overwhelming are the problems of Circle Time for many children on the autistic spectrum that, for them, their parents, their therapists, and even their teachers, simply getting through it—never mind actually getting something out of it—has become an end in itself.

The upshot of all of this is that, where group activities and class discussions can frustrate the unsocial child and confuse the linear thinker, they are several times as frustrating and confusing to our Aspies and HFAs. Too often for these children, such activities amount to little more than spells of wasted time that they must somehow endure without disrupting things or melting down.

THE CHALLENGES OF REFORM MATH

Jared is an HFA from Kansas City. Though mainstreamed at his local public school, he, like a growing number of his autistic peers, now needs to be pulled out of the classroom for math instruction. This, despite the fact that he, like most other Aspies and HFAs, is actually quite good at math. It's just that *Trailblazers*, the Reform Math program that his school uses, isn't working for him. As his mother writes in an e-mail message:

> Our district started using *Trailblazers* two to three years ago. Even though the district was short on funds and had to cut around sixty teachers and staff in the district, they spent a huge amount of money to switch to *Trailblazers*. The people behind the switch lobbied the special ed teachers for support by claiming that the new curriculum would be appropriate for all children. How the special ed teachers bought into this is a big question. It is hard to believe that they did not preview *Trailblazers* before it was adopted. Anyway, all the special ed teachers I

have talked to say they are unable to use *Trailblazers* for their kids with autism and language disorders.

For Aspies and HFAs, one of the biggest problems with Reform Math is its resistance to explicit teaching, which we discussed at length in chapter 3. Even more than other left-brainers, Aspies and HFAs struggle to pick things up incidentally amid all the social dynamics, informal conversation, noise, and visual clutter of student-centered activities. Indeed, autism specialists now view the most promising pedagogy for Aspies and HFAs—whether for language, social skills, or academics—to be direct, explicit instruction, even of material that other children are able to learn informally and haphazardly. That is, what these children most need pedagogically is the diametric opposite of what they get from Reform Math.

This holds not just for teaching but also for content. As we saw in chapter 3, Reform Math is organized more around hands-on activities and multiple, case-specific strategies than according to any logical sequence of mathematical concepts and general procedures. Meanwhile, more than other children, Aspies and HFAs do best when they learn one concept, or practice one strategy, exhaustively before taking on the next. Indeed, among autism therapies, one skill at a time is one of the most successful and commonly used protocols. As one mom puts it, "My son needs to learn and focus on one skill until he has it mastered before moving on to another skill." By middle school, she reports, he was performing so poorly in Reform Math that "the school started a special math class for him using the old math books."

More general concerns come from Gretchen Andrews, a special education teacher at a public school in Philadelphia. She faults the district-mandated *Everyday Math* curriculum for "jumping around all over the place and not giving kids enough of a foundation." It's "drive-by math," she says, adopting a phrase coined by one of her colleagues. The curriculum particularly ill suits her autistic student, who "really didn't understand *Everyday Math* at all." Once she obtained some more traditional texts and worksheets for him, his performance improved significantly.

Aggravating Reform Math's deficient organization (recall from chapter 3) is how it clutters the curriculum with nonmathematical material and activities: all the cutting, pouring, and pasting; all the "applied math" of surveys, birthday parties, and coupons; all the interdisciplinary projects that import large chunks of material from other disciplines such as social studies and home economics. Consider, now, our Aspies and HFAs, especially the many who struggle to maintain attention amid distracting details. More than other left-brainers, these children have low cognitive "bandwidths" and are quickly overwhelmed when tackling sprawling or heterogeneous subject matter. Immersed in the Reform classroom's multimedia and interdisciplinary activities, many are completely unable to do the math.

Recall, for example, Abby Eckhoff's Aspie son, Richard, whom we discussed briefly in chapter 3. As Abby explains, "He can't process information from twenty different disciplines at once," nor can he "multitask" his way through the math assignments. So distracted was he by all the extraneous details of *Everyday Math* that he learned very little actual math and ended up in a remedial class. And yet, like many of his peers on the autistic spectrum, he turns out to be a math whiz. Left to his own devices, this thirteen-year-old boy fills blackboards with equations and solves mathematical puzzles—such as Rubik's Cube patterns—that completely elude his teachers.

Much of the extra-mathematical material that Reform Math mixes in, remember, involves language arts, or "communicating about math." In chapter 3 we saw this encumbering the many analytic children who gain nothing from journal writing and who solve math problems automatically, nonverbally, in their heads. Even more stymied are HFAs such as Ethan and Jared, who can solve hard problems but struggle to put words together.

For the many HFAs with language difficulties, the most prohibitive problems are ones whose intended answers involve so much verbal description and explanation, and so little math, that there's little or no room for numerical solutions for which one can receive partial credit. Fine-motor control and penmanship problems only make matters worse. Scott, an Aspie with a shaky hand grip, was nonplussed by an *Investigations* exercise that asked him to draw six cows with all their twenty-four legs displayed.

Some of Reform Math's written assignments are so linguistically subtle that they create obstacles even for Aspies, who generally have no problem putting words together. Many problems, for example, ask students to convince a hypothetical, typically less mathematically capable, audience why their answer is correct. Recall the third-grade *Investigations* assignment, discussed in chapter 3, that asks students to decide which of two fractions is larger and then "write a letter to a second-grader" that tells "why you are right," reminding them that "a second-grader must understand what you write."

Convincing a second-grader is no trivial task. Doing so means first imagining what he does and doesn't know, as well as what he is capable of understanding. But one of the fundamental deficits of those on the autistic spectrum is in grasping the perspectives of others well enough to draw these inferences. Then there's the added rhetorical challenge of how, given your conclusions about your hypothetical second-grader, you can best make your case. For a third-grade HFA or Aspie, these communicative challenges far exceed the mathematical challenge of comparing $1\frac{1}{3}$ with $1\frac{1}{4}$.

It's interesting to contrast the linguistic demands of such problems with those from the more traditional McGraw-Hill third-grade curriculum (still used by some schools and parents). Here we see exercises such as "Sean had 95 cents. Then he spent 45 cents. How many cents did he have left?" Not only does this seek a more straightforward numerical answer, it also uses the simpler, more direct language of basic words in short sentences.

Indeed, besides demanding much more written explanation than traditional math exercises do, Reform Math's word problems are much more linguistically elaborate, presupposing a significantly higher level of reading comprehension. Some programs even tout reading as one of their cornerstones. The *Trailblazers* website mentions its "many original stories, called *Adventure Books*, that show applications of concepts being studied or sketch episodes from the history of mathematics and science."

In some cases, the greatest challenge is in understanding what you're supposed to do. Reform Math problems often contain multi-step directions, some of them rather involved. Recall this problem from third-grade *Investigations*, discussed in chapter 3:

> Draw several groups of an item that comes in groups of some number between 2 and 12. Describe the picture in words. Then, on the back of the student sheet, use that information to make a riddle.
>
> In your description, remember to identify the three key pieces of information: the number of groups, the number of items in a group, and the total number of items. In your riddle, remember to use only two pieces of information from your description. Your riddle is the question you ask about the missing third piece of information!

"Draw . . . describe . . . make a riddle . . . remember . . . identify . . . ask. . . ." Such multistep directions are even more challenging for Aspies and HFAs than they are for other one-thing-at-a-time left-brainers. Imagine, furthermore, what it takes for someone with reading-comprehension problems to sort out such contortions as "that comes in groups of some number between 2 and 12" and "the question you ask about the missing third piece of information." Compounding the comprehension challenge is the open-ended nature of the questions—another hallmark of Reform problems. It's much easier to understand a question that solicits a specific numerical calculation than one that asks for *any* item that comes in groups of a certain range of sizes, or *any* riddle that specifies two out of three properties about the item and its group. The open-ended tasks solicited by open-ended questions, furthermore, lack the explicit structure that many Aspies and HFAs depend on. As Gretchen Andrews remarks about her student, "I don't think he understood the language of the [*Everyday Math*] book. He just didn't understand what they were asking him to do."

Another reading-comprehension challenge emerges from the hypothetical "real life" situations on which the exercises are based. These are typically much more elaborate than those of traditional word problems and presuppose a background in worldly knowledge that many autistic kids lack—whether about speed limits, fines, coupons, or fundraising tactics. All of this stymies the many Aspies and HFAs who are too absorbed in their own private universes, and too baffled by what goes on around them, to have internalized these worldly entities.

Particularly confusing to them are social and psychological factors. In the "make a riddle" problem, for example, there's the concept of a riddle. To grasp this, you must appreciate another person's perspective and determine which clues might help him deduce an answer. Still more socially and psychologically fraught is a sample problem from the second-grade *Trailblazer*'s teacher's manual:

> I used $1 to buy a 29-cent pretzel, and I got 2 quarters and 1 nickel back. My change should have been about 70 cents. How do I know they gave me the wrong change?

Buying things and getting change back is a social exchange that HFAs often don't grasp until well beyond second grade. Even more challenging is the question "How do I know?" This presupposes a capacity for self-reflection that many young HFAs completely lack. For a second-grader like Jared, with whom we opened this section, the *Trailblazers* problem is prohibitive in its psychological complexity, and trivial in its mathematics.

In a final challenge for reading comprehension, Reform Math problems, more than their traditional counterparts, often deliberately bulk up their exercises with superfluous detail. The goal: to train children to tease out the relevant information. This, of course, is an important skill, but it is not specific to mathematics, and need not be the focus, specifically, of math class. When it is, the extraneous material can distract the more susceptible children to a point where they, like Gretchen Andrews's student, Abby Eckhoff's son, and lots of other Aspies and HFAs, are unable to get to the punch line.

Speaking of her Aspie son, Scott, one mom sums up the problems that Reform Math's exercises pose for children on the autistic spectrum: too elaborate, too much extraneous information, multiple perspectives, and open-ended questions that allow too many possible answers.

The strongest evidence of how poorly Reform Math suits Aspies and HFAs comes from those children who have experienced both it and traditional math. Remember, for instance, how Gretchen

Andrews's student, baffled by Reform Math, did well with traditional materials. When Scott's mom put him in a more traditional classroom in fourth grade, he likewise improved; she worries, however, about middle school, where the Reform program *Connected Mathematics* is mandated throughout Seattle. Abby Eckhoff describes her son, Richard, as having "really blossomed" during a one-semester hiatus from *Everyday Math* in which the teacher used traditional materials. Halfway through the school year she was fired, her replacement reinstated *Everyday Math*, and Richard began floundering anew.

Carolyn, a contributor to Kitchen Table Math, a group blog for parents and educators, describes her HFA son as "flying independently with Saxon Math" (a traditional program popular with many parents) and then "hitting a mountainside when we encountered *Everyday Math* in fourth grade." The result: "Math, formerly my son's strongest subject, became an everyday struggle for him and for us."

As for mathematical challenge, the decline in rigorous, analytical material that we discussed in chapter 3 shortchanges the many mathematically gifted HFAs and Aspies as much as it does their nonautistic, analytical counterparts. In fact, it tends to shortchange them even more. For, with their highly skewed cognitive profiles and their severe weaknesses in communication and social interaction, their best hopes for gainful employment may be in mathematics or other highly analytical fields, such as engineering and computer science, that depend on a mastery of mathematics far greater than what Reform Math supports. Indeed, it is precisely in these fields that we currently find the highest proportion of people on the autistic spectrum, and it would be a terrible shame if their numbers were to decline for lack of proper classroom training, or from the disengagement and mediocre grades that they experience as a result of Reform Math's nonmathematical challenges.

THE CHALLENGES OF CLASSROOM DISCOURSE AND LANGUAGE ARTS

Beyond the word problems of Reform Math, there's the language of the classroom. Increasingly, right-brain practices have rendered certain aspects of this language—both oral and written—all the more problematic for those on the autistic spectrum.

Consider, first, the stories students read in class. In our emotion-ally and culturally sensitive society, these increasingly center on emo-tions and on social and cultural interactions. Fewer fairy tales and adventure stories; instead, books with titles such as *I'm Gonna Like Me*, *A Rainbow of Friends*, and *When Sophie Gets Angry*. The more socially clueless HFAs may find them so demanding and unreward-ing to work through that they make little or no progress in overall reading comprehension. But even the higher-functioning Aspies, with their large vocabularies and fluent reading skills, may find these sto-ries so disengaging and socially confusing that they quickly grow dis-gusted with classroom reading. Both groups would fare much better with the more fact- and plot-filled texts that characterize more tradi-tional reading materials.

Additional comprehension challenges come both from the narrow interests of Aspies and HFAs and from the difficulties they have pick-ing up information incidentally from everyday conversation (which, for their nonautistic peers, is a primary resource for general informa-tion). Their resulting deficits in "commonsense" background knowl-edge, discussed above in connection with word problems, are even more debilitating in the longer, more involved readings of grade-school language arts and, even more so, of high school English. You won't get much out of *The Great Gatsby* if you don't know about social class, upstarts, and the Roaring Twenties.

Then there's the problem of assessment. Increasingly, teachers gauge reading comprehension, in part, by soliciting inferences about characters' emotions, interactions, and motivations—all areas of weakness for the child on the autistic spectrum. Today's oral and writ-ten "text-to-self" connections presuppose that the reader can empa-thize with characters and articulate personal feelings—additional weak points for those on the spectrum. Were the child instead que-ried about the facts of a nonfiction text, and asked to make inferences about these, she would look much more advanced. Instead, many Aspies and HFAs place at the lowest possible reading level, further impeding their progress.

Besides reading comprehension, there's comprehending direc-tions. In today's student-centered, hands-on, activity-driven classroom, directions have become increasingly difficult for language- and attention-impaired HFAs and Aspies to follow. The elaborate, multi-step instructions of Reform Math are just one example. Because the goal of today's teacher—"the guide on the side"—is to take a backseat once students start working, she tends to give them their directions all at once, up front. The activities in question, increasingly lengthy and involved, require a correspondingly lengthy and involved set of instructions of the sort that many Aspies and HFAs find extremely difficult to attend to, comprehend, and internalize. Observing that "whenever directions were given . . . with multiple parts, Scott would remember only the first two parts," Scott's mom could be describing a whole host of children on the autistic spectrum.

Further complicating the teacher's directions, today's emotionally affirming classroom protocols have her using the sort of indirect language that dogs many Aspies and HFAs. Direct commands such as "Please put the stapler back" or "Stop kicking the table," considered overly curt, are commonly reworded as questions such as "Is that where the stapler goes?" or "Do you need to keep kicking the table?" This, superficially at least, may soften the impact on most students. For the Aspie or HFA, it ultimately backfires. When he fails to read between the lines and simply answers the question, "No, it isn't," or "No, I don't," the teacher, herself reading too *much* between the lines, may conclude that he's being cheeky and disrespectful.

Our child's own conversational gambits, meanwhile, tend to be too direct, and he ends up being reprimanded for such statements as "That's too easy," "That's wrong," or "That's boring and stupid." Of course, it was never acceptable for students to speak this way to their teachers, but in today's emotionally affirming, student-centered class-rooms, our children are increasingly taken to task for what they say to their peers.

Their lack of diplomacy, combined with all their misunderstandings—of multistep directions, redirections, and reprimands—is fuel for antagonism with teachers and classmates, and for getting into trouble without knowing why.

Compounding the linguistic challenge in today's classrooms are assignments that ask students to discuss their feelings—in journal entries, responses to readings, autobiographical stories, or even science or social studies assignments. For many Aspies and HFAs, however enthusiastically and fluently they write about how cars and clocks work, such tasks are prohibitive. One HFA boy who could describe, effortlessly, the formation of igneous, sedimentary, and metamorphic rocks was stumped by an assignment to write about his favorite rock and why he liked it.

THE NEED FOR STRUCTURE AND PREDICTABILITY

Besides teaching directly and explicitly and working on one skill at a time, the most successful pedagogical therapies for autism involve large doses of structure and minimal distractions. Unfortunately for our mainstreamed child, these are sorely lacking, not just in Reform Math but in the many other hands-on, group-centered activities of the contemporary classroom, including those of science, social studies, and language arts. Assaulting his senses are a half-dozen simultaneous conversations; handling, cutting, pouring, and pasting; bustle; students moving around from activity to activity. Others can understand the directions and filter out the commotion; many left-brainers, as we saw in chapter 3, have more difficulty; the HFA or Aspie might see only chaos. Totally at sea, she stands motionless in the middle of it all, eyes glazed over. Or, as Scott's mom observes, he runs around aimlessly, attempting to join in on what seems like mere anarchy.

Besides the confusion and sensory chaos of the hands-on, group-centered activity, there's the more conceptual and informational chaos of the sprawling, interdisciplinary project. We've already seen this posing problems for many analytic children; imagine an even more left-brain, one-thing-at-a-time Aspie or HFA trying to work his way through a multimedia presentation of the First Thanksgiving, complete with skits, dioramas, and Power Point. For those with difficulties with executive function and maintaining attention, such projects are an organizational nightmare.

Projects and other open-ended assignments raise another challenge for Aspies and HFAs: lacking concrete guidelines, they may follow their own idiosyncratic interests, and produce material that clashes with their teachers' implicit expectations. Thus, one HFA earned a D for a time line of his personal life that included, as milestones, revelations about the workings of fan switches instead of experiences considered important by his English teacher.

Heightened expectations about organizational skills have teachers increasingly counting on students to hand in work on their own; formative assessments, meanwhile, have them increasingly downgrading students for late or missing homework. An HFA or Aspie who is too distracted or disorganized to turn in his work on the designated day may end up with drastically reduced grades. One mother reports that despite her frequent attempts to ensure that his science teacher was collecting her son's homework, he got an F for failing to turn it in, even though he had completed all of it on time.

WHY THE ANALYTICAL SKILLS OF AUTISTIC CHILDREN ARE UNDERAPPRECIATED

Their weaknesses in communication and social interaction have always made children with autism tough to evaluate. How can you assess someone who struggles to understand your questions and directions, struggles to express his answers, and feels little or no motivation to cooperate with you? When you measure the cognitive skills of an Aspie or HFA through the prism of language and social interaction, only certain skills shine through. As a result, people in general, and professionals in particular, have grossly underestimated these children's analytical talents, writing off their most obvious skills as "splinter skills"—that is, islets of exceptional ability in what is, everywhere else, a vast sea of impairment. Current practices in education and developmental psychology have reduced even further people's appreciation of the intellectual capacities of children on the autistic spectrum.

We've already discussed how educators downgrade left-brain math skills as mindless calculation, particularly when students don't explain their answers. As we've seen, giving verbal explanations is particularly challenging for Aspies and HFAs. Considered even more mindless is a child who can't do word problems or applied math activities —additional areas of weakness for many on the autistic spectrum.

School-based math assessments, as we've observed, now treat word problems as the gold standard of mathematical comprehension. In the minds of today's teachers, a child who cannot answer them, even if he can do the calculations they solicit, must not truly understand the underlying math. Ditto if he can't correctly apply the math in a hands-on activity. Thus, even more than with other left-brainers, today's educators marginalize the math skills of HFAs and Aspies as isolated aptitudes for mindless, meaningless calculation.

It can therefore be awfully difficult to convince teachers that our child is smarter than he appears to them. Many of us parents of Aspies and HFAs are all too familiar with the condescending smiles of psychologists and educators who think they're hearing yet another mother or father coping with the autism diagnosis by naively touting his or her child as a prodigy. Ethan's mother, Rebecca, reports having one meeting after another in which she tried and failed to convince teachers that her son understood complex math despite his difficulty with simple word problems.

Further belittling the analytical skills of the HFA or Aspie is the notion, popular among developmental psychologists, that a certain level of social and emotional development is prerequisite for abstract reasoning. The prominent child psychologist Stanley Greenspan, for example, claims that even the autistic math genius struggles to make connections between her world and the world of abstractions. Children can't abstract, Greenspan claims, until they understand emotions. Citing the abstract notion of causality, he asserts that "the first lesson in causality is not pulling a string to ring a bell. . . . [but] pulling your mother's heartstrings with a smile in order to receive one back." Even basic math concepts, he argues, are derived from such emotional reasoning: "When a child is learning concepts of quantity, he doesn't understand conceptually, he understands emotionally . . . . What is 'a lot' to a toddler? It's more than you expect. What is 'a little'? It's less than you want." A child cannot leap into the conceptual world, Greenspan concludes, until he understands the interconnections among emotions, actions, and ideas.

There are, of course, numerous abstractions that require such social and emotional understanding—specifically, the numerous abstract concepts that are *about* emotions and social relationships. But consider, say, such concepts as "asymptotes" (a line that a curve gets arbitrarily close to), "recursion" (when a function being defined occurs within its own definition), and "friction." The many math, computer, or engineering geniuses in the autistic population are fully capable of mastering such concepts, and of entertaining all sorts of abstract thoughts about them, however unaware they are about how emotions interact with actions and ideas.

In the world of education, we see a similarly right-brain reconception of so-called higher-level thinking skills, which increasingly entail a measure of social and psychological awareness, combined with the capacity to translate this awareness into words. In math, it means reflecting upon and communicating about the strategies you used to solve a problem; in reading, it means expressing inferences and predictions about characters. The weak performances of many Aspies and HFAs on such tasks have led educators to further underestimate and marginalize their cognitive strengths. But what about the HFA who figures out, on his own, the asymptotes of a hyperbola, or how to use HTML to code a Web page, or which direction the blades on a clockwise-turning fan should point for an upward draft? Who's to say that his thinking level isn't as high as the child who can convince a second-grader that 1⅓ is greater than 1¼, or explain why Toad got angry at Frog?

The cognitive deficits in HFA and Asperger's syndrome are quite specific. As we've discussed, many HFAs and Aspies struggle to process auditory information and to maintain attention. But there is just one core deficit that they all share: an impaired ability to relate to people. This problem, while severe, can make HFAs and Aspies look more handicapped than they really are, even to those who don't adhere to right-brain versions of higher-level thinking. This is because it's in interacting with others—particularly family members—that children acquire most of their early knowledge and, in particular, their knowledge of spoken language.

The more limited a child's interactions, therefore, the more impaired her language. In particular, lots of children on the autistic spectrum struggle with pronouns (confusing *I* and *you*), articles (confusing or omitting *a* and *the*), and grammar (e.g., verb endings). But this does not mean that they are inherently incapable of mastering linguistic concepts.

Nor does any of this diminish their capacity for abstract reasoning and higher-level thinking. In fact, reasoning, analyzing, finding patterns, solving logical problems—these are areas in which Aspies and HFAs excel. It's just that, under today's right-brain practices, too many teachers are underestimating these children, and too many classroom activities are drawing out their weaknesses rather than harnessing their strengths.

ADVOCATING FOR ENRICHMENT

As with other left-brainers, one route around the analytical short-comings of the classroom curriculum, particularly in Reform Math, is educational enrichment. Unfortunately, the IQ cutoffs for enrichment programs may disqualify many of our children, particularly our HFAs with their typically below-normal verbal scores. Furthermore, as we have already seen, it can be even more difficult to convince educators of the untapped intellectual potentials of Aspies and HFAs than it is with other left-brain children.

In particular, a child who struggles with word problems and never explains his answers, or who can't stay focused, follow directions, cooperate in groups, and hand in his work on time, does not, in the eyes of most educators, look like a good prospect for enrichment. All the more so if it entails having this child spend time in a classroom intended for older, more mature, students.

Take Timothy, an extremely precocious math and science whiz with Asperger's syndrome. By age two he was spending hours with math toys intended for school-age children, solving 3-D puzzles and the like. By first grade he was writing "poop" across all his classroom math sheets. When Margaret, his mother, told the teacher that her son was probably misbehaving because the math was too easy for him, her response was all too familiar: "I don't see it. What he's good at, if anything, is rote computation."

Eventually Timothy's parents turned to an outside evaluator, a veteran psychologist specializing in IQ testing. And it was only her assessment—which noted that Timothy had obtained the highest math score she had ever seen in twenty years, and that he was, in her words, a "math genius"—that convinced the school to accommodate him.

They accommodated him not only in math—pulling him out for special tutoring—but also in science, where by fifth grade he was doing physics with ninth-grade honors students. His performance in this classroom, however, made his teacher decide against recommending tenth-grade chemistry for the following year. The problem wasn't academics: in his evaluation, the teacher remarked on Timothy's interest and engagement; his thoughtful, articulate responses; his strong grasp of concepts; and how this ten-year-old, with his final grade of B, was performing at an academic level equal to the majority of his talented and significantly older classmates.

What gave the teacher pause, rather, were all those nonacademic quirks particular to Aspies and HFAs. Timothy, he notes, "has trouble processing verbal instructions." He was often "disengaged in the classroom, or would become distracted by the equipment and perform his own experiments." He didn't get his class work done on time, and his written responses "tend to be brief and incomplete." But the biggest problem was that much of the school's science curriculum was centered on groups of students discussing things and that Timothy wasn't participating appropriately. He preferred to work alone, and when he did join in, he tended to dominate the discussion, sometimes "becoming agitated if he perceived that the group members were not 'listening to him.'" His frequent isolation from groups, the teacher noted, "limits Timothy . . . to his own observations and interpretations." His conclusion: "Given the above observations, it is my recommendation that Timothy be placed in middle school science as opposed to high school chemistry."

In this case, outside testing failed to sway the school. On the Spatial Test Battery, which Johns Hopkins University uses to determine eligibility for its Center for Talented Youth science classes, and which is the closest thing there is to a standardized test of science aptitude,

Timothy received a score of "outstanding." Describing him as "an exceptionally gifted young man in the areas of global intelligence, as well as in math and science," the evaluator recommended high school chemistry. But the school stuck to its guns, and Timothy ended up struggling through sixth-grade science, significantly more disengaged and disruptive than he had been the previous year in ninth-grade honors physics.

In the worst cases, our schools' right-brain practices end up completely undermining the goal of mainstreaming our mildly autistic child. As we've seen, some Aspies and HFAs are so confused and disengaged by the dearth of explicit teaching, the group work, and the sprawling, multimedia, interdisciplinary jumble, that they have to be pulled out of their classrooms for core subjects that often include even math. Some become so disruptive that they cannot remain in school without support from an aide assigned especially to them. Being thus shadowed by an adult both isolates them further from their peers and diminishes their prospects for learning to function independently in classrooms—something they must master before they can proceed to higher education.

The most successful mainstreaming of HFAs and Aspies occurs in traditional classrooms such as the one that Scott, the HFA who struggled with multistep directions in Reform Math, attended in fourth grade, by far his best year of school. These classrooms use pedagogies that parallel those of the most effective autism therapies: direct, streamlined instruction, lots of structure, and one subject or one concept at a time, drilled until it is mastered. But in a society so slanted toward social priorities and so averse to structured teaching, these classrooms are becoming all too rare—even though this very same society is constantly publicizing its alarming rise in autism diagnoses and touting its goal of fully including all children.

WHAT TO DO ABOUT THE PROBLEMS AT SCHOOL

The strategies we discussed in chapters 1 and 3 for meeting the scholastic needs of unsocial and analytic children apply, as well, to the mildly autistic child. The essential goals, even more than for other left-brainers, are: uncluttered, structured environments; clear directions; and explicit, individualized instruction. Crucial as well is a protocol that ensures that they complete and turn in their work on time. As for the major additional academic challenge faced by many HFAs and Aspies, namely their difficulties with reading comprehension, we should request more subtle assessments and teaching strategies that separate fiction from nonfiction, don't require personal connections, and take into account any deficits in social reasoning or general knowledge that impede comprehension. In making these requests, furthermore, we should exploit as much as possible the Americans with Disabilities Act (ADA) and the Individuals with Disabilities Education Act (IDEA). These legally obligate public schools to make "reasonable accommodations" in the "least restrictive environment" for any child diagnosed with special needs, and to agree with parents on an Individualized Education Plan, or IEP, a legally binding document that details educational goals and how to meet them.

The IDEA puts far less pressure on schools to enhance our children's strengths than to remediate their weaknesses. To the extent that our school resists challenging our child academically—and to the extent that we can afford it—one-on-one tutoring is perhaps the most promising venue for enrichment. If we live near a college or university, the best tutoring candidates are math, science, and engineering majors who are linguistically sensitive enough to handle the communicative challenges of Asperger's and HFA. Many college students enjoy teaching bright children with autism, and many parents report that hiring them is a more promising way to spend money than suing their school districts.

"WHAT ABOUT THE AUTISM THERAPIES PEOPLE KEEP RECOMMENDING?"

In a society as enamored as ours is with unstructured play and child-centered learning, it's inevitable that at least some of the more prominent autism therapies wholeheartedly eschew the structure and explicit teaching that, as many who work closely with Aspies and HFAs can testify, is absolutely essential. The most popular of the unstructured therapies is Floortime, the brainchild of Stanley Greenspan, who, as we saw above, claims that autistic children can't learn abstract concepts until they understand emotions.

Which autism therapy we are told best suits our child often depends on the personal philosophy of the psychologist or psychiatrist who evaluates her. So great is the partisanship among autism clinicians that our psychotherapist may give short shrift to the therapies that compete with the one with which he is associated. In particular, if he is an acolyte of Floortime, he may leave us thinking that the best therapies for autism necessarily use right-brain strategies. However much this clashes with our intuition about what our child most needs, we may hesitate to question someone who is professionally qualified to know more about autism than we do. Let's therefore take a closer look at Floortime and how well it suits our HFAs and Aspies.

Floortime, essentially, is a variety of play therapy. It asks us to join our child on the floor, follow his lead, build on his games, be firm but affectionate, tempt him to communicate, and interact joyously with him. The goal: to gently insert ourselves into his world in order to woo him, over time, into ours. For example: "When your child is rolling a car across the floor and you put a doll inside, talk for the doll. Say, 'I want to go to the zoo! Can we go to the zoo? Can we go home?'" In general, "Keep trying different scenarios . . . until you engage his interest."

Of course, all this sounds very good, and it is; the problem with Floortime is that it doesn't go much beyond what most of us parents are already doing with our children. Furthermore, because HFAs and Aspies are weakest at this kind of informal social and emotional interaction, and easily distracted and disengaged from it, it takes them only so far. Floortime will not teach them the subtler aspects of English grammar—for example, *a* vs. *the*—or how to take the floor politely in a large group conversation. For these, some sort of explicit teaching is crucial.

The main competitor to Floortime, and the one with the most comprehensive curriculum, is Applied Behavioral Analysis, or ABA. But it, too, only goes so far and, as far as explicit teaching is concerned, offers little more than rote drills that harness the autistic child's skills in categorization and pattern recognition: for example, having him sort objects by shape and color, or map words to objects. With one exception that we will discuss below, there's little in the therapy world that harnesses the autistic child's left-brain strengths in deductive reasoning and abstract analysis.

ALTERNATIVE APPROACHES

The left-brain strengths of our Aspies and HFAs offer the most promising route to mastering both language—particularly the systematic rules of grammar—and the myriad and complex rules for social interaction. Harnessing these strengths means completely inverting Greenspan's right-brain paradigm. Instead of first fostering emotional connection, then language, then abstract, symbolic thinking, as Greenspan recommends, we should instead begin with symbolic skills and abstract concepts.

Consider, for example, the meaning of *maybe*. It is a key word and concept for us all, but particularly for children on the autistic spectrum, who crave predictable routines and need to be warned ahead of time whenever uncertainty lurks. Greenspan might claim that *maybe* is an abstract concept that children grasp only once they have learned about the *feeling* of uncertainty.

But what about a six-year-old HFA who simply can't recognize an uncertain face or voice but can add multidigit numbers and knows the words *plus* and *equals*? Perhaps he can learn what *maybe* means through math: yes + no = maybe. It's a crude formulation, but let's see where it leads. We repeat it to him. We have him repeat it until he knows it by heart. Then we start using *maybe* in paired sentences whenever it comes up: "Maybe it will be sunny tomorrow. Maybe it will rain." "Maybe we will go to the pool tomorrow. Maybe we will stay home." We watch our child's face as it fills with recognition and delight. In one small victory in the game of life, he is certain, now, about uncertainty.

As for social interaction, all the explicit teaching strategies and structured learning opportunities we discussed for unsocial children in chapter 2 apply as well to those on the autistic spectrum: the social skills groups, the Mind Reading program (for learning to read facial expressions), the books about conversational dynamics, and the videos showing peer interactions. We sometimes need, however, to start at a more basic level and luckily, there is a structured curriculum out there specifically designed for HFAs and Aspies, namely, Carol Gray's "Social Stories." Her *New Social Story Book* and more recent *My Social Stories Book* include personalized narratives about how to help others, greet someone, make someone happy, and play fair, as well as when to say "thank you" or "excuse me." Some collections of Social Stories are available online, for example at the website of the Flemington-Raritan Autism Program in New Jersey (www.frsd.k12.nj .us/autistic).

PARENTING ADVICE

As seen in the popularity of right-brain autism gurus such as Stanley Greenspan, society's prevailing parenting ethos extends to parents of children on the autistic spectrum. The route to healthy relationships is through the emotions. Parents should favor emotional validation, emotion processing, and "positive discipline"—praise, negotiation, and redirection—over strict, structured, disciplinarian parenting. The problem is that for children with autism and Asperger's syndrome, even more than for other left-brainers, validation and processing are often completely ineffectual, as are negotiation and redirection. Indeed, autistic children may not even understand emotional vocabulary, let alone respond to it. They can be oblivious to emotions and unresponsive to praise, and their good behavior often depends on negative consequences, material rewards, explicit teaching, and critical feedback. A parent can validate, process, negotiate, and redirect until the cows come home without modifying an inappropriate behavior, subduing an unproductive fixation, or aborting a relentless tantrum.

Sometimes the only way out is to deploy precisely the sort of direct, emotionally dismissive, punitive firmness that "positive" parenting completely renounces: "If you don't stop screaming and crying, then you can't have dessert." But, given our society's near-ubiquitous condemnation of such tactics—on the playground, in the school yard, at the family reunion—deploying them takes confidence. Indeed, every time we attempt to discipline our autistic child in public, we risk being judged as hard-hearted. No matter how obvious we think it is that the normal parenting strategies won't work, most people simply don't get it. When they make their critical remarks, as they invariably do, the best we can do is to prepare a ready comeback. Why not say, out loud, that which we're constantly replaying in our minds: "Would you like to take my autistic child for the weekend?"

Luckily, however, there are often other, less punitive options that the right-brain world of child psychology doesn't even consider, options that we parents must therefore pursue on our own. As mentioned in the previous chapter, left-brain activities such as math problems, strategy games, and construction projects can serve as occasions for bonding between parents and analytic children. So, too, with Aspies and HFAs. Furthermore, by giving our child our focused attention, and something engaging and productive to do, we can help him calm down and better regulate his behavior.

Many parenting gurus, trained as they are in the psychodynamic approach to human psychology, are eager to read deep emotional needs into every act of defiance. As we discussed in the previous chapter, they forget that one of the most common causes of misbehavior is boredom. In this respect, Aspies and HFAs are no different from other children. It's just that because most social environments don't engage them, and because most environments are social, they get bored much more often—indeed, they can get bored any time they are not absorbed in some sort of structured activity.

Particularly deadly is standing in line, or sitting on the bus, or waiting to be served at a restaurant—places where other children might happily chat away or improvise games but where autistic children commonly act up. We can preempt this simply by handing our child something engrossing: a clipboard with math problems; some sidewalk chalk; a magnetic puzzle. Or, if we forget to bring these along, we improvise. During an excessive restaurant wait, one mom had her son reading the ingredients of the salt, sugar, and sugar substitute packets and conducting blind taste tests. Another mother believes that one reason her son—Timothy, the Aspie math and science whiz we discussed above—became so precocious in math was his restlessness during car rides: the only way to keep him from unbuckling his seat belt and exiting the car, it turned out, was to pile up the backseat with challenging math toys.

Besides boredom, the other major behavioral challenges shared by most HFAs and Aspies are their lack of sociability, narrow interests, and resistance to change, all of which we discussed in connection with other left-brainers. In this, mildly autistic children are simply more extreme versions of these other children; more extreme versions of the strategies we suggested in chapters 1 through 4 are thus applicable here as well. They include carefully choosing and monitoring our child's playdates; making his obsessions more interactive by joining in or having him teach us about them; broadening his interests with related ventures out of the house; providing him with maps or checklists to help him stay engaged on outings; and giving him calendars and flowcharts to prepare him for changes in routine—making full use, all the while, of that key concept "maybe."

Beyond helping them through their behavioral difficulties, we want to bond with our Aspies and HFAs in any way we can. As with other analytic children, this is most likely to happen over the analytical ventures that excite them the most: chess games, chemistry experiments, the mechanics of ceiling fans.

We want, as well, to foster the skills our children need to interact happily and productively with the world at large. Because they're often so uninspired by the informal, open-ended play opportunities that so many parenting books insist on, they, even more than other left-brainers, depend on the very tactics that these books discourage, namely, structured play and direct instruction by parents. Recall "yes + no = maybe." As suggested above in connection with teaching therapies, direct, structured instruction, even at home, and especially in abstract, systematic, left-brain topics such as math and logic, may be the *only* activity that initially engages them with the outside world, helps them make sense of it, and expands their horizons toward creativity and sociability.

How to Change Right-Brain Attitudes
Useful Talking Points

In the Introduction, we suggested that our classroom's right-brain prac-tices reflect a broader bias in contemporary American culture, a bias against traditional math, science, and analytical thought in favor of holistic learning, gut reactions, social skills, and the arts. The breadth of this bias makes it especially difficult for us not only to make our case with the education establishment, but also to enlist other parents as allies. To begin making inroads into the dominant right-brain para-digm, we must know its premises and be prepared with ready replies.

THE BIG PICTURE

For starters, we need to realize why the dominant paradigm is so broadly appealing. At work are three key factors. First, many of us are biased by outdated and negative stereotypes about schools. Movies and sitcoms that portray contemporary classrooms—such as *Election*, *Mean Girls*, *Life as We Know It*—keep these stereotypes vividly alive, with their scenes of bored students slumped over desks in rows facing teachers who drill them on inane facts. The combination of No Child Left Behind testing and cuts in recess, art, and music have convinced many that schools are increasingly focusing on reading and math at the expense of everything else.

With such impressions filling our collective unconscious, it is the calls to make classrooms even more child-centered and discovery-oriented, not more structured, rigorous, and academic, that resonate.

In teacher training programs, in particular, professors and students alike regularly allude to the rote drills and spoon-fed facts that purportedly still predominate. Outside the education establishment, academic celebrities such as Jordan Ellenberg, the mathematician and *Slate* columnist, and Brian Greene, the best-selling physicist, characterize classroom math and science as "abstract," "remote," and removed from students' lives. Meanwhile, the mainstream media gets far more worked up about cuts in school arts programs than about academic losses within the math and science curricula.

Second is the bombardment of claims by education experts that "research supports" that children learn things best through hands-on discovery; that communicating about math helps them learn math; that working in groups fosters the social skills that most jobs require; and so forth. Hear these claims enough times, and they start sounding like common sense. Ever fewer people think to question whether the evidence is actually out there.

Most compelling of all, however, is the underlying philosophy, reflecting as it does all those right-brain biases we discussed in the Introduction: intuition over analysis; social and emotional skills over book smarts; art over science. Both reflecting this philosophy and reinforcing it are popular theories such as Howard Gardner's multiple intelligences, and best sellers such as Daniel Goleman's *Emotional Intelligence*. How refreshing to hear an expert proclaim that three-quarters of human intelligence—the musical, spatial, bodily-kinesthetic, interpersonal, and intrapersonal—is distinct from the verbal and logical reasoning skills that traditional classrooms and conventional measures of intelligence have deemed so important. Or that social and emotional skills are at least as crucial as traditional IQ.

Indeed, many right-brain teaching philosophies appeal, at least in the abstract, to *all* of us—even to the most academically inclined among us, right- and left-brain alike. Who, for example, wouldn't rather let children discover things on their own, in their own way, if only all things could thus be learned, and learned efficiently? Who wouldn't happily dispense with rote drills, if only drills weren't so indispensable to arithmetic and foreign language mastery? Who wouldn't prefer, ideally, to have students working together in harmony, rather than competing against one another, if only such harmony were always possible, and if only cooperative groups were always the most efficient, inspirational medium for learning?

Throughout our arguments, therefore, we need to expose the outdated stereotypes, question the empirical evidence, and, perhaps most importantly, distinguish between wishful thinking and practical reality. On the one hand, wouldn't it be nice if we could successfully rear our children without worrying about book smarts, and without ever deviating from our ideals of freedom and harmony? On the other hand, quite simply, we cannot. Indeed, all of us, to some degree, start learning this almost as soon as we become parents.

In making our arguments, we should be careful not to gravitate too far to the opposite extreme. Some incidental learning, some focus on practical, real-life problems, some cooperative group learning, some attention to emotional issues, some requirements for class participation, and some avoidance of rote learning in favor of thoughtful reflection can benefit, to varying degrees, most, if not all, students. But, we must repeat, the intensity and uniformity with which these things are now practiced in America's primary and secondary schools ultimately shortchange everyone.

THE COMMON ARGUMENTS SUPPORTING TODAY'S TEACHING METHODS—AND HOW TO COUNTER THEM

In this chapter I'll list sixteen claims that you might encounter as you advocate for your child in school—assertions that reflect what most teacher training programs have taught today's teachers. You'll also hear these claims from learning specialists, principals, and other professionals who are invested in today's right-brain classroom practices and curricula. Below I'll review these claims one by one, offering specific counterarguments you can make in advocating for your left-brain child. (The counterarguments are presented in a first-person voice to suggest the kinds of things that might be useful to say in a school meeting with teachers, school counselors, and other school staff.)

1. *Children learn best through hands-on, child-centered discovery rather than explicit instruction.*

The noise and clutter of child-centered learning overwhelm my child, and he is probably not alone. According to the educator Vicki Snider, author of *Myths and Misconceptions about Teaching*, activity-centered classrooms pose attention problems for all young children. She points out that youngsters have trouble knowing what to pay attention to, and that "activity-based instruction can make it difficult for learners to focus on what it is they are supposed to learn."

At home I've found that my child learns many things best when I teach him explicitly, and again, he's probably not alone. Informal surveys show large numbers of parents so concerned about what today's classrooms are no longer explicitly teaching that they provide extra tutoring after school. What about children whose parents can't do this? As Lisa Delpit has argued in *Beyond Silenced Voices: Class, Race, and Gender in United States Schools*, students from poor homes or disempowered cultures often enter school less academically prepared than their peers, and therefore are especially in need of explicit teaching by teachers. Their parents and other advocates—whose voices are too often ignored by the powers that be—expect schools to provide such instruction. The more our schools resist this, the more they widen the achievement gap between the underprivileged and the privileged.

When it comes to Reform Math, however, nearly all those affected are failing to thrive. Mathematicians estimate that the inefficiencies of discovery learning ultimately delay Reform Math students, relative to their non-Reform peers, by up to two whole years, and many children are telling their parents that school math is way too easy.

2. *Oral participation is an integral part of classroom performance that grades should reflect.*

Because of her social insecurities and trouble following group discussions, my child finds it extremely difficult to participate orally. That doesn't mean she's not involved: I know from what she tells me about class that she's actively listening to everything that others are saying and making all sorts of evaluations and connections in her head, just as people do when they read. Nor are she and other shy kids the only ones who approach class this way. As Heejung Kim and Hazel Markus argue in *Beyond Silenced Voices*, there's a whole subculture of school-children, namely first-generation East Asians, who tend to be quiet in classrooms. These authors ask an important question: "Is this a problem that needs to be fixed?" In East Asian cultures, they point out, "listening and not hastily talking are highly valued as ways of demonstrating sympathy and trying to understand what others are feeling." In embracing students from other cultures, shouldn't we avoid discriminating against students who tend to be quiet in classrooms?

3. *Children learn best when relating things to their personal lives.*

If you ask my child, he'll tell you that he finds it far more interesting to immerse himself in new and exotic material than to relate things back to his personal life. Having to ponder his personal connections to the latest developments in *The Chocolate War* actually interferes with his enjoyment of the book. Also, because his linear mind works best when focusing on one thing at a time, thinking about himself while reading diminishes his ability to fully digest and comprehend the words on the page.

And he's probably not alone. Some college professors have observed a marked decline in reading comprehension among their recent undergraduates. Students, they report, are inserting more and more digressions about their personal feelings and experiences into their reading-based writing assignments, apparently letting their own perspectives distract them from those of the authors. Professors have also observed a decline in analytical writing skills. Here, too, students appear to be injecting more and more personal feelings, personal anecdotes, and unsupported opinions rather than defending their own arguments or analyzing someone else's.

4. *Group work enhances learning by fostering communication and exposing students to multiple perspectives and strategies.*

My child finds group work intimidating and confusing, and learns much better on her own. She absorbs multiple perspectives and strategies more readily from textbooks than from classmates. While she may be unusual, other children report having their own problems with group work. Try polling the kids in the classroom. Many students complain that working in groups actually reduces their learning. In the more harmonious groups—friends, for example—students report wasting many long minutes goofing off. In the mixed-ability groups that today's classrooms favor, brighter students report spending significant time trying to explain things to weaker ones. Here especially, one or two children often end up dominating the discussion and doing most of the work, reducing everyone's exposure to multiple perspectives and strategies.

5. *Mathematicians and other people who solve complex problems mostly work in groups; group work in the classroom prepares children for group work on the job.*

Ask any mathematician, and he'll tell you that when mathematicians collaborate, they do so by divvying up the problem and working separately. This characterizes many professional collaborations: participants divide things up, and then reconvene to assess progress and combine results, but typically—unlike what students in school math groups are supposed to do—they complete the bulk of their work on their own. As a writer who has coauthored three books, mostly by working alone, puts it, "How many projects are ever created by people sitting in the same room together for hours on end?" In more corporate settings, a single person is typically in charge, assigns specific tasks, and sends people back to their cubicles. Indeed, it's the cubicle, not the conference table, that predominates at most offices. Finally, compared with schoolchildren, adults are more likely to end up working with like-minded peers—for example, those who have chosen the same line of work.

Looking beyond our borders, we see few other countries spending anything like the amount of class time that we do on student-centered group work. And we see no evidence from advocates of cooperative learning that foreign professionals are less able to collaborate than we are.

6. *Working in groups makes classrooms more harmonious and less competitive.*

In my child's experience, group work is far from harmonious and noncompetitive. Communal activities may reduce academic competition, but they bring out *social* competition—over who gets the floor and who should be in charge—however much teachers insist that no one dominate. Worse, the more socially vulnerable or awkward kids often find themselves teased, ignored, or otherwise ostracized whenever their teachers are out of earshot.

7. *Children learn best in noncompetitive environments.*

My child learns best when competing academically. While not all children depend on competition for learning, he's probably not the only one who does. In *The War Against Boys*, Christina Hoff Sommers points out that boys in general are languishing in today's classrooms, and argues that one reason is that they tend to learn best in the competitive environments that our schools have renounced.

8. *Students learn best through integrated, interdisciplinary projects.*

My child currently lacks the organizational skills that interdisciplinary projects demand. Nor is she alone in this. Consider a 2003 *New York Times* Science Section article on executive function (EF), the cognitive mechanism that helps us see the big picture and plan things out. According to the article, because most executive functioning occurs in the frontal lobes, and because these are the last part of the brain to mature, EF is not fully developed until people hit their thirties. When executive function falls short, the article adds, "the person approaches large projects haphazardly and without all the needed materials" and "is easily overwhelmed by details while missing the big picture."

Projects challenge, in particular, not just the linear, one-thing-at-a-time thinkers, but also the many children with suspected or diagnosed ADD, ADHD, and Nonverbal Learning Disabilities, who struggle to stay focused on tasks that are broad in focus. They challenge, as well, the many others, some of them labeled with OCD, who get stuck in a subtask and can't move on, or who struggle with transitions from subtask to subtask, or who have trouble putting it all together.

A 2007 brain-imaging study by the National Institutes of Health and McGill University found that children with ADHD are simply delayed relative to their peers. A 2008 article in the *Journal of Experimental Psychology* (Naomi Friedman, lead author) suggests that executive function is almost entirely genetic and varies among individuals along many dimensions. Eventually, it's probably safe to assume, most children will develop brains that can handle broad assignments. But there's no evidence that tackling these assignments prematurely accelerates EF maturation.

Instead, big projects end up penalizing a subsector of kids for largely inborn, developmental idiosyncrasies that most of them will eventually outgrow—kids who, in the meantime, either flounder or become overly dependent on their parents to help them get much of their work done.

9. *You shouldn't push your child ahead of his or her developmental timetable.*

The deep influence of Jean Piaget and his followers on the American education establishment has many of our teachers believing that cognitive development follows stages that limit what children can learn at different ages. Observations by the Piaget disciple Constance Kamii, for example, have convinced educators that children under eight aren't capable of understanding place value—specifically, the ones, tens, and hundreds places. But cognitive psychology has largely discredited Piaget's and Kamii's assumptions about developmental readiness. Simply put, academic skills such as arithmetic and phonics aren't developmental skills like walking, talking, and executive function, and are at least somewhat independent of general cognitive milestones.

Thus, students in other countries start learning place value in first grade, and Montessori programs, even in America, start teaching it in preschool. In *The Schools We Need and Why We Don't Have Them,* E. D. Hirsch cites data showing that in France, Japan, and other developed countries, first-graders "perform written operations with two-digit numbers and have an at least implicit understanding of place value to two places," and second-graders "know the multiplication table through 9 times 9, and can add and subtract three-digit numbers . . . thus demonstrating an operational understanding of place value." This education, Hirsch reports, occurs "without great strain on them [the students] or their teachers and without any known harmful psychological effects."

10. *Math is most meaningful when grounded in daily life.*

My child also finds it distracting and limiting that so much school math is grounded in concrete, daily-life scenarios. Again, he's probably not alone. A new study by Jennifer Kaminski at the Center for Cognitive Science at Ohio State University suggests that too much of a focus on real-world math obscures the underlying mathematics, such that students are unable to transfer concepts to new problems. Also, not all math readily relates to daily life. The kind my child most enjoys is highly symbolic and abstract; abstract math, as any mathematician will tell you, is at least as meaningful as applied math, and often essential for it.

11. *Students who can't explain their thinking don't really know what they are doing.*

My child finds school math easy enough to do in her head, and has nothing to say as explanation. She does the problems automatically and subconsciously, and therefore doesn't even know how she solved them, let alone how to describe this in words or pictures. But that doesn't mean she doesn't grasp the math—after all, she almost always gets the right answer. It's one thing to say how you solved a complex algebra problem, where there are multiple steps that you have to think through, consciously, in your head; it's quite another to say how you added two one-digit numbers. How many of us adults can honestly say how we solved 7 + 8, beyond simply saying that we know it's 15?

My child isn't alone. If you ask other children, you'll hear many report that explaining their solutions to easy problems is pointless, tedious, and often has them making up methods that they didn't actually use. Also, requiring verbal explanations disadvantages those with autism and other language impairments, as well as nonnative English speakers and students with penmanship problems. Requiring pictographic explanations, meanwhile, disadvantages nonvisual thinkers and children with poor drawing or draftsmanship skills.

12. *A child who can't do word problems or applied, hands-on activities doesn't understand the underlying math.*

My child is struggling not with the actual math, but with the language of the word problems and directions. Try giving him just the math, and see how he does. Those who understand math most deeply, namely, mathematicians, will tell you that their focus, and the focus of the tests they give students, isn't real-life word problems and applied math activities, but abstract, symbolic math.

Again, my child isn't alone. Any child with language delays or nonnative English skills will struggle with word problems and multistep directions. Some teachers recognize this and adjust their materials accordingly: one reports "stripping math of as many words as I could" so that his class could be "the one place . . . where immigrant Korean kids did not have to suffer for their limited English fluency." Word problems and written directions also challenge students with reading difficulties such as dyslexia. All of these populations contain many who do understand the underlying math, and find word problems and activities with multistep directions challenging for purely linguistic reasons.

13. *Reform Math reflects the standards of state tests mandated by No Child Left Behind.*

It's reasonable for teachers to spend some time ensuring that students can handle the content covered by the state-mandated tests. But many of these tests set an extremely low bar over which most students can sail. The more the material covered in class limits itself accordingly, the more those parents with resources will provide supplementary instruction at home, thus widening the gap between their children and those for whom No Child Left Behind was originally intended.

14. *Formative assessment is a more valid measure than traditional assessment.*

Traditional assessments, today's educators claim, bias the curriculum toward tests, favor children who test well, and fail to capture much of the learning process. Purportedly more valid are formative assessments of students' work and class participation. But what if my child is so shy, underchallenged, overwhelmed, or distracted in the classroom that she isn't able to demonstrate, during most in-class activities, her true academic potential or her eagerness to go above and beyond expectations? What if she finds the homework so easy that she's unmotivated to put much effort into it? What if her potential, ambition, curiosity, and work ethic surface only during solo assignments that are much more academically challenging than what she's typically asked to do? And what if, in her case, tests are a much better measure of aptitude and achievement than class participation? While it's true that some children don't test well, others actually perform better in quiet, individualized testing situations than in the noisy, cluttered environment of the hands-on, group-centered classroom.

15. Past experience shows that explicit teaching and traditional math don't work for most students.

The past experience most people remember is the Back to Basics movement, in full force in the 1970s and 1980s, when many of us parents and teachers were students. Inspired by a backlash against the New Math of the 1960s, and reinvigorated by the publication of *A Nation at Risk* in 1983, it featured large amounts of drill and memorization at the expense of conceptual understanding. Back to Basics classrooms are the kind best remembered not just by many current parents and teachers but also by many current film and TV writers, which is why tedious teachers, inane facts, and bored students star in the classrooms that most commonly appear, even today, in movies and TV shows.

But the Back to Basics classroom is not the only form that traditional, teacher-centered, explicit teaching–focused classrooms can take—or have taken in the past. Browse through an antique bookstore and you'll marvel at the conceptual challenge of many of the old word problems, and at the liveliness of the long-out-of-print readers and social studies texts. Visit classrooms in East Asia, where students routinely outperform us in math and science, and you will find, as Harold Stevenson and James Stigler do in *The Learning Gap*, that teacher-directed, call-and-response instruction can be "a very lively, engaging enterprise."

16. Current educational practices are supported by experts and empirical research.

In making our case against current practices, we must bear in mind three other trends in contemporary American education: an increasingly centralized control of our schools by our towns and cities, the state-mandated testing required by No Child Left Behind, and a growing deference to the advice of specialized professionals, including organizations such as the National Council of Teachers of Mathematics (NCTM), the National Science Teachers Association, and the education division of the National Science Foundation.

Reform Math is largely a reflection of the NCTM's new *Standards*; so are the state-mandated tests to which many teachers now feel they must teach. What all this means is that superintendents, school boards, curriculum consultants, and the leaders of national organizations of teachers are wielding ever more influence over textbooks and tests, giving little or no say to individual teachers and principals. Even those hands-on educators who are convinced that the new materials are effective may have simply trusted the experts—for why should the experts be untrustworthy?

Thus, to make any real headway in the education world, we must either win over or discredit the education experts. And to do this, we must confront their ultimate trump cards: the scientific expertise and empirical studies that purportedly support their claims.

Education professionals readily cite empirical evidence and endorsement by outside experts. Once again, Reform Math takes center stage. As far as expert credentials go, *Everyday Math* has it best. As part of the University of Chicago Math Project, it evokes Chicago's world-class math department. But all Reform Math programs can claim expertise and funding from the National Science Foundation (NSF).

The University of Chicago Math Project is a product not of the university's math department but of its now-defunct education school. The NSF expertise and funding comes, specifically, from the NSF's education division (the Directorate for Education and Human Resources). The developers and funders of Reform Math, in other words, aren't scientists and mathematicians, but those who have always been its greatest supporters, namely, our education professionals.

What about the empirical claims: "research shows" that children learn concepts best when constructing them on their own, through incidental, hands-on learning activities; "studies show" that math scores rise after schools introduce Reform Math.

School test results are notoriously fickle. The student body, the teaching staff, the external supports, the tests themselves—all of these can change significantly from one year to the next. You can always find schools in which scores are currently rising, regardless of the math program. Just as readily you will find schools with falling scores, some of which use Reform Math and which Reform's supporters either don't mention or try to explain away (perhaps the program wasn't "properly implemented"). In general, there are too many variables for firm conclusions.

Among the more confounding variables are, first, the Hawthorne effect, or the tendency of people to improve their performance in the short run in response to any change—for example, a change in wall color, or a curriculum change, even one that turns out to be a bad idea. Second, there's the effect of parental intervention—for example, alarmed parents tutoring their children in response to perceived shortcomings in the curriculum. But Reform Math's greatest defenders don't acknowledge either of these factors; some go farther, distorting the statistics and then stonewalling. In fact, there's no unequivocal evidence that shows Reform Math programs outperforming traditional ones.

As far as empirical data go, therefore, Reform Math remains, at best, an inconclusive experiment. As for the traditional curriculum, although the statistics are just as slippery, at least it has been around longer (and thus been subjected to more scrutiny and revision), and more closely resembles programs used successfully in the many countries that are outperforming us in math.

What about the empirical claims that education experts marshal in support of the incidental, hands-on, group-centered learning philosophy, now known as Constructivism, that underlies not just Reform Math but contemporary classroom practices in general? How "research-based" are these? When pressed, some defenders concede that the "research" in question is merely a theory about how children learn. In other words, even the experts will acknowledge that their arguments aren't based on empirical data—results, for example, from neurological or psychological experiments—but only on someone's untested hypothesis. In fact, there appear to be no reputable empirical studies in cognitive science that support the Constructivist learning models employed by our schools.

———

In a nutshell, the points to stress in making our case with teachers and other educators are as follows. Neither test scores nor cognitive science supports today's classroom practices over those of the past and those in other countries, and neither do real-world vocational requirements. Current practices are shortchanging not only our child but many others as well, including those with learning disabilities and those from different linguistic and cultural backgrounds. If the teacher checks in with other students and their parents, he or she will probably discover that many have resorted to supplemental instruction at home. Current practices, given all this, are widening the gaps between the privileged and the underprivileged, those inside the dominant culture and those on the outside, the cognitively typical and the learning disabled, the developmentally typical and the developmentally skewed, and, finally, the socially normal and the socially eccentric—leaving altogether too many children behind.

Conclusion

The Best of Both Worlds

The first five chapters of this book may leave the impression that the world consists of two distinct types of people with diametrically opposed sets of needs and talents. On the one hand, there are the afflicted left-brainers, seen throughout these chapters under tremendous pressure to speak up in class and work in groups, confronted with material that both confuses them and fails to challenge them intellectually. Then there are the fortunate right-brainers, happily discussing and cooperating, engaged by a hands-on, interdisciplinary math and foreign language curriculum that comes much more easily to them than place value, long division, and the declensions of foreign nouns.

Of course, many children aren't unequivocally right-brain or left-brain, but lie somewhere in the middle—in some ways suited, and in other ways ill suited, to current educational practices. But even supposing a polarized society of only extreme right-brainers and extreme left-brainers, might it be possible, somehow, to create an educational system that embodies the best of both worlds? Keeping in mind that some right-brain practices shortchange left- and right-brainers alike, can we strike a balance that doesn't simply shift the pain rightward? Indeed, as we will see, accommodating all children—right-, left-, and middle-brain—is not as difficult as it might at first appear.

THE FALSE DICHOTOMIES

To begin with, many of our schools' current practices are based on false dichotomies. Consider the question of explicit teaching vs.

incidental discovery. On closer inspection, their incompatibility is more apparent than real. As we've discussed, when reading a textbook or listening to a lesson we might—indeed, we should—be drawing all sorts of inferences and connections on our own. These inferences and connections are things that we are discovering incidentally *while* being taught explicitly. Even drills and the mechanical use of explicitly taught procedures, even if not yet fully understood, can spawn incidental discovery, for example, about patterns in the multiplication tables or about how long division works. Indeed, the best lessons combine both explicit teaching and incidental discovery, with books and teachers presenting material both explicitly *and* in a way that inspires further student-centered revelations.

What about the virtues of *purely* incidental discovery, where there's no guiding authority in the background? As we've discussed, this need not compete inside the classroom with explicit teaching. People, particularly professional educators, too often forget that children learn all kinds of things incidentally outside of school. And too often they fail to consider that the outside world might, in fact, be the best place for most incidental learning, while the more structured, artificial environment of the classroom might best suit explicit teaching.

Precisely this division of labor can apply, as well, to academic vs. practical skills. The classroom doesn't lend itself to many of the practical skills that modern-day educators would like it to teach. But even if it did, how valid is the purported dichotomy between academics and real life that underpins this preference for the practical? However much our educators dismiss traditional academics as overly abstract and irrelevant to students' lives, many academic skills, and many secondary aptitudes that develop when one does academics, in fact, are key to practical success. These include not just skills that schools still consider important, such as literacy and numeracy (numerical literacy), but others that, under the new curricula, we've seen them marginalize: mathematical reasoning, rigorous analysis, and diligent practice with conceptually challenging material. These are all skills and work habits that employers expect from candidates for high-level jobs. Indeed, many businesses, including investment banks, management consultants, and law firms, prefer to conduct the more practical, vocational training themselves, and expect schools to provide the more theoretical and academic basics.

Employers also prefer candidates who readily accept high standards and critical feedback—people who can make it through their annual performance review without falling to pieces. As we saw in earlier chapters, however, educators, favoring compliments over criticism, believe that holding students to high standards and critiquing their shortcomings is incompatible with fostering their self-esteem. Again, how valid is the dichotomy? The most dependable source of self-esteem is the confidence gained by actual achievement, for which high standards and critical evaluations are often crucial.

Perhaps the most entrenched of our false dichotomies, because it extends far outside the world of education to pervade the entire culture, is that between creativity and analytical rigor, reflected in our vision of the free-spirited artist vs. the rigidly logical scientist. In fact, creativity and analytical rigor aren't mutually exclusive. Art, music, and literature require structure as well as creativity: clearly constructed sentences and organized prose; carefully worked-out chord progressions; meticulous calculations of perspective, lighting, color, and balance of objects on canvas. Mathematics, science, computer programming, and engineering require creativity as well as logic. Logic alone does not build bridges across broad rivers with unstable banks. Nor did mere logic give Einstein his theory of general relativity, which, overturning a several-hundred-year-old paradigm, accounts for gravity by bending the very fabric of the universe. Indeed, thinking outside the box, in science as much as in the arts, is what distinguishes the great from the merely proficient.

THE RIGHT-BRAIN SKILLS THAT EVERY CHILD NEEDS

What all this implies is that there are both right- and left-brain skills that every child needs. On the right-brain side, as suggested above, there's creativity. While it's unclear whether schools can actually teach or objectively evaluate it, they can provide opportunities for students to develop it, whether in canonically creative subjects such as music and art (too often the victims of school budget cuts); in more analytical ventures such as engineering, robotics, and computer pro-gramming, which likewise invite creativity; or in the more inspiringly open-ended of core academic assignments.

Also crucial are social skills. As we've seen, our world, for better or for worse, is one in which such skills are increasingly paramount. They are key not just to avoiding ostracism and making friends but also to more intellectual accomplishments for which parents might assume that left-brain skills would suffice. Charisma, leadership, get-ting along with others, and forging interpersonal connections are what "makes friends and influences people." As we've discussed, such skills can determine a student's college admissions. They can also deter-mine her career success, as Daniel Goleman argues in *Emotional Intelligence*. Even though many jobs don't require group work, and can be performed perfectly well by those who lack social skills, those with social skills will more readily get promoted, especially into posi-tions of leadership. Social skills affect even the careers of the quintes-sential left-brainers who staff university science departments—careers that depend more and more on large grants, the securing of which can hinge, in turn, not just on scientific credentials but on network-ing and self-promotion.

Finally, there's big-picture thinking or executive function (EF)—a key ingredient of common sense, as well as of the many life skills that involve long-term planning, organizing large amounts of unstruc-tured material, or transitioning between disparate activities. While EF thus benefits everyone greatly, cognitive science suggests that it's largely genetic and developmental, and that in some people—as we've observed with many of our left-brainers—it simply develops later than in others. How much its development can be accelerated through explicit intervention—say, by training children to make lists and flowcharts—remains unclear.

THE LEFT-BRAIN SKILLS THAT EVERY CHILD NEEDS

The most obviously important left-brain skill is numerical literacy. This includes the ability to perform precise arithmetic calculations on arbitrary numbers. How many of us, when we calculate tips or receive change, have pocket-calculators in hand? When the cash register breaks down, wouldn't we prefer to know whether the cashier gave us exactly, not just approximately, the right change, and wouldn't we like him to be able to compute it? Most real-life arithmetic is not restricted to the simple calculations, "friendly fractions," and short-cut-conducive problems of Reform Math. The traditional procedures are sometimes indispensable.

Another cornerstone of numeracy is basic probability and statistics. Whether the issues are risks and benefits, test results, political assertions, scientific predictions, or the odds of winning the lottery, we are constantly bombarded with ratios, rates, percentages, conditional probability, and margins of error. One virtue of Reform Math is that it includes more of this than traditional math does. However, in stressing intuitive judgment over precise calculation, Reform's statistics do not prepare students for the more slippery statistics of daily life, which often are counterintuitive, especially when manipulated by people with political agendas, or where unlikely events are concerned. Think how many people at low risk for HIV, for example, panic unnecessarily when they get a positive HIV test result because they don't know how to use statistics to override their faulty intuitions about the false-positive rates for relatively rare conditions. More generally, whether the issue is health, safety, personal finances, or politics, think how many people react irrationally or make irrational decisions based on assumptions that better training in basic statistics would help them override.

Beyond equipping all students with such numerical literacy, there's another pragmatic reason for rigorous mathematics: giving as many people as possible the opportunity to pursue careers that require sophisticated math, statistics, and computer skills. These include not just quintessentially left-brain disciplines such as science, engineering, accounting, economics, finance, and programming, but also fields like architecture, contracting, design, medicine, psychology, and sociology—to which as many right-brainers as left-brainers may aspire. With more and more companies using sophisticated computer models, jobs requiring quantitative skills extend to business administration, marketing, stock trading, risk management, and quality-control management. Our increasingly quantitative world requires quantitative skills even of journalists: Nicholas Lemann, dean of the Journalism School of Columbia University, who is said to have taught himself how to do linear regressions, reportedly plans to introduce statistics courses for journalists.

In our global economy, preparing our students mathematically has become ever more important, for they are now competing against ever larger numbers of students from overseas, most of whom, even before Reform Math took hold, went through much more demanding math programs. This competition begins with higher education: a growing number of applicants from other countries is one reason why our top colleges have become so much more difficult to get into. Recent admissions statistics suggest that around 10 percent of Ivy League undergraduates now come from other countries. Even though admissions committees, as we've observed, often discount math and science whizzes as insufficiently well rounded, they still expect math proficiency and high SAT scores. Reform Math hasn't been around long enough to have served as the primary curriculum for many current college applicants; given how poorly it prepares students for algebra, we should be concerned about how well our children will perform on their math SATs and compete against college applicants from other countries in the next ten years.

Algebra, of course, is crucial, not just for the SATs but also for higher math and science. Indeed, some studies show algebra mastery to be one of the strongest predictors of college success. Because mathematics is so cumulative, few people are able to major, or even minor, in math or science without having mastered algebra in high school. Similarly, few earn advanced degrees in mathematics or science without majoring in math or science in college. Even now, more and more international students are filling the ranks of our country's most competitive math and science graduate programs, with approximately two-thirds of our top mathematics doctoral candidates coming from overseas.

Increasing numbers of international students are also beating out their American-born counterparts over the many jobs that require strong math skills. Others are returning to their countries of origin, raising more worries about our country's intellectual capital and future competitiveness in science and technology. As a 2005 report by the National Academies notes, our public school system "compares, in the aggregate, abysmally with those of other developed—and even developing—nations . . . particularly in the fields which underpin most innovation: science, mathematics and technology."

Beyond fostering numeracy, preparing students for the job market, and keeping our country competitive, rigorous math instruction may yield more subtle rewards. Mathematics is the one logically cumulative subject that follows students throughout their thirteen years of primary and secondary school. Taught properly, it provides long-term practice in logical analysis and deductive reasoning that no other subject can match. It's not at all clear whether this mental workout extends beyond mathematics, and beyond the many fields for which mathematical thinking and knowledge are crucial, to enhance the general intelligence of our children. But unless and until research shows otherwise, caution dictates yet another reason for preserving and reinvigorating these thirteen years of mental calisthenics.

Beyond math and science, another crucial left-brain skill is rational debate. All children can and should learn how to argue effectively, present opposing sides fairly, and assess competing viewpoints. In the world of today's classrooms, with their open-ended problems with multiple solutions and their preference for compliments over criticism, too few students are developing these skills. Our world, it seems, is one of increasingly polarized politics, politically ghettoized neighborhoods, and online political echo chambers, a world in which like-minded individuals intensify their beliefs rather than hearing out the other side. And so it is a world that cries out more than ever for cool-headed, rational argumentation and skepticism toward knee-jerk partisanship.

Moving beyond the analytical, consider, finally, that much-disparaged left-brain trait of introversion. So much does our society value sociability that it rarely encourages children to spend time in solitude. But all people, not just the left-brainers, need from time to time to shut out the pressures of the outside world and look inward. As both David Riesman and William Whyte, respectively, observed a half century ago in *The Lonely Crowd* and *Organization Man,* inward-directed thinking is our society's best defense against mindless conformity and the mediocre decisions that too often result when everything is done by committee.

THE IDEAL WORLD: THE CLASSROOM AS A MICROCOSM

Our goal should be to help all children develop social skills and creativity, on the one hand, and analytical skills, on the other. But we will not achieve this using uniform teaching methods. As is suggested throughout this book, different children require different approaches. In particular, educators need not, and in some cases should not, teach right-brain skills through an exclusively right-brain pedagogy, any more than they should use an exclusively left-brain approach for left-brain skills. Remember from chapter 2, for example, how the best way to teach social skills to left-brainers is to spell out explicit, systematic rules for social interaction. Similarly, recall from chapter 3, the best way to encourage left-brainers to be creative in open-ended assignments is to provide more specific guidelines than right-brainers require. In general, even for right-brain activities, left-brainers need structure.

Right-brainers, on the other hand, tend to fare better, even when the topic is an analytical one, in the more free-form environments of incidental, experiential learning. The problem is that a laissez-faire pedagogy, taken to the extreme that many of today's classrooms practice, risks either leaving out or being too inefficient a learning medium for certain crucial concepts—especially when it comes to abstract, logically cumulative subjects such as math and foreign language grammar. When teaching these subjects, even to a highly right-brain student body, educators must therefore tailor the hands-on, group-centered activities for maximum efficiency, use them in moderation, and both introduce them and follow them up with a fair amount of explicit teaching. When the more abstract rules and concepts arise, teachers should consider dropping such activities entirely and resorting to direct instruction and structured practice. Good instruction and structured assignments can still encourage incidental discovery by inspiring students to notice patterns, make connections, and draw inferences. Too much laissez-faire, on the other hand, can unmoor class discussions and group activities, diluting the academics for everyone.

Although even right-brainers need some structure, left-brainers need much more. How, then, can one teacher simultaneously accommodate everyone? In fact, the complementary needs in the classroom can be an advantage.

Let's start with sociability. For most children, it develops naturally. Consider, for example, interactive play, the art of conversation, empathy, diplomacy, and making friends. Assuming they have competent parents and the usual opportunities to interact with peers, most children will acquire and hone these skills without the intervention of their classroom teachers. Beyond providing and enforcing basic guidelines for social behavior in the classroom (e.g., sharing, apologizing, waiting your turn), it's not clear that teachers need assume any responsibility for the social skills of the sociable majority, especially given how much these children practice being social after hours in more natural settings. But even if a teacher does want to enhance their sociability, all she needs to do is put them in groups and let things unfold. This then frees her to work directly with the more unsocial, left-brain students, perhaps with a couple of right-brain extroverts as models. Or, perhaps more appropriately, the left-brainers can develop their social skills outside the classroom, in one of the many specially designed social skills groups that more and more specially trained psychotherapists are running.

As far as encouraging creativity in open-ended assignments goes, teachers can easily accommodate both right- and left-brain needs by providing optional parameters and specific suggestions that students can follow if they need to, and that the more right-brain students can simply ignore.

What about analytical skills? Rebalancing hands-on activities vs. explicit teaching, as discussed above in connection with right-brainers, obviously improves things for left-brainers as well. Indeed, in kindergarten and first grade, where the math is simpler, more concrete, and captured relatively efficiently by hands-on activities, such a balance may work for all students. The only modification that the left-brainers might require is the option to do the hands-on work independently;

indeed, given the questions we raised about group work in chapter 6, this option is perhaps one that all students deserve.

By the time they reach second or third grade, increasing numbers of left-brainers are mature enough to learn math independently, at their own rates, through appropriately challenging texts, software packages, or online programs (some of which are available for free). They must be properly set up from the get-go, though, and might require periodic supervision or guidance, but usually are highly self-sufficient and self-motivated. Letting a portion of the class do math independently may strike some teachers as a radical, unworkable idea: what's to guarantee that the children will actually stay focused, do their work, and learn the material? In fact, some very successful math classes have had all students, of all different aptitudes, working independently, at their own individually optimal rates. I've observed some of these myself. Allowing this option to the left-brainers in particular frees up the teacher to focus on the more right-brain students, for some of whom the math might be much more challenging, and for many of whom the group-based, hands-on activities may still be quite appropriate.

What about the math curriculum? Is there a single one that suits every child? Many of the serious shortcomings of Reform Math affect all students. More traditional textbooks, for example those of McGraw-Hill and Saxon Math, are still being published. Especially for the more right-brain students, however, much of this curriculum can be unnecessarily dry and repetitive. Another option, however, has recently become readily and cheaply available to American students: Singapore Math, which we discussed in chapter 3. This curriculum, designed in part by professional mathematicians, manages to train proficiency in the standard procedures through a relatively small number of carefully chosen exercises. The Singapore word problems, with their interesting twists, are at once mathematically to the point (with multiple layers of math concepts in place of Reform Math's excess verbiage) and open-ended (in that it's often not obvious how to begin). The most challenging Singapore problems combine, within mathematical parameters, the best of both right- and left-brain worlds: analysis and creative problem solving.

Many parents of left-brainers have found that Singapore Math suits their children perfectly. But even if it turns out that a different curriculum works better for other students, the ability of left-brainers to do math independently allows them to follow one curriculum while everyone else uses another.

The ideal curriculum, as we suggested above in connection with numerical literacy, also includes, for left- and right-brainers alike, some rigorous probability and statistics. Here both Reform Math and Singapore Math come up short; a better resource is Saxon Math, in which the middle school curriculum includes such topics as representative samples, bias, dependent and independent events, and identifying misleading graphs.

The most serious challenge for proper math instruction comes not from the logistics of addressing left- and right-brain needs simultaneously but from the dwindling number of prospective teachers who are able to teach the more challenging concepts to anyone. This is a vicious cycle that our country has faced for decades, as the quality of the mathematics training of each new generation of K–12 students affects the mathematics teaching skills of those students who later go on to become K–12 teachers. Accelerating the cycle, most new teachers, as the New Commission on the Skills of the American Workforce reports, come from the bottom third of high school graduates, as measured by their SAT scores. As for their math credentials in particular, the National Academies' 2005 report estimates that half of those teaching fifth- through twelfth-grade math have neither majored in nor been certified in mathematics.

The National Academies' statistics for science instruction are even more unsettling: approximately two-thirds of students studying physics and chemistry are taught by teachers with no major or certificate in these subjects.

We need, therefore, to recruit more mathematically and scientifically skilled adults, whose ranks, of course, include many left-brainers. As an October 2007 article in *The Economist* reports, the main obstacle isn't salaries: countries such as Japan and Singapore, whose teachers come from the *top* third of high school graduates, actually pay less than we do. It is, rather, the relatively low professional status enjoyed by America's schoolteachers as compared with their counterparts from these other countries. Another obstacle may be our teacher certification programs which, with their right-brain proselytizing and low tolerance for skeptics; their right-brain pedagogies (practicing what they preach, education professors often ask prospective teachers to work in groups); their omission of academic, or "content area," training (e.g., in math and science); and their right-brain reconceptions of mathematics, are turning off many left-brain math and science buffs.

Indeed, fast-track programs, such as Teach for America and Alternative Routes to Certification, that bypass or speed up the usual certification process attract students with superior academic credentials—higher SAT scores, higher grade-point averages, bachelor's degrees from more rigorous programs, and more academic training in the subjects that they aspire to teach. But, few in number and (in the case of Alternative Routes) small in size, fast-track programs admit a much smaller proportion of applicants and prefer candidates with teaching experience. Recently, for example, a friend who is a computer software engineer with a BA in math from Harvard but no background in classroom teaching was rejected from Connecticut's Alternative Routes program, which admits only 125 applicants per year.

What we need, then, is a broader system of Alternative Routes or fast-track certification programs that have the latitude to pursue two key strategies. First, they should specifically seek out anyone who has majored, minored, or done high-level course work in mathematics and science—or perhaps anyone who has scored in the top third on the SAT or GRE math test. Second, they should exempt these candidates from the teacher training courses that would otherwise deter them. As the principals and headmasters of private primary and secondary schools have known for decades, many talented, dedicated teachers have never taken a single education course. As public school principals have noted in surveys, novice teachers from Teach for America, mostly straight out of college, rate well above average in their motivation and teaching skills as compared with novices from traditional certification programs.

Principals, for their part, should select teachers more for their academic credentials than for their education course work, and assess their teaching skills directly through real-life demonstration lessons. If she shows enough promise, hire her—if not as a general classroom teacher, then as a math or science specialist. Just possibly, the more we value—and have reason to value—their academic skills, the more the professional status of our schoolteachers will rise, and the vicious cycle in our math and science instruction will reverse itself.

Let's turn now to more general pedagogical issues, such as projects, cooperative learning, and class participation. Once again, how can we accommodate all students? Consider, first, the unstructured, interdisciplinary project that increasingly dominates the homework assignments. For some right-brainers it is highly inspiring. However, as we've seen, it assumes a degree of organizational sophistication and focus, or executive function, that lots of children haven't yet attained. Those with so-called attention deficit disorders, in particular, may struggle as much as their left-brain counterparts. For many students, therefore, teachers need to do what we parents have ended up doing in their place: break the projects down into smaller pieces and provide step-by-step guidelines and feedback. None of us busy adults— most of whom received little help from our parents on *our* school projects—should be walking our children laboriously through all the myriad steps of *their* projects.

Another modification that benefits everyone involves ensuring that the projects don't end up diminishing students' exposure to math and science. To the extent that math and science projects include social studies and art, social studies and art projects should in turn include math and science. For example, if a linear algebra project includes the history and geography of the Oregon Trail, along with clay models of the landscape, then a coloring project might include a discussion of the physics of the color spectrum; and a social studies project about an upcoming election might include the mathematics of opinion polls, complete with questions about sampling and standard deviation.

As for cooperative learning, teachers, as suggested above, can easily give left-brainers the ongoing option to work independently. Indeed, where the more outspoken, unsocial left-brainer is concerned, teachers may find that it's in fact easier not to force him to work in groups. Similarly easy is exempting the shy student from mandatory participation in class discussions and, in another accommodation suggested in chapter 1, allowing her to contribute through written responses or formal presentations.

Given their independence and affinity for textbooks, workbooks, and software programs, left-brainers are not difficult to accommodate. For the most part, all teachers must do is allow them to work on their own, give them analytically challenging materials that they can progress through independently (whether for math, science, or foreign language), provide alternatives to personal connections and reflections assignments and specific guidelines for assignments that solicit creativity, and allow them more private or structured options for class participation. Finally, teachers should be open to advancing them to higher grades, particularly when their current environments, like those of the more cacophonous, early elementary school classrooms, overwhelm them for nonacademic reasons.

Consider, then, the ideal classroom, a microcosm of the best of both worlds. One corner—at least in the lower grades—houses Circle Time, with the usual trappings of rug, mats, and easel. Another corner, with bookshelves, chairs, and a computer or two, serves as a quiet retreat for the less social children. Its shelves hold science, math, and foreign language textbooks that students can work through independently. Alongside these are more literary works, only some of which showcase material that relates to students' personal lives. Other books favor the exotic over the familiar, engaging the many left-brainers and others who prefer, at least on occasion, to immerse themselves in faraway worlds.

Sometimes the teacher stands in front, with chalk, pointer, or whiteboard marker in hand, walking students through the more challenging material. Here, while doing most of the talking and keeping the discussion streamlined and focused, he sometimes solicits questions or answers. At other times he sits among the students and facilitates a more free-form discussion, stepping in whenever the conversation stalls, goes off topic, or is taken over by the more charismatic kids, and encouraging, but not pressuring, all students to participate. At still other times he circles the classroom while students work. Some work in groups, others on their own. Sometimes they cut, paste, and bundle up Popsicle sticks, especially in the lower grades, or do hands-on science experiments;

sometimes they stick with pen and paper. Sometimes a math specialist comes in—a math whiz who may lack any official teaching credentials but knows how to engage students and explain things clearly. At other times the students go out for special classes such as art, music, and computer programming, which give all of them opportunities, in their different ways, to be and become creative.

THE WORLD AT LARGE

What about the world at large? Accommodating left-brainers better than we do now need not worsen things for right-brainers. Most of all, we must broaden our criteria for psychological health and normality. We must include introverts as well as extroverts, and allow that some children follow developmental trajectories in which cognitive development soars way ahead of what we think of as normal emotional and social maturity. We should think, and think again, before concluding that this pattern of development is a problem or disorder that needs to be fixed.

We must also recognize and value the analytical talents, creativity, and contributions to society of our left-brainers, as much as we recognize and value the talents, creativity, and contributions of their more social, artistic, and emotional counterparts. We should value, in particular, those left-brain contributions that help our society stay sane, smart, competitive, and tolerant: cool-headed rationalism and skepticism; the drive to challenge and educate others; advancement in math, science, engineering, and technology; openness to fellow eccentrics. We must especially appreciate left-brain talents if we have the authority to determine grades, qualification for enrichment, or admission into selective schools. Finally, while always being sensitive to their idiosyncratic intellectual and social needs, we should, more than we do now and increasingly as they get older, leave our left-brainers to their own devices, looking on in appreciation as they march through life to their own refreshingly idiosyncratic beat.

Resources

SOCIAL SKILLS

Books

Bardovi-Harlig, Kathleen, and Rebecca Mahan-Taylor. *Teaching Pragmatics*. Washington, D.C.: U.S. Department of State, 2003.

Gabor, Don. *How to Start a Conversation and Make Friends*. Rev. ed. New York: Fireside, 2001.

Garner, Alan. *Conversationally Speaking*. Third ed. New York: McGraw-Hill, 1997.

Genzel, Rhona B., and Martha Graves Cummings. *Culturally Speaking*. Second ed. Boston: Heinle ELT, 1996.

Gray, Carol. *The New Social Story Book: Illustrated Edition*. Arlington, Tex.: Future Horizons, 2000.

Tillitt, Bruce, and Mary Newton Bruder. *Speaking Naturally*. Cambridge, U.K.: Cambridge University Press, 1985.

White, Abbie Leigh, Carol Gray, and Sean McAndrew, eds. *My Social Stories Book*. Philadelphia: Jessica Kingsley Publishers, 2002.

DVDs and Software

Fluent American English, www.theseabrightgroup.com/videos.html. A video series on conversational styles, produced and directed by Susan Steinbach.

Mind Reading, www.jkp.com/mindreading. Software that trains users to read facial expressions and tones of voice, featuring a library of over four hundred emotions.

The Transporters, www.thetransporters.com. A British television series, available on DVD, for four- to seven-year-olds that teaches emotions in context, featuring trains, trolleys, and trams with human faces.

Websites

American Speech-Language-Hearing Association, www.asha.org. Includes listings for social skills therapists.

Association for Play Therapy, www.a4pt.org. Includes listings for social skills therapists.

Flemington-Raritan Autism Program (New Jersey), www.frsd.k12.nj .us/autistic. Samples of Social Stories.

Shy United, www.shyunited.com. A website and chatroom for shy people.

Wrong Planet, www.wrongplanet.net. A website for people with Asperger's syndrome.

EXTRACURRICULAR ENRICHMENT

Math Curricula

Saxon Math, http://saxonpublishers.harcourtachieve.com/en-US/ sxnm_home.

Singapore Math, www.singaporemath.com.

Educational Software

Cognitive Tutor, www.carnegielearning.com. Interactive instruction to supplement secondary math courses: Algebra Readiness, Algebra I, Geometry, and Algebra II.

Math Blaster, www.knowledgeadventure.com/mathblaster. A futuristic adventure-game series teaching math basics for ages six to twelve.

Maths Quest: 3-D. An adventure game teaching and testing children
ages 8 through 14 in essential math.
Zoombinis, www.venturaes.com/zoombinis. An adventure-game
series featuring logic puzzles.

After-School Programs

Kumon, www.kumon.com. A system of after-school learning centers
offering a self-paced math curriculum from preschool through
college.
Mathnasium, www.mathnasium.com. A system of after-school learning centers for students in pre-K through twelfth grade, designed
to boost math skills by fostering "number sense."
The Russian School of Mathematics, www.russianschool.com. An
after-school program providing mathematical education for children K–12, with branches in Boston and San Jose.

Distance Learning

Drexel University Math Forum Problem of the Week, http://math
forum.org/problems_puzzles_landing.html. Students submit
solutions to weekly problems and receive feedback from mentors.
Johns Hopkins University Center for Talented Youth, http://cty.jhu
.edu. Offers assessment, programs, services, publications, and
resources for academically talented precollege students.
Stanford University Educational Program for Gifted Youth, http://
epgy.stanford.edu. Provides e-learning courses for gifted and talented students in mathematics, English, physics, computer science, music, and political science.

Summer Camps

Hampshire College Summer Studies in Math, www.hcssim.org.
PROMYS, Boston University, www.promys.org.
The Ross Mathematics Program at Ohio State University, www.math
.ohio-state.edu/ross.

Additional math camps listed at www.ams.org/employment/
mathcamps.html.

For academic camps in general, find additional listings by region at
http://kidscamps.com.

Math Competitions

AMC (American Mathematics Competitions), www.unl.edu/amc/
index.shtml. An individualized, nationwide math competition for
high school students.

Continental Mathematics League, www.continentalmathematics
league.com. A team competition for students in elementary
through high school.

MATHCOUNTS, http://mathcounts.org. A team competition for
elementary and middle school students.

Math Olympiads for Elementary and Middle Schools, www.moems
.org. A team competition.

USA Math Talent Search, www.usamts.org. An individual, online
competition for middle and high school students.

Additional listings at http://homeschoolmathcontests.com.

ACHIEVEMENT TESTS

*High scores on achievement tests may help your child gain entry into
academic enrichment programs at his or her current school and raise his
or her chances for admission to competitive high schools and colleges.*

Advanced Placement Tests. Advanced subject-area exams in about
thirty subjects.

Independent School Entrance Examination (ISEE). A verbal and
math achievement test, used by some private schools in admissions decisions, for students in fifth grade and above.

Johns Hopkins Spatial Test Battery. A test of spatial reasoning that
predicts success in mathematics, natural sciences, engineering,
and architecture, for students in fifth grade and above.

SAT-9. A standardized aptitude test in reading and math for students through high school.

Wechsler Achievement Test. A standardized test of verbal and mathematical achievement for children ages four through thirteen.

Woodcock-Johnson. A variety of comprehensive tests measuring general intellectual ability, specific cognitive abilities, scholastic aptitude, oral language, and academic achievement for students of all ages.

Index

abstract concepts, 4, 89, 90, 95–97, 118, 120, 131, 178–79, 185, 210
academic camps, 141–42
academic vs. practical skills, 204–5
accommodation of learning styles, 43–47, 132–34, 183
affirming classrooms, 112–13, 175
after-school opportunities. *See* extracurricular activities
age of playmates, 72, 73
algebra, 98, 101, 130, 208
aloofness and being hard on others, 153–55
Americans with Disabilities Act (ADA), 50, 183
analytic children
   appreciating, 129–31
   cases, 1, 86–87, 94, 101, 103, 104, 105, 107, 124–25, 127
   characteristics, 88–90
   helping them at school, 129–42
   prospects for competitive high schools and colleges, 126–28
   reasons for getting low grades, 113–21
   trends across academic disciplines that may hinder them, 108–13
   See also specific topics
analytical assignments, 133, 216
   decline in, 26, 90, 105, 115, 125, 173
analytical rigor vs. creativity, 110, 122–23, 130–31, 133, 205–6
Anderegg, David, 7, 10, 22

antisocial behavior, reports of, 39. *See also* behavior problems
Applied Behavior Analysis (ABA), 184
"applied" math. *See* Reform Math: "applied"
argumentativeness, 149–50. *See also* critical attitude; debate
art, 67, 86, 96, 100, 105, 107, 109, 110, 130, 133, 190, 215
Asch, Solomon, 41
Asperger's syndrome, 31, 55
   disability and, 50–52
   DSM and, 31, 49, 50, 162
   nature of, 31, 89
   symptoms and diagnostic criteria, 31, 49, 50, 89, 161–62
   See also autistic/Asperger's syndrome children
attention deficit disorder (ADD), 169, 175, 179, 195, 215. *See also* executive function
attention deficit/hyperactivity disorder (ADHD), 169, 175, 179, 195, 215. *See also* executive function
autism therapies, 183–85
autistic/Asperger's syndrome children
   alternative approaches for, 156, 185–86
   cases, 49, 51, 52–53, 53–56, 163, 165, 167–69, 171–73, 180–82, 187–88
   challenges of classroom discourse for, 173–76

autistic/Asperger's syndrome children
(*continued*)
  challenges of group-centered learn-
    ing for, 165–67
  challenges of Reform Math for,
    167–73
  challenges of language arts and lit-
    erature for, 173–76
  deficits, 179
  generalizations regarding, 51
  helping them at school, 182–83
  need for predictability, 176–77
  need for structure, 71, 176–77
  parenting advice and, 186–88
  poor behavior and disengagement in
    classroom, 165
  reasons for underappreciation of
    analytical skills of, 177–80
  See also specific topics
autistic spectrum disorders, 30–31, 60
  diagnostic criteria, 30–31, 40, 50,
    160–62
  See also autistic/Asperger's syndrome
    children

Back to Basics classrooms, 199
Balanced Literacy, 103
Bardovi-Harlig, Kathleen, 79
Baron-Cohen, Simon, 2, 8, 11, 80, 164
behavior problems, 28–31, 39–40,
  52–56, 111, 157–58, 165, 186–187
Beyond Silenced Voices (Delpit), 192, 193
big-picture thinking, 115, 129, 131, 132–
  33, 152, 195, 206
birthday parties, 60, 61, 71
Bon Voyage (French text), 106
Bruder, Mary Newton, 77

calculation 92, 93
  "mere calculation," 118, 123, 129, 177,
    178
  skills, 121, 129–30, 163, 178, 206–7
call-and-response model, 18, 19, 23,
  45, 199

cases
  Benjamin, 14–16, 29, 101
  Brian, 57–58
  Caleb, 14–15
  Daniel, 124–25
  Ethan, 163, 178
  Gretchen Andrews' student, 168, 171,
    172, 173
  Hannah, 87–88
  Janet, 16–17
  Jared, 167
  Joseph, 123–24
  Josh, 86–87
  Justine, 94, 103
  Lisbeth, 33–39, 74–76, 104, 105, 107,
    127
  Marc and Jessica, 51–52
  Mark, 165
  Max, 29, 31, 49, 52–53, 81
  Miranda, 58–59
  Monica, 13–14
  Ms. Grant, 14–16
  Ms. Johnson, 1
  Oscar, 14–15
  Richard, 94, 169, 173
  Rose, 53–56
  Scott, 165, 169–70, 172, 173, 175, 176,
    182
  Timothy, 165, 180–82, 187–88
Catholic schools, 136–37
chat rooms, Internet, 84
child-centered discovery vs. explicit
  instruction, 44, 92, 106–7, 132, 134,
  168, 183, 192, 199, 203–4, 210, 211.
  See also "discovery learning" and
  incidental discovery
Circle Time, 15, 17–18, 29, 166–67, 216
circular seating in classroom, 18. *See
  also* Circle Time
classroom discussion, 18–23, 35–36,
  108, 167
  vs. call-and-response model, 18, 23
classroom groups. *See* group activities
classroom participation, 20, 24, 27,

35–37, 39, 40, 44, 121, 198–99, 215–16. *See also* oral participation
classroom(s)
group work, harmony, and competition in, 22–23, 35, 112–13, 194–95
as microcosm, 210–17
See also specific topics
clubs, school, 48. *See also* extracurricular activities
Cohen, Cathi, 74
collaboration vs. cooperation, 42, 194
colleges. *See* high schools and colleges, competitive
communication, 161, 175, 193–94. *See also* conversations
competition
and learning, 195
social, 35, 194–95
conformity. *See* peer pressure
Connected Mathematics, 91, 95, 96, 173
connecting with your child, 63–64, 66–70, 154–55, 187–88
connection to self. *See* personal connections and reflections
Constructivism, 90, 94–95, 201–2
conversations
books on, 76–79
difficulty with, 33, 39, 164, 166
encouraging, 68–69
teaching rules for, 75–80
"cookbook math," 98
cooperative learning, 34, 166, 215–16. *See also* group activities; group-centered learning, challenges of; group work
"cooperativeness" in class and cooperative behavior, 27, 42, 166, 194
difficulty cooperating in groups, 40, 125, 180, 181
creativity, 115–17, 211. *See also* analytical rigor vs. creativity
crisis story books, 156
critical attitude, 4, 19, 79, 89, 112, 150, 154

criticism, 205
classrooms that avoid, 112, 113, 117, 205, 209
Culturally Speaking (Genzel and Cummings), 77
culture, American. 10, 63, 66, 77–79, 82–83. *See also* right-brain world, overview of
Cummings, Martha Graves, 77
curiosity, 76, 78, 198
"curiosity" in class, 27, 28, 120

debate, 88, 209
student, 113, 141, 159
See also argumentativeness
Delpit, Lisa, 192
developmental timetable
pushing children beyond their, 123, 125, 196
readiness to learn and, 134, 146–47, 178, 196, 217
Diagnostic and Statistical Manual of Mental Disorders (DSM), 30, 31, 49, 50, 160, 162
diagnostic labels. *See* psychiatric diagnoses
directions, comprehending, 174–75
disability, concept of, 49–51. *See also specific topics*
"discovery learning" and incidental discovery, 95, 103, 174, 192, 203–4. *See also* child-centered discovery vs. explicit instruction
discussion. *See* classroom discussion
disruptions, 29, 53–55, 155. *See also* behavior problems
drawing, 67, 96, 114, 197
Dumbing Down Our Kids (Sykes), 113

Eckhoff, Abby, 93–94, 95, 169, 173
Ellenberg, Jordan, 190
Einstein, Albert. *See* scientists, famous
Emotional Intelligence (Goleman), 6–7, 21, 190, 206

emotional problems, 28–31
emotionally affirming classrooms, 112–13, 175
emotions, 154, 178–79, 186
    alternative ways of processing, 66–68
    teaching your child to read, 80–81
English class, 21, 26, 35–37. *See also* language arts and literature
enrichment programs
    advocating for, 133–34, 180–82
    reasons children may not qualify for, 121–26
    See also extracurricular activities
"enthusiasm" in class, 27–28, 114
equity principle, 133–34
European model. *See* international schools; Unified Math
evaluation of children. *See* grades; intelligence testing; psychiatric evaluation
Everyday Math, 91, 93–94, 95, 96, 97, 124, 125, 168, 169, 171, 173, 200
everyday tasks, difficulty with, 151–53
executive function (EF)
    delays/impairments in, 131, 132, 152–53, 164, 176, 195, 196, 206, 215
"experiential learning," 95. *See also* "discovery learning" and incidental discovery; hands-on activities
explicit instruction. *See* child-centered discovery vs. explicit instruction; teaching, explicit
extracurricular activities, 32–33, 38, 47, 48, 62, 139–40, 148, 159
extroversion vs. introversion, 8–9, 23, 40–41, 209–10

family, helping your unsocial child open up and connect with, 66–70
Feel-Good Curriculum, The (Stout), 113
Floortime, 67, 184
Fluent American English (Steinbach), 79

foreign language, 89, 105–8, 121, 135
formative vs. summative assessment. *See under* grades
French schools, 46, 136
friendships, helping your child develop, 71–75, 153–55

Gardner, Howard, 132, 133, 190
"geeks," 7, 10
gender differences, 2, 8–9, 72–73, 164
Genzel, Rhona B., 77
German schools, 46, 136
Gladwell, Malcolm, 10, 32, 38
Goleman, Daniel. *See Emotional Intelligence*
Golinkoff, Roberta Michnick, 146
Gottman, John, 65–66
grade compression, 28, 116, 126, 136
grades, 87–88, 131, 144, 146, 192
    attitude and, 27–28
    autistic children and, 173, 176
    college admissions and, 31–32, 47–48, 126–28, 140–41
    formative vs. summative assessment, 24, 25, 27, 114, 116, 118, 198–99
    reasons analytic children get low, 113–21
    reasons unsocial children get low, 24–28, 37–38
graduate programs, competition for, 128, 208
    improving your child's prospects for, 140–42
graphic arts skills, 89, 100, 109, 115
Gray, Carol, 186
Greene, Brian, 190
Greenspan, Stanley, 67, 146, 178, 184, 185
group activities, 18, 22, 34–35, 106, 111, 112, 114, 176, 210, 212. *See also* classroom participation; group work

group-centered learning, challenges of, 95, 165–67, 176
group work, 14–16, 42–44, 92, 95, 100, 113, 190, 193–95, 215. *See also* group activities

hands-on activities, 89, 91–93, 95–96, 109, 110–11, 176, 178, 192, 197–99
    vs. abstract symbols and concepts, 95–96
    vs. explicit teaching, 211–12
    See also Reform Math
handwriting, 89, 100, 115, 169, 197
Harris, Judith Rich, 63
high-functioning autism (HFA). *See* autistic/Asperger's syndrome children; autistic spectrum disorders
high schools and colleges, competitive, 37–39
    children's prospects for, 31–33, 126–28
    improving your child's prospects for, 47–48, 140–42
higher-level thinking, 119, 125, 129–130, 179–80. *See also* relational vs. procedural/instrumental understanding
Hirsch, E. D., 196
Hirsh-Pasek, Kathy, 146
homeschooling, 46, 137
homework,
    challenges of managing at home, 143–45
    modifying, 137–38
    supplementing, 145–48
Howe, Roger, 130

independent learning, 34, 89, 95, 132–33, 137, 193, 211, 215–16
    of mathematics, 100, 136, 212
Individualized Education Plan (IEP), 50, 51, 52, 183
Individuals with Disabilities Education Act (IDEA), 50, 51, 183

inflexibility, 155–56. *See also* predictability, need for
"initiative" in class, 27, 28, 36, 114
Input Processing, 105
instrumental/procedural vs. relational understanding, 118–19, 129–30
intelligence testing, 122–23, 181. *See also* standardized tests
intelligences, theory of multiple, 132, 133, 190
interdisciplinary projects, integrated, 92, 93, 102, 109, 110, 115, 132, 133, 195–96, 215. *See also* Project-Based Learning
interests, narrow and obsessive, 153, 157–59
international schools, 45–46, 136
Internet. *See* chat rooms, Internet; online charter schools
interviews and interview skills, 32, 38, 47, 126
introversion, 30–31, 41, 209–10. *See also* extroversion vs. introversion
intuition/"following your gut" vs. logic/analysis, 2, 7, 8, 9, 102, 190
Investigations, 91, 95, 96, 97, 99, 170, 171
IQ tests, 122, 181
ISEEs (Independent School Entrance Exams), 126

Kamii, Constance, 196
Kaminski, Jennifer, 197
Kim, Heejung, 193
kindergarten, 39–40, 54, 111
King, Jayne, 90–91
Klein, David, 130
Kumon, 139

Lane, Christopher, 30–31
language arts and literature, 20–21, 102–5
    challenge for autistic children, 173–76

leadership skills, 32–33, 38, 47–48, 127, 136, 140, 206

learning disabilities. *See* autism/Asperger's syndrome children; executive function

Learning Gap, The (Stevenson and Stigler), 199

learning styles, 43
  emphasizing accommodation and, 43–47, 132–35, 183

lecturing, 61, 126, 150–51, 154

left-brain children, 3, 40
  general characteristics, 3–5, 88–90
  meaning of the term, 1–2
  overlap with "Systemizers," 2
  portion of children who are, 2
  and the world at large, 217 (*see also* right-brain world, overview of)
  See also analytic children; autistic/Asperger's syndrome children; unsocial children; *and specific topics*

left-brain skills that all children need, 206–10

linear thinking and learning, 89, 110, 111, 143, 164, 167, 193, 195. *See also under* Reform Math

logical organization and hierarchy, need for, 89, 94–95

Lonely Crowd, The (Riesman), 41, 209

magnet schools, 135–36

Mahan-Taylor, Rebecca, 79

mainstreaming, 55, 163, 165, 167, 182

Markus, Hazel, 193

math camps, 141–42

math teams and competitions, 140–41

mathematicians, 42, 98, 130, 138, 192, 194, 197–98, 200, 212

mathematics
  economic value of, 208–9
  ideal curriculum, 212–13
  ideal teachers, 213–14
  independent learning of, 212

precise calculation, value of, 129–30
  probability and statistics in, 207
  society and, 7–8
  traditional math, 199
  See also left-brain skills that all children need; Reform Math; Saxon Math; Singapore Math; Unified Math

"maybe," understanding the meaning of, 185

Milgram, James, 94, 98, 130

Mind Reading program, 80, 185–86

Montessori programs, 46, 136, 196

multiple-intelligences theory, 132, 133, 190

multiple solutions, 23, 92, 97, 134, 209

multisensory learning, 105, 110–12. *See also* sensory overload

multitasking, 169

mutism, selective, 5, 50

Myths and Misconceptions about Teaching (Snider), 192

"nerds," 7, 10

National Academies, 209, 213

National Council of Teachers of Mathematics (NCTM), 200
  Standards, 91, 117, 133

National Science Foundation, 90, 200

National Science Teachers Association, 200
  Standards, 101

National Standards for Foreign Language Learning, 105, 108

No Child Left Behind (NCLB), 9, 115, 117–18, 122, 126, 189, 198, 199–200

nonconformity. *See* peer pressure

nonverbal learning disability (NLD), 89, 129, 131, 195

Nurture Assumption, The (Harris), 63

obsessive interests, 153, 157–59

online charter schools, 46–47, 137

online courses, 139
online venues for older unsocial children, 83–85
open-ended assignments, 90, 92, 106, 110, 115, 133, 137, 144, 145, 164, 171, 176–77, 210, 211
open-ended questions, 19, 36, 171, 172, 209
oral participation, 20, 40, 43, 44, 45, 192–93
    grading children on, 26, 114, 193
    voluntary vs. required, 19–20, 36
    See also classroom participation
oral presentations, 20
organizational skills. See executive function (EF)
outings, handling problems with, 156–59, 188

parenting advice, 65–66, 146–47, 158, 186–88
parochial schools, 45, 136–37
peer pressure, 4, 6, 21, 41, 75
penmanship. See handwriting
personal connections and reflections
    in class discussions and school work, 17, 20–21, 23–27, 35, 43–44, 90, 101, 103–5, 106, 108, 109, 115, 117, 120, 174, 183, 193, 216
    with friends and relatives (see relationships)
    with parents (see connecting with your child)
personality differences, 40, 41, 84. See also under left-brain children; and specific traits
pervasive developmental disorder (PDD), 162, 164
phonics, 103, 196
Piaget, Jean, 196
playdates, 60–63, 71–74, 188
    mishaps, 73–74, 150, 154
playmates

finding, 71–73
    See also friendships, helping your child develop
practical vs. academic skills, 204–5
    in math, 91, 105
predictability, need for, 154, 155–56, 157, 176–77, 185
probability and statistics, 207, 213
procedural/instrumental vs. relational understanding, 118–19, 129–30
Project-Based Learning, 90, 101, 109–10
projects, 35, 86–87, 92, 93, 100–2, 109–10, 115, 121, 125–26, 131–33, 136, 137, 144, 145, 169, 176–77, 195, 215. See also interdisciplinary projects, integrated
Prose, Francine, 103–4
psychiatric diagnoses, 30–31, 48–51, 162. See also specific disorders
psychiatric evaluation, 48–56
psychiatric problems, 28–31
psychotherapists, selecting, 45

questions, 76
    call-and-response model, 18, 23
    open-ended, 19, 35, 36

reading, 25, 67, 102–3, 170, 174, 193
reading-response journals, 20, 25, 105, 176, 179, 183
Reform Math, 90–101, 117–19, 167–73, 192, 207, 208, 212
    "applied," 93, 96, 100, 169, 177, 197–98 (see also hands-on activities; word problems)
    challenge for linear thinkers distracted by sensory clutter, 92–94
    challenge for autistic children, 167–73
    challenge for those better suited to abstract symbols and concepts, 95–96

Reform Math (*continued*)
    challenge for those needing logical organization, 94–95
    challenge for those who calculate numbers in their heads, 98–99
    challenge for those who excel in math, 96–98
    challenge for those who need and strive for precision, 99–100
    challenge for those who struggle with handwriting, graphic arts, and visual representation, 100
    challenge for those who work best independently, 100
    "daily life" connections, 90–91, 95–96, 196–98
    enrichment programs and, 125
    experts, empirical research, and, 200, 201
    foreign language instruction compared with, 106, 107
    intelligence testing, and, 122–25
    No Child Left Behind and, 198, 199–200
    reasons for disliking, 90–92, 100–101
    reasons for low grades in, 117–19
    requiring students to explain their answers, 27, 98–99, 117–19, 134–35, 169, 197
    vs. Singapore Math, 138–39, 212
    See also *Everyday Math*; *Investigations*; *Trailblazers*; *Connected Mathematics*
relational vs. procedural/instrumental understanding, 118–19, 129–30
relationships, 71–75, 153–55
    parent-child, 63–66, 70, 186–87
    with peers, 31, 161–62
    with relatives, 68–69, 155
    See also connecting with your child; playdates
Riesman, David, 41, 209

"right-brain," connotations of the term, 2
right-brain skills that all children need, 205–6
right-brain world, overview of, 6–11

SATs, 126, 208
Saxon Math, 138, 173, 212, 213
school
    alternative, 45–47, 135–37
    helping your unsocial child at, 39–56
    helping your analytic child at, 132–35
    helping your autistic/Asperger's child at, 182–83
    reasons for disliking, 17–24, 100–101
    See also high schools and colleges, competitive; *and specific topics*
school yard dynamics, 22–23, 35, 113
Schools We Need and Why We Don't Have Them, The (Hirsch), 196
science, 7–8, 21, 101–2
    reasons for low grades in, 119–20
scientists, famous, 8, 42, 131, 205
Senator, Susan, 156
sensory overload, 89, 93, 111, 114, 164, 166–67, 168, 192, 199
sequential learning. *See* linear thinking and learning
sharing, personal. *See* personal connections and reflections
shyness, 19, 20, 21, 23–28, 30–31, 32, 40, 44–45, 50, 68, 78, 84, 198, 215–16. *See also* cases: Lisbeth; unsocial children
Shyness: How Normal Behavior Became a Sickness (Lane), 30
siblings, interactions with, 64, 68
Singapore Math, 138–39, 212–13
Singal, Daniel, 108–9
Snider, Vicki, 192
sociability and social skills, 6–7, 15, 32,

38, 40–42, 43–44, 49, 50, 63, 68, 74, 85, 188, 206, 209, 211. *See also* conversations: teaching rules for; social skills groups, enrolling children in; social dynamics of youth culture, teaching the

social anxiety disorder, 30–31. *See also* shyness

social dynamics of youth culture, teaching the, 82–83
    through fiction, 81
    through movies and TV shows, 82

social skills groups, enrolling children in, 81–82

Social Stories, 186

social studies, 18, 20–21, 26, 104, 109, 169, 215

Sommers, Christina Hoff, 195

Speaking Naturally (Tillitt and Bruder), 77–78

spiraling, 94, 125

splinter skills, 177

spontaneous participation, 19–20

standardized tests, 122–24, 126, 141, 181

statistics, 207, 213

Steinbach, Susan, 79

Stephenson, Neal, 7

Stevenson, Harold, 199

Stigler, James, 199

story problems. *See* word problems

Stout, Maureen, 113

structure, need for, 68–69, 71, 74, 81, 94–95, 145, 164, 171, 176–77, 182–83, 185–86, 187, 188, 205, 210, 211

summative vs. formative assessment. *See under* grades

summer camps, 141–42

summer projects, 144

Sykes, Charles, 113

Systemizers vs. Empathizers, 2, 9

systemizing, 164–65. *See also* analytic children; linear thinking and learning

Tannen, Deborah, 8

teacher certification/training programs, 191, 214

teachers
    accommodation of learning styles, 43–45, 132–35
    credentials and competence, 213–15
    negotiating with, 43–45, 132–35

teaching, explicit, 192, 199, 211–12
    in autism 182–86
    See also child-centered discovery vs. explicit instruction

teaching methods, today's, 17–19
    expert opinions and empirical support for, 190, 199–202
    false dichotomies and, 203–4
    how to counter arguments supporting, 191–99, 202
    See also Constructivism; "discovery learning" and incidental discovery

Teaching Pragmatics (Bardovi-Harlig and Mahan-Taylor), 79

temperament,
    argumentative, 149–50 (*see also* critical attitude)
    shy (*see* shyness)

tests, 122, 198
    school-based, 24, 114, 116, 117–18, 199
    See also psychiatric diagnoses; standardized tests

"text-to-self," 20, 25, 103, 174. *See also* personal connections and reflections

"text-to-world," 103

thinking, explaining one's, 27, 98–99, 117–19, 134–35, 169, 197. *See also* personal connections and reflections

Tillitt, Bruce, 77

Total Physical Response, 105

Trailblazers, 91, 96, 99, 167–68, 170, 172

tutoring, 48, 52, 139, 159, 183, 192, 201
   achievement gap and, 192, 198, 202

Unified Math, 136
unsocial children
   cases, 1, 13–14, 14–16, 16–17, 29, 31,
      49, 52–53, 53–56, 57–58, 58–59, 81
   helping them at school, 39–56
   helping them open up and connect
      with family, 66–70
   at home, 60–63
   online venues for older, 83–85
   See also conversations: teaching
      rules for; social skills groups,
      enrolling children in; shyness;
      social dynamics of youth culture,
      teaching the; and specific topics

virtual schools, online, 46–47
visual creativity, 110, 115, 130
   vs. analytical creativity, 133, 205
visual representation, 89, 95, 100, 109,
   114

Whole Language, 102–3

word problems, 93, 96–97, 163, 170–
   71, 177–78, 197–98, 212. See also
   Reform Math
workforce, preparing children for, 204,
   207–8
   importance of social skills for, 42, 75,
      194, 206
writing, 20, 43, 67, 68, 103, 104, 120,
   130, 133, 193
   analytical/essays, 28, 193
   creative, 93, 130
   journal, 20, 21, 25, 98, 100, 103, 105,
      106, 169, 175–76
   in math, 91, 92, 93, 97, 98, 118, 163,
      169
   in science, 101, 102
   in foreign language, 106
   reasons for low grades in, 25–26, 120
   See also personal connections and
      reflections
Writing Across the Curriculum, 90,
   101, 108–9
"writing workshop" model, 20
written responses to classroom discussion topics, option of, 44